NINE
ROTTEN
LOUSY
KIDS

NINE ROTTEN LOUSY KIDS

Herbert Grossman

If I could only do one thing for them,
I would love them and not worry about the rest.
WILLIAM JORDANSON

Holt, Rinehart and Winston
New York · Chicago · San Francisco

To Carletta With Love

First Edition

ISBN: 0–03–091386–1 (Trade)
      0–03–085189–0 (College)

Designer: *Sheila Lynch*

Printed in the United States of America

Contents

Preface

This is the story of an experimental school for delinquent boys, and nine of the kids who attended that school instead of the state training schools, mental hospitals and residential treatment centers the courts had already assigned them to. The staff of the school could not accept the courts' decision; convinced of a different approach, they have written this book in the belief that these kids can be helped, not by punishing them for their problems or removing them far from the communities they know, but rather by understanding the conditions that caused their difficulties and by answering their hopelessness with optimism, their alienation with friendship, their suspiciousness with trust, and their anger with love.

Day by day the staff dictated a log of what happened, how it happened, who was present, what they thought and felt about the events, and the actual conversations that took place—as the staff remembered them at the time. This book then, based on the daily log, is as much a measure of adult achievements in a chosen field, as well as of their disappointments and failures, as it is a story of nine kids. For such a story had to be told honestly, if it was to be told at all, and from as wide an angle as the human camera "eye" could see. The staffs' real names are used throughout. The students' names and identities have been changed. The school is a real school in New York City. The story of our nine kids is true.

Although the staff dictated the log and corrected the earlier forms of the manuscript, the author assumes full editorial responsibility for the pages that follow, especially for the selection of incidents and dialogue.

I would like to acknowledge the contributions of all of the staff members to the success of the school: Edward Cain, Constance Dickinson, Henry Detlev Fishel, Marilyn Grossman, William S. Leicht, Norman H. Penn, Natalie Tucker, and John Uhrich. Two staff members were especially instrumental in the founding of the school. As the most experienced clinician and assistant director of the school, Henry Fishel was responsible for the development of the therapeutic approach and the conceptualization of much of the theoretical basis of the program. An earlier article which he co-authored included many of the principles discussed in the first chapter of the book. Norman Penn was the father of many of the creative techniques we used in our daily work. He did much to make the program swing.

I would like to express my appreciation to Phyllis Frishberg, the school secretary, who somehow managed to type the log while taking care of the regular business of the school and to John Uhrich whose unpublished essay provided the idea for the epilogue. Many people read the earlier forms of the manuscript. Wilbert T. Daniels, Ellie Klein, and Mary McKnight contributed comments that were especially helpful.

Finally, I would like to thank Harry Krohn, Hershel Alt, and the Jewish Board of Guardians for conceiving the idea of the school and helping me make their idea a reality.

HERBERT GROSSMAN

Tuskegee Institute, Alabama
January 1972

Prologue

Society usually removes troublesome adolescents, especially if they're poor, black, or different in some way—society usually removes troublesome adolescents who fail to conform to its demands—society usually removes them from their communities and places them in training schools, treatment centers, and hospitals—especially if they're poor, black, or different in some way. Society usually removes them for their own good, in order to better rehabilitate them, but really to protect society.

Society places them in training schools, treatment centers, and hospitals which always cost a lot and usually do little. Something's wrong somewhere. Spending all that dough just to turn rotten kids into rotten adults! That don't make no sense. Maybe we ought to stop a minute, take a look around, and see where we're at.

This is a book about nine rotten lousy kids, failures in school, in trouble in the community, about to be sent away to institutions by society's agents: teachers, guidance counselors, principals, parents, psychologists, attendance officers, policemen, probation officers, social workers, judges, lawyers, and psychiatrists. Nine rotten lousy kids waiting to be shipped somewhere, but who were sent to our school instead.

1

This book is also about us, the adults who loved these kids—therapists, teachers, graduate students, and a secretary. Maybe we all didn't love every boy, but every boy, including Harold and George, had at least one person to love him and sometimes that's a hell of a lot to be able to say.

Our boys were problem kids. Stealing, extortion, shoplifting, drugs, breaking and entering, homosexuality, male prostitution, and assault were among their crimes. Society, that was their problem. We, the adults who worked with the boys, weren't perfect either. We had our "hang-ups," some similar to the boys', others quite different—more mature, more sophisticated, more middle-class "hang-ups."

This book tells what we did—that's good. It tells the troubles we had getting together—that's better. Our book tells about our nine rotten lousy kids—that's best, yeah, that's best.

After you have read our story we dare you to call our boys rotten lousy kids.

1 Getting Our Thing Together

LET'M ALL IN

"Later for techniques. First we have to talk about the kids. We made a mistake last year by taking in every kid referred to us. We can't help every kid," Norman insisted.

"Like which kids?" Herb asked.

"Like the two kids we got rid of," Norman answered.

"I don't know," Herb disagreed. "We were just getting started then. We were too nervous. Maybe we actually could have helped them."

"Both of them? You're kidding, right?" Norman asked sarcastically. "You know one of the kids' mothers was so disturbed, she had him believing there were plots against him. She was telling him we were using him for a guinea pig. There was no food in the house. He stunk cause he only had one pair of underwear and socks to his name. The refrigerator was filled with garbage. He had to sleep on the floor. You really think we should have let him stay in that house?"

It was early in November, 1966. Herbert Grossman, Norman Penn, and three other teachers and clinicians were meeting in Greenwich Village, New York City. Most of us had sat in that same building around the same table almost two years earlier in January, 1965, planning an experimental program for delinquent teen-age boys who were out of school, in trouble with the law, and scheduled to be sent to residential treatment centers, state training schools, or mental hospitals.

It had been some experiment. We had taken a group of boys whom society had just about given up on. Instead of hiding them away somewhere where they and the problems they caused society would be out of sight and out of mind, we had kept them in their homes and in the city.

"Remember!" Herb, the director of the project, had been told when he was given the go-ahead to start, "Society considers the boys you will be working with incorrigible, the bottom of the barrel. People are afraid of them—which is the main reason why they are removed from the community. No one can say for certain that they should not be placed in residential settings because they have never been treated any other way. So forget about what is usually done in the field. Try whatever you want. Be as innovative as you want. Just one thing. Don't take too many chances. If some of the boys are too dangerous to keep in the city, don't hesitate to send them to a residential center or hospital. You do not have to succeed with all of them. This is just a pilot project. Find out what kinds of things work. See if the program is successful. Remember you don't have to keep every boy you accept. No one is assuming that all the institutions can be closed down overnight."

We ran the project for a year and a half, more successfully than any of us had anticipated. And, despite our initial concern and a few very close calls, none of the boys had gotten into trouble. In July, 1966, we terminated the experiment, published our results, and continued to seek the funds needed to establish the school on a permanent basis. By the end of October, 1966, we had received enough support from the New York City public school system, the New York City Community Mental Health Board, and private foundations to reopen an expanded version of the school.

Now almost two years after the initial experiment, six of us, Herbert Grossman, his wife Marilyn, Norman Penn, Henry Fishel, and William Leicht, all of whom had worked in the pilot project, and Constance Dickinson, whom we had just hired, were meeting to plan a program for twenty-five boys. With the exception of Bill Leicht and Connie Dickinson, everyone had worked with delinquent teen-agers even before the pilot project. Experimental work with the boys had taught us many things we hadn't known before. So we wanted to use the five or six weeks before reopening to review our experiences during the pilot project, redefine our theory, and make changes in our techniques.

There we were in the middle of our first meeting. We had just agreed on a research design. We had also promised to use the dictating equipment daily so that we would have a record of our program which we hoped to share with others in book form. With that out of the way, Norm, as one of the teachers, was pressing Herb, a psychologist and our director, to agree to set some limits on the kinds of boys we would accept.

Norm had been brought up in the tenement-enclosed slum streets of New York City. So he was very sensitive to the culture of the streets and especially sensitive to the effects slum living conditions had on our boys. In fact he almost seemed more comfortable with that culture than the culture of the middle-class professionals with whom he worked.

The argument continued: "I don't mean he was better off at home than in a residential program," Herb answered. "I meant we were too quick to decide we couldn't help him. Our research design was to find out which kids we could

help without removing them from their homes. We didn't
give ourselves a chance with him. So we can't say anything
definite."

Like Norm, Herb had grown up in the streets of New
York City. However, unlike Norm, Herb had left the city
for a Harvard education, and he had received a Ph.D. from
Columbia. So he was more interested in research.

"Dammit, we can say something definite," Norm answered. "You can't just take in any kid. We can't help every
kid. Everyone else is sending these kids to institutions and
you want to help all of them."

"I disagree," Constance Dickinson said. "If this is an experimental program, it appears to me that it's our job to determine which boys do not have to be sent away. Norman,
you want to exclude them before they have a chance. If we
do, how can we find out if they could have succeeded?"

It was Connie's first day on the staff. Although she was
an experienced teacher, she hadn't worked in the pilot project before, and she had never worked with delinquents. So
she had no experience to call upon to judge whether Norm
or Herb was right. Connie wasn't taking Norm's sugges-
tions seriously because of his street language, his bushy
hair, hippie clothes, and arty appearance—Norm was a
painter. However, she was making a mistake, because Norm
had credentials. He had taught in private schools, schools
for disturbed students, and a community college. Connie
was also upset by Norm's unwillingness to accept Herb's authority as director, because she didn't realize that policy was
set by majority rule. Norm was quick to answer her argument.

"You weren't here last year, Connie," he pointed out.
"You're new. Even though you taught for five years in regular school, you don't know our kids. We can't act like we
didn't learn anything from the pilot project. Some kids
should be removed from their homes. And wild kids like

Charlie. He could have killed one of us last year. It was crazy to let kids like him loose in the community. What if he had shot someone with that zip gun he was shooting off?"

"Okay," Herb agreed. "Kids like Charlie shouldn't be in the program. I remember when he went after me with the steel pipe. I ran scared. But we can't keep out kids just because they *might* turn out to be a Charlie. We have to give them the benefit of the doubt if we can't predict in advance."

Herb was exaggerating. Henry Fishel, our other clinician, corrected him.

"No one is suggesting rejecting large numbers of boys. I'm certainly not. I'm talking about a few minimal criteria for admission. We could easily learn quite a few things from a boy's record which would enable us to judge how helpful we might be to him."

Henry knew what he was talking about. He had been trained in psychology and social work. The oldest and most experienced member of our staff, he had also worked with disturbed kids for years. Born in Germany and raised in various parts of Europe as his family kept one step ahead of the Nazis, Henry's approach to the boys was a mixture of European Freudian orthodoxy and American practicality. Perhaps that was why he wanted us to keep at least a few of the proven-to-be-effective traditional admission criteria.

Herb, however, disagreed.

"Maybe I'm wrong," Herb answered, "but could you predict which kids we can't help?"

"Yeah!" Norm interrupted, accepting the challenge. "Kids who got the hots for their mothers. You *know* they should be gotten out. They're too involved with their mothers to get hooked on us."

Frustration and anger were building rapidly. Connie felt it. All this arguing, she thought to herself, how can they work together?

"That's still just a hunch," Herb answered. "We don't have any real data. I say let them in. If we can't help them, let's find out. Then we have something definite to say."

Herb's mind was made up. He wasn't about to budge, regardless of what Norm and Henry said. If necessary he would insist on his authority as director. Norm, nevertheless, had a point, and knowing it made him feel increasingly frustrated at not having the power to implement it.

"C'mon!" he shouted. "You don't mean we should take in kids we can't help, just for research? Shit on research. You know we couldn't help Charlie. We are all scared he would kill someone. We're lucky he didn't. I don't want any more kids throwing cueballs or going at people with cuesticks and broken bottles. You know that's why we kicked him out."

We were becoming polarized. It was time for a compromise, and Bill Leicht was good at that. Bill was a moderating influence in our disagreements. Quiet, thoughtful, and methodical, he was able to appreciate both sides of an issue long after others had established fixed positions. As the other artist in the program, besides Norm, Bill provided an alternative approach to Norm's infectious spontaneity and competitiveness. Bill's calm I'm-here-if-you-need-me manner and conservative dress reminded us of his mid-western background, while Norm's driving dynamism seemed typical of New Yorkers.

Bill offered his compromise.

"We should be able to combine service and research. I feel we should take students like Charlie but only a few. If we took more, I would be too nervous. And if we didn't take any, I would feel guilty."

"I'll buy that," Norm announced, hoping to gain a compromise.

"That isn't the real problem. We aren't going to have

many Charlies referred to us. It will be the infantile and impulsive boys, not the homicidal boys, that will be the problem." Henry was reminding us of another kind of boy. "During the pilot project we took a youngster who had been rejected from three residential treatment centers because they thought he would be too wild for them. I don't deny that we helped him, but at a tremendous cost to the program. Boys like him will disrupt everything. They are the ones who will tear the school apart before we have a chance to establish it. They will monopolize all of our time."

"Right," Norm added. "They each need their own teacher. Even when they're in the mood to learn you have to teach them differently. They can't read, so you have to do everything orally and visually and start with the very basic things. What do you do with the readers? You can't work with both together. You know I'm right."

Again Norm had a point.

"All right, you reject this kid for this reason and you reject that kid for that reason. Then we're just like everyone else," Herb insisted.

But Norm wasn't buying Herb's argument.

"Bull shit!" he shouted angrily at Herb. "We ain't God. I'm not going to feel guilty about trying to help kids we know we can help. And you're not going to be stuck with a bunch of infants in your class. We'll be the baby-sitters, not you."

"That's bull shit!" Herb shouted back. "I'll be stuck with them just as much as you. You'll be in your class. I'll be taking care of the wild kids so you can teach. So don't give me that shit."

Norm had had it. He wasn't getting anywhere with Herb.

"I vote we limit our intake," he suggested. "Let's have a vote."

"*Vote?* Not on this," Herb answered.

"What do you mean, no vote? I thought we make group decisions."

Norm was right. In the past we had always made group decisions about policies and techniques. But Herb was too committed to his position to be able to give up.

"Yeah, but not about the research design," Herb answered. "That's already written up. It's too late to change."

It really wasn't too late to modify it, but Herb wanted it as it was. Everything had been said. There was nothing left to do but decide. It wouldn't be by general agreement. It would have to be some kind of compromise. It was Bill's turn again.

"We're arguing in the abstract about what we can and can't do," he reminded us. "Why don't we accept the boys as they are referred . . . slowly, one at a time? Test our limits. So we can see whether we can take in more of one kind or another."

"Okay, I'll buy that," Herb answered. "No restrictions until we find we have to."

"Is that okay with everyone?" Henry asked, hoping that we had reached an acceptable compromise.

Connie experienced a sense of relief that the argument had run its course.

"Then it's settled?"

We had made our first decision. We still disagreed, but we had decided. We had many more decisions to make. We didn't know it at the time but we would have only five more weeks to set up the program—five weeks to examine the policies and procedures we had developed during the pilot project, find the boys, order more supplies and equipment, and renovate the section of the building we were using for our school. We were glad that we weren't starting from scratch as we had when we set up the pilot project. Still, with the kind of kids we worked with, five weeks wasn't nearly enough time.

AN OLD-TIMER

Take Harold Stern, for instance; he was one of the boys in the pilot program who would be continuing in the expanded program. Harold was typical of one kind of kid we expected to have referred to us.

When Harold had first come to our school, he was a fat slob. His hair was bushy, wild, dry, and already thin. His face was hairy and pimply, and his eyeglasses hung down lopsided over his nose. His neck and arms were scaly from a rash which he rubbed and scratched in fits and spurts; when he wasn't scratching, he was wiping his running nose with the back of his hand or hacking up phlegm to spit on the floor. His torn sneakers, loosely fitting dungarees held up by a piece of clothesline rope instead of a belt, and dirty long-sleeved shirt kept as unbuttoned as possible to show off his hairy chest completed the effect. The way he looked only a mother could love him and she didn't.

Harold had come to our school when he was fifteen, after he had been caught stealing stamps from a large department store. He had been stealing for a long time, things he didn't really need. He stole for the sake of it, rather than to acquire. Once he had stolen collectors' stamps worth $263, which proved he was smart enough to know which stamps to take.

According to Harold's mother, Mrs. Stern, her troubles with him began when he was "little." He demanded her attention, wanted his own way, and resisted everything she wanted. He had problems immediately after he started in kindergarten. He was transferred from one elementary school to another because of "disruptive behavior" and finally suspended for a year when he was eleven for "extremely antisocial behavior and defiance of authority." He was placed on home instruction and referred to a psychiatric hospital for outpatient therapy.

After the year's suspension, Harold returned to school behaving as poorly as before. Although he wasn't overtly aggressive, he infuriated his teachers by blurting out answers, breaking into other students' discussions, constantly arguing with other children, and assuming an air of righteous indignation whenever his teachers criticized him. The school authorities tried the same unsuccessful approach— more transfers, suspensions, and other forms of push-outs. Finally after two years, Harold stopped going to school. About a year later he was caught stealing and was referred to our school.

Harold was the younger of two sons of a poor white family who lived in a ground-floor apartment facing the street in a section of New York City that was rapidly becoming a black and Puerto Rican neighborhood. In order to prevent break-ins, the family had covered over the windows with heavy screening and corrugated tin which also prevented sunlight from breaking in. The apartment was so dark, so cluttered, and so disorganized that unless you had grown up in it, it drove you out after a few minutes.

Harold's father was a weak, passive man who had little to do with his family. He avoided his whining wife by working late in a tailor shop. When he arrived home, it was often just in time to hear her complaints about how badly Harold had behaved. Mrs. Stern filled in for Harold's father as disciplinarian and practically smothered Harold with supervision until he was suspended from school. At that time the psychiatrist who saw Harold for outpatient therapy helped her let go a little. She even found a part-time job. However, as she worked, she still worried about Harold and waited for the phone call which she expected would tell her that he had been run over by a bus or something. Being busy, she encouraged Harold's slightly older brother to take over as his disciplinarian, to punish Harold as he saw fit, and to report to her whatever Harold had done wrong. Although she smothered Harold less, he was still under her thumb. She still picked out his clothes for him when he was fifteen, and she usually didn't even bother to take him along with her. She really didn't need to as long as the only pants she bought Harold were dungarees, and she simply forgot to buy him the belt he needed instead of that piece of clothes-line rope she had given him.

Harold had a lot to feel angry about, but he couldn't express his anger directly without risking almost certain punishment. So he learned to act passive and innocent while provoking and needling others, always without meaning to, always by accident. He also caused "accidents," which hurt him, so often that his body was covered with scratches, bruises, Band-Aids, and bits of toilet paper which he used for the bleeding pimples he cut on the rare occasions he shaved.

Harold's experience in school was as painful as his home life. The extreme self-doubts and feelings of helplessness he had developed because of the rejection and abuse heaped on him at home and his disruptive behavior interfered with his school work.

Harold also had a speech impediment which made it difficult for him to pronounce certain sounds or to differentiate them when he heard them. He avoided words with sounds he couldn't pronounce or left the sounds out when he spoke. He said, "It there" and "Thmoking ithin't bad for your health," instead of "It was there" and "Smoking isn't bad for your health." Harold also tended not to notice these sounds and word endings when he read. He read as if such things as past, present, future, singular and plural were non-existent, and he misunderstood almost as much as he understood. Rather than admit his difficulties to himself, he developed an extremely uncritical attitude about his work, to the point that his misunderstandings seemed logical and correct, and even his grossly distorted spelling looked right to him. He also acted like a scholar to avoid facing his inadequacies. He "read" books about archaeology and philosophy and talked about becoming an archaeologist after college. These defenses worked pretty well. But every so often his hopelessness and feelings of inadequacy broke through and drove him to outbursts of violent temper or depression.

When Harold started in our school, his passive but aggressive obnoxious behavior drove everyone wild. When he sat in class, his feet poked out just a little too far, so they accidentally tripped someone walking by. He poked people a little too hard while trying to attract attention. And he smeared people with clay as he patted them friendly-like on the back, forgetting that he had just been working on the potter's wheel. Believing that these things had happened accidentally, he acted like the victim when his victims got angry. That infuriated them more and made things worse.

Harold had made progress in the pilot school as well as at home during the year and a half he was with us. He began to see that his mother had been mistreating him. He became less dependent on her low opinion of him and somewhat more able to see himself as a worthwhile person in his own right. Since he saw himself more realistically he understood, to some small extent, why people got angry at him, and he was a little more willing to deal fairly with us and the boys. He was no angel, but he became a lot less obnoxious.

Harold also made academic progress. He raised his reading level from sixth to tenth grade and improved his spelling. He became more self-accepting, more able to tolerate frustration, and just a little less unrealistically rosy about his future. To someone who hadn't known Harold before, that may not have been much, but to us it was great.

TOO OLD?

Back to our first planning session. Just as we had decided who we were going to accept, someone asked whether we thought we should enroll fourteen- and fifteen-year-old boys instead of sixteen- and seventeen-year-olds.

It was a good suggestion. We realized that fourteen-year-olds had a better chance of making it. They were "into" fewer things. They hadn't been in trouble quite as long. They trusted adults more. At least they were less suspicious of us. They could get back into regular school after they had been with us a year or two. Take in a sixteen-year-old, keep him for a couple of years, and you know they won't take him back into high school when he's eighteen.

On the other hand, we realized that the older boys needed us more, because hardly anyone was taking older adolescents. Everyone wanted the under-sixteens—sometimes for the same reasons that we did, sometimes because they were easier to handle. If we closed our doors to the older boys, we would be joining the crowd that was keeping them out in the cold.

Well, could we take some of each? Sure, but how would they fit in a small program for twenty-five students? Could our small staff provide the variety of educational activities their different ages and experiences required? It was a problem, but we decided to tackle it anyway. We just weren't in an excluding mood.

OLD-TIMER NUMBER TWO

It was time for a lunch break. Stanley Burns, the other boy from the pilot project who would be coming back, was coming to see us. He had sounded nervous when he called Herb the night before about some home problems.

Stanley was brought to court by his father when he was fifteen because he had ordered a pistol through the mails to shoot his mother. Mrs. Burns also complained to the court that Stanley beat her black-and-blue, threw knives at her, and forced her to give him money. Mr. Burns claimed that his son had been running away from home, refusing to attend school, staying out extremely late, sleeping until three or four in the afternoon, and acting like the "king" of the house. At first they had tried to protect themselves by locking him out of the house, but each time he had gotten back by breaking the windows. When Stanley ordered the gun, his father decided to get the court's help to keep him out of the house.

After hearing Mr. Burns's complaints, the judge wanted to send Stanley to a residential treatment center. However Stanley's mother refused because she was sure he had learned his lesson and would be good. Stanley was placed on probation and seen in outpatient therapy for a year. He did better for a while, but a short period of better behavior at home and regular attendance in school was followed by the old story. When his mother tried to wake him or refused to give him money, he threatened to stab her or burn her with his cigarette lighter. He refused to go to school, to get out of bed, or to wash himself. Mr. Burns went to the probation officer once again and demanded that he remove Stanley from the house. However, at the court hearing, Stanley's mother again testified that Stanley had "learned his lesson," had undergone a "miraculous change" and didn't need any more help. It was at that time that he was referred to us.

When Stanley first came to our pilot project, he was a way-out-looking sixteen-year-old. He wore tight-fitting black clothes—black pants, black shirt, black leather motorcycle jacket, and pointed high-heel black boots. He kept his curly hair shoulder length before it was in style. His face, which looked like he never washed it, was covered with pimples and blackheads, and he had a sleepy, dopey expression with eyes that seemed too tired to stay open. We thought we had seen the last of Stanley after he said that he didn't want anyone to think he was smart; he was sure he wouldn't be able to wake up in the morning for school; and he didn't want to come anyway. We were wrong. Stanley decided to come to the school.

During the first week Stanley attended school regularly and even arrived on time every day. But by the end of the week he had beaten up his mother again. His father kicked him out of the house and threatened to move out if Stanley was allowed to return. During the second week of school Stanley told us that he was having problems in the subway on his way to school. "Homosexuals" with bumps under their chins entered the train, winked at him, followed him from car to car, and stroked him on his legs. Stanley carried a stiletto in his pocket to protect himself, and forced "one of them" off the train at knife point because he was sure the man was about to attack him sexually.

When the people who had referred Stanley to us learned about what he said he was doing, they urged us to send him to a mental hospital, but we didn't. We thought he needed a cooling-off period. We told him to stop coming to school for a while, to leave his knife at home, to remain in his neighborhood, and to go out with his girl friend. We advised his parents about how they might deal with his behavior and persuaded them to allow him to continue to live at home. After eight or nine days Stanley returned to school, although he had to travel by bus rather than train for a few days in order to avoid the "homosexuals" he imagined were after him.

Stanley changed during the pilot project. His fears of homosexual attack and physical assault disappeared, although he still felt embarrassed about being nude in front of other men whom he imagined stared at his penis. He stopped assaulting his mother, and he was able to get up in the morning. He raised his reading level from sixth to ninth grade and completed a year of high school academic subjects. However, he was not really interested in finishing high school.

As our pilot project was drawing to its close in June, we were trying to encourage Stanley to think about entering a vocational training program. He was much too insecure to follow through. Yet after the summer vacation, Stanley seemed ready to begin vocational training. He was willing to enroll in some program if he could study in the evenings for his equivalency diploma. Herb, who was his "shrink," referred him to the Institute for Vocational Rehabilitation in October. However, we weren't certain that they would accept him, or that if accepted, he would attend. While he waited, Stanley was supposed to continue to see Herb and attend our school when it reopened. He and Harold would be the two old-timers from the original pilot project.

Stanley was a little late for his appointment with Herb because he had overslept—because he was depressed, because his parents were "bugging" him to forget about the Vocational Institute, because they wanted him to find a job, because they didn't want him to be a bum, because he was down to his last shirt and pair of pants, because he needed money and his parents wouldn't give him any, because they wanted him to contribute money, not to take it. Stanley told us that he wanted to attend the Vocational Institute but he felt hard-pressed by parental pressure and his own financial needs. He needed a solution to his problem soon. If not, he hinted, he might have to find a job instead, just to exist. We decided to give Stanley a small weekly allowance for his personal needs, to buy him some clothes, and to meet with his parents.

HALF A SCHOOL

During the following weeks we continued to set up the school, admit new students, and decide policy simultaneously. We had evolved a general approach to the boys during the pilot project which we intended to continue. Our first goal was to get them into the school. All of the boys in our pilot project had been out of school for a year or more. They were three-, four-, and five-time losers in school. Many of them had had their heads "shrunk" time after time. We realized that we couldn't expect them to come for another dose just because *we* knew we could help them. We had to do things to make sure they would come. We could have told them to come or be sent away, but we didn't want to use coercion. Instead we tried to create a place with people and a program that would attract them.

The environment we had created for our kids during the pilot project was tailored to where they were at when they first came to us. The original school was designed so that it could conform to whatever made the boys comfortable. The classrooms looked like regular school rooms—desks, blackboards, books, maps, lab equipment . . . the works. However with the classroom doors shut, the school looked like a recreation center with a pool table, a basketball court, and a shop. The classrooms were used when the boys were relatively ready to apply themselves to learning tasks and conform to some of the demands of a learning situation. The recreation area including the gym, art studio, and shop, on the other hand, could be used when they were unable to adjust to the classroom setting.

During the pilot project, the different sections had all been on one floor so we had difficulty isolating the boys engaged in productive work in "school" from the disruptions and temptations of the boys who were looking for company while they were "hanging around." When the school re-opened we would have three floors in the building we were sharing. We would have the gym and recreation area, the shop, the art studio, and the music room on the second floor. The third floor would contain the secretary's office, the academic classrooms, and the remedial and therapy offices. We would try to keep the boys who wanted to play disruptive games on the second floor where they could be handled better.

With the space divided up, we could begin decorating the school. Norm was given the responsibility of making the school attractive, light, bright, and colorful. He helped us choose color schemes for our rooms. Red, yellow, orange, and white soon replaced institutional green and gray. Norm's taste was magnificent. It came out beautiful. The plans for the physical facilities moved along without a hitch until Henry made a suggestion.

TO LOCK OR NOT

"It's about time we talked about how we can keep the kids out of my office while I am interviewing, and away from the confidential material in the secretary's office. We could have avoided much disruption last year if we could have secured some of their places with locks."

"Man, you know our kids can get into anything. There's no sense lockin things up," Norm answered.

"That's not the point," Henry replied. "True locks will not stop thieves, but they do discourage honest people. If things were locked out of sight then the boys wouldn't be tempted. When they are open, it's an invitation, especially tools and art equipment, which are like toys to the boys."

That sounded like a direct challenge to Norm, who an-swered, "C'mon, you know you can't run a shop with tools locked up. What's the big deal if they steal a tool? What are we talking about? There was hardly any stealing."

"It's not the stealing," Henry explained. "It's the taking and teasing—the disruptive playing. It's spending valuable time coaxing boys to give us back the things they took, time which could be used other ways."

"If you want to lock your room that's your thing," Norm answered. "You lock your closets, let me keep mine open."

Herb interrupted their two-way discussion.

"Wait a while! You two can't act independently. We have to establish a common policy for everyone."

Henry continued: "Herb, if you insist that we accept infantile boys like Sam, we will have to be able to stop them from penetrating our rooms and offices. We won't be able to teach, dictate, write letters, or even make telephone calls without locks."

"I just don't see lockin doors against kids," Norm answered. "Man, if they're upset and need TLC, stop what you're doing and give it to them. What are you gonna do? Make an appointment?"

"That's an exaggeration, Norman," Henry replied. "Of course when they are upset they should be seen. However there are times when not being allowed to see us may be even more therapeutic."

"Then where do you want them to go when they're lookin for contact? They'll spill over into the classrooms!" Norm said.

"We can lock the classrooms and allow them to enter the shops," Henry replied.

"There you go with that shop shit again. We don't want disruptions either. The impulsive kids are already on our floor in the rec room. Now we should let all the kids into our shops to screw around?"

Herb interrupted them again. "Wait a while! What does everyone think?"

"I'd like a lock on my door to signal kids about my availability," Bill answered. "If the door's open it will mean come in. If I lock it, that will mean we're busy with work that shouldn't be interrupted."

Connie had her own opinion.

"It seems to me," she said, "if any rooms should be locked up, it should be the classrooms. Aren't the therapists supposed to see the boys when they are upset?"

"That's just theory," Norm told her. "You never know what'll calm a kid down. It doesn't have to be a therapy session. They could just sit and rap with a teacher or throw a pot. You guys know that."

"There's some merit to that, Norman," Henry agreed. "However we will still have a great need for time for more formal psychotherapy, and if we don't install locks on the therapy offices, the more demanding boys will monopolize the time."

"So let's not take them in," Norm suggested, catching Herb's attention.

"UH! UH! We already decided against that," Herb reminded Norm.

"You made that decision," Norm answered. "Remember whose idea it was. You take them in . . . okay! You baby-sit with them, not me."

We weren't getting anywhere. We needed time to let things settle down. Instead we talked about the new student Henry had seen in Youth House, the court's detention center.

UN MUCHACHO NUEVO

The new boy was Manuel Martinez. He was in Youth House waiting to be sent to a state training school. It was Manuel's second trip to Youth House. When he had been caught stealing, he had gone there; then he had been placed

on probation, sent home and returned again because he refused to attend school and extorted money from the other
students.

Manuel was the kind of kid it was a shock to see locked
up. He was too young, only fourteen years old. And he was
too quiet and timid-looking, like a beautiful helpless frightened deer ready to run at the first sign of danger. Why
would anyone want to lock him up behind heavy iron
doors? He looked so innocent—tall, sleek, creamy brown
skin, long lashes, fine face. He was almost too pretty. Outside, he would be handsome. Locked up inside, he had the
kind of looks that would cause him big problems.

The court psychiatrist who interviewed Manuel described
him as a somewhat withdrawn and depressed, pleasant-
looking fourteen-year-old. Manuel told him that his main
problems were that he was nervous, got angry easily, lost
his temper, felt like hitting anything that came near his
hand, threw things around, and broke things at home. But,
he added, he had never hit anyone in anger. He said he saw
"punching ghosts," people who weren't there, and often
heard voices of ghosts who wanted him to go to the grave-
yard. He often felt confused, he told the psychiatrist, especially when he traveled on the subways. Sometimes he
wasn't able to find the place he was going to and had to return home instead. The psychiatrist thought that Manuel
would not be able to benefit from any educational
experience because "his bizarre thinking dominated his
functioning."

Manuel was a puzzle to us. When Henry visited him in
Youth House, Manuel said almost nothing about himself despite Henry's coaxing and questioning. And he had an odd
way of answering questions. When Henry asked him where
his parents were, he told Henry they were in the living room
eating supper. It wasn't a language problem. Manuel under-

stood English well enough even though he had been born in Puerto Rico. It was something else.

Then Henry visited the Martinez' at home. Their apartment was old and bare but much cleaner than the slum they lived in. The family was supported by the Welfare Department because, according to the department, Mr. Martinez was unable to work. He had undergone an operation about four years previously and had developed a nervous condition. He became violent, threw things around the house, assaulted his wife repeatedly, chewed shoes, and ate garbage. Since Manuel's mother couldn't speak English and his father's English was garbled and almost incoherent, it was very difficult for Henry to communicate with them. Henry described our school to them. They seemed pleased and said they would do whatever they could to help if Manuel were accepted.

After Henry had summarized all of the information about Manuel, he told us that the court wanted an immediate decision about him. Manuel seemed like a promising candidate. Even if he hadn't, we would have accepted him because he fit our minimum criteria. That made three students: Harold, Stanley, and Manuel.

AN ARGUMENT CONTINUED
With the decision about Manuel out of the way, we continued our discussion about locks. But we were still much too involved in our own preferences to understand each other's positions. We continued to argue on and off for another few days, but couldn't resolve our disagreements. All we could do was agree that we would each decide for ourselves whether we wanted to lock our own closets and doors.

The intensity of our disagreements and the emotional way we expressed ourselves upset Connie. She had never experienced our kind of frankness on the job. To her it was destructive, but she wasn't sure, because she could see that most of us didn't think so. So she asked Bill, who appeared to be as uncomfortable as she was, what he thought.

Bill told her that he appreciated our openness. He felt it was good for him because he had always been too passive and close-mouthed.

"That's surprising," Connie answered. "Then I would have expected you to say more during the meeting."

"I would say more. But I only worked in the pilot project during the first term," Bill explained. (Bill had left after six months to take a job as a professor of art in a New Jersey state college. Norm had been his replacement.) "So many things have changed during the year. I want to listen for a while, then I will have more to say."

"That may be true," Connie answered. "Still you seem uncomfortable about the arguing. Why else would you always be the one to suggest the compromises?"

"You're right," Bill answered. "I am uncomfortable. But not nearly as much as I once was. When I first started, I used to feel the way you do, because I couldn't understand what was going on. Gradually I came to understand that we were getting our feelings out into the open. That way we didn't have to be defensive about what we felt. Sometimes we would change our attitudes. Even if we couldn't agree, at least we all knew what to expect from each other. You can't possibly understand the unorthodox methods they use because you haven't had the experience. You were hired because of your teaching competence and personality, not because of your experience with delinquents. We all feel you have what it takes to work with delinquents. It will come out in time. You weren't chosen haphazardly. We don't hire anyone unless everyone on the staff agrees. One vote against you would have prevented us from offering you the job. We interviewed more than twenty people for the two new positions we have, and so far you are the only one we offered a job to. Herb is going to run seminars for you and the other new teacher and the two interns who will be working with us. Everything will make sense sooner than you think."

HAROLD RETURNS

Harold came back to school and Connie tutored him in English and social studies. Before she started, we told her a little about our educational approach. We informed her that the boys were encouraged but not required to attend class. We told her to find out Harold's strengths and weaknesses, without assigning him grades which were symbols of his past failures. Since Connie had never taught problem students before, we tried to prepare her for Harold's provocative behavior—yet we knew she would have to experience him firsthand.

At the beginning of their sessions, Harold was more concerned about Connie than about his work. First he tried to get her to act like the male teachers. He asked her to play pool with him, to be "one a the guy." He saluted her and said "Yes her" when she told him to do things. Then he told her that he was crazy, no one could like him. To prove it he told her he had gotten a ticket for "Thmokin" in the subway, and his friend didn't, even though he was "thmokin" too. As Connie took notes about his reading, he asked if she was writing it down for his "headthrinker" who "were intre'thted in it." He asked why she was going "ta put curtain on the window like a woman," commented that women always try "ta change things," and then drew moustaches on the pictures of the women in his textbook.

Harold also tried to avoid the academic difficulties Connie wanted to help him overcome. First he tried to impress her with his intellectual ability by telling her about his collections of stamps and newspaper clippings of articles on missiles and UFO's and his interest in archaeology. However, as Harold began having difficulty with the work he quickly changed his tune. He said he couldn't remember what they had done the day before, complained she was giving him too much work in class, sidetracked the sessions into unrelated discussions, spent a lot of time in the bathroom, and tried to manipulate her by telling her "I get nervouth in thkool. That my big problem. I can't do a lot at a time. My thpeech problem thopth me from reading. Ath Herbie. It'h true."

Connie tried to reassure Harold and talked to him about not feeling defeated before he started. It helped, but only a little.

As we expected, Connie was extremely frustrated by her inability to help Harold face up to his academic problems and even more upset because of Harold's constant cracks about women. We explained why Harold did what he did and advised Connie not to take his cracks personally. It helped, but only a little.

FREE MONEY?

Although we were busy ordering equipment, renovating rooms, interviewing students and prospective staff, we still wanted to discuss the therapeutic approach central to the pilot project. Time was short, too many things were pressing for our attention. We could only discuss the most imperative issues.

During the pilot project we had given our boys the lunches, carfare, clothing, allowances, and other things students need in order to attend school. We had two reasons for doing so. Some of the boys' parents couldn't provide these things. Other parents wouldn't. In either situation the boys needed what we gave them. However, for these deprived boys, getting what they needed helped make up for the frustrations of their childhood when they had been deprived of meaningful expressions of love.

We all agreed that giving was important, too important

to do in any but the most efficient way. However, we disagreed about what the most efficient way was. Some of us, especially Herb and Henry, felt we should give the boys such things as food, clothes, and money without strings, independent of the boys' behavior and progress in school. Others were not so sure. Norm, especially, believed that we should use such things as money as a way of helping the boys develop a sense of responsibility.

During the pilot project we had given the boys allowances without using the money to get them to change their behavior. Norm wanted us to change the policy.

"We're not helping the kids mature," he contended. "We have to ask for something in return to help them grow up. They'll feel better if they earn their money, self-satisfied. People feel good when they earn their own way."

Henry agreed partially but added, "We also give money to demonstrate our concern and affection. Unconditional giving, without strings, is a much more effective symbol of our affection."

"Besides," Herb joined in, "it's against our basic approach to force kids to behave. Do you want to change the whole thing?"

The discussion continued without resolving anything. As our discussion turned into a debate, a disagreement, and then a dispute, we became less reasonable and more emotional.

"Giving a dollar up front is one thing but seven dollars without asking for something back—that's stupid," Norm insisted.

"You're still making the same point. Okay, you want us to change our permissive approach? No dice," Herb countered as their two-way argument continued.

"They don't have to be good to get the money. No one's talking about that. I'm talking about letting them earn the bread by helping out around the school, doing whatever they can, maybe cleaning up the shops, fixing things. You can't have chicken soup forever. It's a hard world out there. They hafta be able to earn their own way."

The longer Norm continued to hold out, the more support he received. Bill, then Connie, joined him. That made a complete split. Teachers against therapists. It was time for a break. Connie went upstairs to check on Harold. The rest of us talked about the intercom system.

SWING OUT

After a while Connie came downstairs trembling but under control. She told us that she had been having a bad time with Harold. He had persuaded her to let him paint her bookcases while the painters were working in her room. There had been an argument, Harold had swung twice at one of the painters and missed, knocked the bookcase over, thrown the books off the table, and then had threatened Connie. Connie had told Harold to leave her room. He had refused. So now she wanted our help to get him out.

By the time we got upstairs, Harold had calmed down and was leaving Connie's room of his own accord. We left the two of them out in the hall. He apologized and told her he was upset because he wasn't able to take his driver's test. Upset or not, we had to do something to help him regain his self-control.

HOW MUCH IS TOO MUCH?

Our discussion about allowances continued on and off for a few more days. Finally, we decided not to change the policy. The boys would receive their allowances unconditionally. The next decision was how much. A dollar a day seemed like a reasonable amount to some of us. Henry and

Herb suggested that each kid should be guaranteed seven dollars a week between the school and his parents. If his parents gave him three dollars regularly, we would give him the other four. If they gave him nothing, we would give him the full seven. That didn't sit too well with Norm and others who thought each boy should receive what he needed, with seven dollars the maximum. Some kids had never seen seven dollars in their lives, they argued. The boys would lose it gambling or waste it some other way. Give the boys only what they could use profitably, they advised.

Henry, Herb, and Connie disagreed. During the pilot project we had given all the kids the same amount of money. Besides, seven dollars wasn't a hell of a lot for cigarettes, spending money, food, and movies, not to mention a date in New York, they contended.

"You talk about treating kids individually," Norm pointed out, "but you want to give kids money they'll waste, money they don't need, money to buy pot. That's anti-therapeutic. That's your own need to be Mister Superfair."

"Just how would you work it out?" Herb challenged him. "Could you decide which of them need less, *and* could you get them to agree?"

Getting the boys to agree would definitely be a problem.

"Okay," Norm agreed, "they all get the same, but we give them supervision on how to use the money."

Herb half agreed with Norm. "Fine," he said, "but don't expect miracles. It'll be their money. We'll only advise. It's going to take a while for them to learn to manage their money."

"Then give it to them slowly," Norm suggested. "Some Monday, some in the middle of the week, then some Friday for the weekend."

That sounded like a good compromise. We all bought it. We started talking about clothing.

STANLEY'S DRAFTED

Phyllis, our secretary, interrupted. Stanley was on the phone and wanted to talk to Herb. The intercom hadn't been connected yet, so Herb had to take it in the office.

"Hey, Stan, how are ya?"

"You can forget about me an the Vocational Institute. I'm gettin drafted."

"Getting drafted?"

"Yeah. I got my draft card in the mail this morning."

"Look, why don't you come down to the school so we can talk about it, and bring your draft card with you."

"I just woke up."

"That's okay, we'll be here."

Stanley couldn't possibly have been drafted, Herb realized. He had just turned eighteen. He hadn't even had a physical. We would have to make him see the reality of his situation.

When Stanley walked into the dining room where we were meeting, he really looked like he thought he had just been drafted. He walked up to us, greeted everyone, and waited for Herb to excuse himself.

"See," he said, handing Herb the draft card.

"What?" Herb asked.

"It's my draft card. It means I'll be drafted to Vietnam."

Herb asked him what made him think he'd be drafted immediately.

"Everyone gets drafted when they're eighteen because the army needs men for Vietnam. All my guys was drafted."

"Everyone?"

Silence.

"Do you want to go?"

"I ain't chicken but I don wanna get killed. If ya don wake up on time they throw ya in jail."

"Maybe you can be deferred."

"What's that?"

"That you can stay out of the army."

"How?"

"We could explain to your draft board that you're still in a special school and still have problems which would make it difficult for you to adjust to the army. A lot of guys like you are deferred because they wouldn't be able to adjust."

They continued talking. Stanley wasn't reassured.

"It's too late. I got my draft card. They're takin everyone. They lowered the requirements. They said I got five days to get the letters in, and two days are up."

"You still have three more to go."

"You sure I won have to go?"

"Don't worry, you just turned eighteen. You probably won't be called down to the draft board for a physical for six months or more. The army doesn't take everyone, especially if they believe you aren't ready for it yet. Henry'll send a letter to your draft board. The final decision is up to them. But since you really aren't ready for the army yet, and they wouldn't want to take anyone who wasn't ready, it's unlikely that they'd draft you."

Stanley liked what Herb said, but he wasn't ready to believe it. So Herb explained some more. At the end of the session, Herb, unsure what effect the discussion had had on Stanley, asked him: "How do you feel about it now?"

"I still know I'm gonna be drafted. I know what you said, but it won make a difference what you and Henry do. They need everybody. All my guys went."

Stanley needed a lot more reassurance. Herb asked him to come back to school in a couple of days so he could see that we had sent the letters to the army and they could talk some more.

NUMBERS FOUR AND FIVE

As the days passed, Henry got two more students. During his second trip to Youth House, he interviewed Willie Smith, a short, slender, very black sixteen-year-old whose out-of-style and ill-fitting, hand-me-down clothes couldn't conceal strikingly handsome features.

According to his probation report, Willie had been in court before because he "stole repeatedly, refused to attend school, and was involved in an actively delinquent gang." His latest arrest occurred in the spring after he and his friends had stolen almost three thousand dollars worth of phonographs, projectors, tape recorders, and athletic equipment from his school. At the time, the court had considered paroling Willie to his mother. However, Mrs. Smith has insisted that he be sent to an institution, so he had been staying in Youth House awaiting placement.

When Henry visited Willie in Youth House, he was impressed by his quiet, clearly over-controlled manner and his expressionless face, which remained masklike except during those few instances when it was punctured by a smile— more forced than real—designed more to disarm Henry than to express true feeling. Willie told Henry that he wanted to attend our school not only to get out of Youth House, but also because he thought the program would be good for him. Willie obviously knew how to play the game with social workers. Yet he was pitifully concerned about being poor. When Henry asked him about his truancy and stealing, Willie said that he didn't go to school because he didn't have the clothes and things the other students had. He especially wanted money to buy music books and a mouthpiece for an instrument that had somehow "fallen into" his hands. He seemed to think it was all right to steal from school. The school had a lot. If they gave things to him, fine, if not, and he had to steal it, that was okay too.

Willie still wasn't a criminal. He was just a dirt-poor kid making it in his own way, and not very successfully.

Henry also arranged for Mrs. Smith to visit our school. Mrs. Smith had come to the city from the South in the forties and married her husband a few years later. They had lived together for a few years until he was arrested for selling narcotics. He spent five years in prison, came home on probation, violated his probation the same year, and was sent back to prison.

With her mouth curled into a hint of a snarl and in a voice full of the hatred and contempt she felt for her husband, Mrs. Smith told Henry during her visit to us, "The next time he's out, he ain't gettin his butt inside my door."

When Henry asked her why she had refused to allow Willie to come home from Youth House, she said because Willie had made sexual advances to one of his sisters. One of the girls had awakened at night and found him in her bedroom with his hand on her cover. She had cried out and Willie had run out. "If I was to let Willie come back, there's no telling what he might do," she insisted. When Henry said that Willie had denied approaching her daughter, she replied she couldn't believe anything Willie said.

When Henry tried to convince Mrs. Smith to let Willie come home, she refused. Finally she said she would let him stay home if she had to, but she needed our help because she didn't know how to manage him. She gave her permission so unwillingly that Henry wasn't sure he could count on it.

Henry also visited Mrs. Smith and two of her daughters in their home. Their apartment and their building, which was in an extremely run-down slum section, reeked of poverty, deprivation, and dead rats. Mrs. Smith's favoritism toward her daughters was obvious. She and each of the girls had their own rooms, small, dirty, and dilapidated, but still their own. Willie slept in the living room on an old broken couch behind a curtain. There was another room, an empty room that had been used by the oldest daughter, which Willie couldn't use just because the daughter hadn't yet removed all of her clothes and belongings.

The other student Henry visited was Don Russo. Don was a fifteen-year-old Caucasian youngster who was awaiting placement in a state training school when we accepted him. He looked like every other runaway teen-ager who walked MacDougal, Bleecker and the other Village streets trying to find the action, except he seemed a little wilder, a little more explosive, and a lot older than his real age. His long hair, heavy mutton-chop sideburns, and clothes conformed to the Village scene. But the frantic look in his eyes, the apelike way he swung his long arms at his sides, hunched over his wide shoulders, and stuck out his angular chin, and above all the explosiveness in his tense tall body set him off from the rest. Despite the peace buttons and the flowers, Don could never pass for a flower child.

According to Don's probation report, his mother, Mrs. Russo, who was Jewish, had quit high school in order to marry her first husband who was Catholic. They had four children including Don. Her husband drank heavily and stayed away from home for long periods of time. They were divorced after a two-year separation during which the family was supported by Welfare. A year later she married her present husband who adopted the four children. Mrs. Russo told Don's probation officer that her son's problems were caused by a poor relationship with his stepfather who, she thought, was too strict with Don and set a curfew that was too early for him. She also said that she felt that Don would disobey any curfew and that he was not entitled to any liberties because he was not ready to accept any responsibilities.

Mrs. Russo told the probation officer that Don had been promoted to tenth grade in school in September but was sent back to the ninth grade because he truanted too much. She claimed that Don was extremely intelligent but just wouldn't go to school. He ran away from home, used drugs, and spent most of the time staying with addict friends in Greenwich Village. She asked the judge to set a curfew and provide the discipline her husband could not. She wanted Don to remain at home. If he ran away again, she said, then she might want to place him.

When he was interviewed, Mr. Russo promised to do anything to help Don, even leave the house temporarily. However he felt that Don had never adjusted to his marriage to Don's mother. Like his wife, Mr. Russo wanted the court to get tough with Don and make him listen to them.

During his interviews with his probation officer, Don said he liked his friends in the Village because they didn't make demands on him. They were older than he was and had dropped out of college. They worked at odd jobs one or two days a week just to make food money. When Don went to the Village he slept on benches or stayed at their apartments. They would spend their time "rapping" about philosophy and listening to music in incense-filled rooms or "messing" with the girls in the neighborhood. He said he felt that he was doing the right thing and didn't care what his parents thought about him. He wanted to go to live in Greenwich Village with his friends because that was the only place he could go and not be bothered.

After his investigation, the probation officer recommended that Don be placed on probation. The court agreed. A short while later, Don disappeared for ten days after he had been beaten by his stepfather. When he returned, his parents brought him back to court. The judge sentenced him to a state training school, but we accepted him in our school instead.

We were able to get Don released from Youth House so that he and his mother could visit the school and meet with Henry and Herb. Mrs. Russo was a young, seductive, "on-the-make-looking" housewife. During the interview, she and Don sat together holding hands, giggling, nudging each other with their elbows, sending private signals to each other, behaving more like teen-agers going steady than mother and son.

Mrs. Russo apparently felt left out. She asked Henry if she could call the school and talk to him about her son. Henry asked her if she was jealous and she replied, "Yeah, why can't I be treated nicely too?" Henry told her that he would see her as often as she wanted to see him and she could call the school, but she wouldn't really be a part of the school and she would have no power over what happened to Don in our program. Yet it was clear to us that it would be no easy task to break up the romance between the two of them or to substitute our influence for her tremendous influence over Don. We guessed it was an inconsistent influence from the way she acted in the interview—alternating between attempting to dominate Don totally and yielding to him helplessly as if he were beyond her control —first saying she was pleased that he would be coming to our school, then saying she felt that our program wasn't tough enough.

Don ran away from home the next day and Mr. Russo decided to send him back to court. Henry telephoned Mr. Russo to convince him to change his mind. Mr. Russo flew into a rage that Henry was interfering. He told Henry that he didn't care what happened to Don. He was too angry to think about it. He didn't want to have to "spend even one minute worrying about the kid." After a few minutes, he said he might be able to talk about it later and Henry arranged to visit their home that evening.

By the time Henry arrived, Mr. Russo had calmed down quite a bit. He spoke about his great efforts to have a better relationship with his adopted son, and how disappointed he felt when their relationship worsened. He complained that his wife consistently took Don's side when arguments developed between the two of them. Mrs. Russo disagreed and assumed an air of innocence, which angered Mr. Russo even more than her relationship with her son. After a while they dropped the pretense that they couldn't get in touch with Don, and agreed to ask him to return home and meet with us. We were on our way to gaining our fifth student.

FOOLPROOF PLAN

With a group of students chosen and the school just about ready to reopen, we had one final task to complete—scheduling the first week.

Starting time for school was set for ten. Morning coffee, milk, and cake would be served until ten twenty when the first class would start. Latecomers could have a snack when they arrived. Lunch would be at twelve thirty. The day would officially end at three. Since many of the boys would want to stay after three, we would keep the school open until four.

The last thing we had to do was to plan the first few days of school. Most of us would be working part-time. Henry and Herb, the two clinicians, were part-time. Henry would be working three and a half days and one evening. The remainder of Henry's time was taken up by his work in a nearby consultation center. Herb would also be working three and a half days a week. The rest of his time was devoted to his duties as director of the training program for teachers of emotionally disturbed students at Hofstra University. Henry and Herb would arrange their schedules so at least one of them would be present each day. Bill and Norm, our two artist-teachers, would also be part-time. Marilyn, Herb's wife, would be our music teacher, would come in a day and a half on the days that Norm was out. Connie, our English teacher, and Phyllis, our secretary, were both full-time. We had still not hired a social studies teacher because we could not all agree on anyone.

We decided to have a short school week Monday, Wednesday, Thursday, and a short day, ten to two during the first week of school. There would be no scheduled periods. The boys would be able to float from room to room and staff to staff without committing themselves to any program right away. By keeping the program unstructured at the outset, we hoped to determine just how much the boys could tolerate and thereby help them avoid program commitments which they might not be ready for.

We and the boys would have coffee in a small area so we would all be close together. We would leave a small table off in the corner where someone could retreat if he wanted to. Lunch would be served family style, by pushing a few tables together and eating in one area. The key concept was intimacy. We wanted to encourage an intimacy between us and the students through the closeness of the physical situation in which we would break bread together. Again, provisions would be made for anyone who preferred to eat by himself.

SI DIOS QUIERE

It was Friday afternoon. The planning time had come to an end. We were all eager to get started. We had the weekend to wait out, then the school would open. *Si Dios quiere.*

2 Honeymoon

ON THEIR BEST BEHAVIOR

The first day was a quiet one. Harold, Willie, and Don arrived on time. Manuel was late. Stanley came after lunch to talk about the draft. During the warm-up the boys ate little and said even less. The air was tense, like two people on a blind date with nothing to say at the start. Actually the boys didn't seem to mind it as much as we did. We kept trying to start conversations—unsuccessfully—but the whole scene was strained.

Around ten thirty we went into the gym.

The morning dragged on. Herb spoke to Willie out in the hall about what he wanted to do in the school. Willie mumbled that he wasn't too interested in regular school work. Later Henry asked him about his home life. Willie complained about his sisters and his mother. Henry thought he was telling him what he figured "headshrinkers" wanted to hear.

Don took pretty much the same approach with Henry. He said he was happy to be in the school and promised to work hard in class. Henry tried to get Don to talk about his

40

parents, but Don wouldn't bite. All he would say was that things were better, at least for the moment.

Herb got the same story from Don. The school was great. He wanted a full academic program—no shop because he didn't want to waste his time there. Herb smiled to himself thinking, "Sure, Don, sure," then advised Don to try different classes before making up his mind.

Manuel came late. He looked just as Henry had described him: terrified, eyes down, chest in, chin on his chest. His parents had come with him to help him find the school. Henry thanked them for coming, then politely ushered them out.

Manuel nervously asked what he should do. He wanted to be told what to do; he wanted structure. We hadn't planned the day that way, but Manuel needed it. So Henry suggested that Herb give him a program for the day.

Herb asked Manuel what he had liked in school. Speaking in a whisper, with his eyes down toward the floor, Manuel said he liked social studies and shop and he especially wanted to learn how to read. Herb assigned him to a period with Norm in the general shop, a period with Bill in the art studio, and separate periods with Connie for reading and social studies. That would provide the additional structure Manuel required.

A BIT OF REALITY
It was almost time for lunch. The boys had been acting like four angels, rather than four delinquents on their way to training schools. Leave it to Harold to bring in reality. Just when we were about to leave the gym for lunch, Harold grabbed the fire extinguisher that was hanging lonely on the wall, tilted it, and let it spray around for a while, as Herb and Norm looked at him with anger in their eyes. After Harold had covered the floor with goo, he stopped, smiled,

replaced the fire extinguisher, and started to sprinkle the goo with the newspaper he had begun to shred. Herb told him to stop. Harold lunged at Herb, grabbing, pushing, and punching—playfully, but annoyingly. The three new boys watched silently. Norm said, "Let's go eat." Norm, Bill, and the three boys left, leaving Herb and Harold alone.

"Why da the thkool haf ta be different?" Harold asked.

"What do you mean?"

"It were better lath year when there were juth a few thudent."

"But we had more students last year."

"Yeah but it were different."

[Harold was jealous of the new boys. He was trying to get our attention in the way he used to get it at home. We would have to accept a lot of grabbing, leaning, and bear-hugging from him until he was able to express his affection in less physical and less provocatively attention-seeking ways.]

PIG'S FOOD

When we went down to lunch, Manuel looked at the food and said it was disgusting pig's food. We offered to buy some other food from one of the nearby restaurants for him, but Manuel wouldn't eat anything at all. Don gobbled down as much food as he possibly could. Harold ate some and played with the rest, making comments about how ugly it looked. Willie took a big plate of food like he hadn't eaten in days, but left most of it untouched. Just before lunch was over, Harold poured milk and soda over the leftover food and plates on the table, leaving a sickening mess.

After lunch Norm and Bill organized a basketball game with Willie and Harold. Connie played Ping-Pong with

Manuel, and Don sat on the sidelines. Herb watched until Stanley arrived.

IBM COMPUTERS?

Stanley wanted to talk about the draft again. So Herb reminded him of the things we had done to help him stay out of the army. Stanley was beginning to believe Herb. What about the Institute, Herb asked. Yeah, Stanley answered. Herb described the various training programs the Institute offered. Stanley didn't like any of them except for "IBM computers." IBM computers? Herb hadn't said computers. He had said IBM key punching.

Stanley was building it up in his own mind. Computers sounded much more impressive than key punching. Herb knew Stanley wasn't even eligible for key punch training without his high school diploma. "Still," he thought to himself, "if Stanley only wants IBM, let him think he can have it, at least until he gives himself a chance to see the other programs. But not computers, complicated IBM machines but not computers."

"For computers," Herb said to him, "you need more math. And remember, you just can't pick out what you want. They run their own program. They'll have to agree with you."

It was just about two o'clock—time to leave. It had been an unrealistically easy day. No fights, no emergencies, no one high on drugs . . . but no real communication.

Wednesday, December 14

STILL ON THEIR BEST BEHAVIOR

The next day Manuel still wouldn't eat anything. Even after we offered to buy him some other kind of cake or a soda during warm-up he refused, saying, "You don need to ax me to buy sonething else. I neva eat breckfis. It jus make me throw up. My mother, she tries ta make me drink milk but I never do."

And the same thing happened at lunch. But it wasn't the food. Henry had gone out early and brought some cold cuts and sandwiches which would have pleased anyone, or almost anyone. However Manuel wouldn't eat anything.

"I don like this stuff here or cheese," he told us. "The meat's funny-looking."

"What kinds of meat do you like?" Connie asked.

"I only eat roas beef. Thas all I eat home. I don eat ugly meat."

Connie wondered whether we would have to buy roast beef if we wanted Manuel to eat lunch. Henry felt certain we would.

After lunch Herb asked Manuel to read for him. As he tried to read, Manuel substituted "b," "d," and "p." Guessing at words he didn't know, using the first letter, the shape, and length of the word as clues, he didn't seem to be concerned about whether his guesses were right. He was satisfied to give any answer just to get through. When Herb asked Manuel to look at the letter he had misread, he was unable to correct himself. He became even more anxious and disabled whenever he was encouraged to reread a word or to sound it out before guessing at it.

Manuel did better in shop where he spent a lot of time just shooting the breeze with Norm, sometimes in English, sometimes in Spanish. When Norm told Manuel that he spoke English much better than Norm spoke Spanish, Manuel smiled proudly but quietly, pleased that he could feel superior to someone about something.

Before he left, Manuel had his first class with Connie. He appeared to know very little about the structure of the world. He didn't know north, south, east, and west, or the difference between countries and continents. He couldn't believe how small Great Britain was because it was such a "strong" country, and he wanted to know why the North and South Poles didn't float away. Even after Connie explained that they were part of the earth, Manuel still couldn't believe that they wouldn't float away.

Don and Willie had an uneventful day. They had their first biology class with Norm and Harold, and spent most of their time in Bill's studio playing with the potter's wheel while they listened to rock and roll. Henry talked to them about allowances, then they left school.

Harold did well in biology, English, and algebra. However outside of class he continued his attention/affection-seeking behavior by setting small fires in ashtrays and grabbing and punching us. Before Harold left, Henry talked to him about his allowance. Harold's mother gave him six dollars a week, but she often forgot to give him the money or made him beg for it when she was angry. So Harold was never sure whether he would get the money or not. We would have given a new boy in his situation more than one dollar. However, Harold wasn't new. Finally, after two years, he was aware that he had not stood up at home for his rights as a person. We wanted to encourage and support his attempts to insist on them. So we decided to give him only one dollar to help him obtain the rest from home.

Although Harold accepted the one-dollar allowance, he wasn't satisfied with it. He followed Henry around during the afternoon asking him for money for clothes, food, and the movies. Before he left, Harold summed up his feelings about the allowance when he told Henry, "If I didn't like you tho much, I could kill you."

Thursday, December 15

CHILDHOOD DAYS IN PUERTO RICO

It was the third day of school. The boys began to come out of their shells a little, so our dictation became a little more interesting.

Manuel's class with Connie was especially revealing. They began by reviewing some of the countries Manuel had identified earlier. Then Connie asked him to tell her about Puerto Rico.

"I use ta live in P.R. till I was three," Manuel told her. "With my granma and her son. But he wasn no uncle a mine cause he wasn her real son. He jus live with her since he was a boy when his ol lady died. So he came ta live up in a mountains with my granma when they kill his folks. My brother he live with people in another mountain. An my folks live in another village. We neva see each other when I'm small. But my brother's bigger than me cause he's older."

Connie couldn't follow Manuel's train of thought. Never having worked with a disturbed student like Manuel before, she had no reason to assume that his thinking was disturbed. She assumed he had a language problem.

"I use ta catch lobster in P.R. in a ocean," Manuel continued.

Connie wondered how a three-year-old could catch lobsters but she didn't ask.

"Man, were they ugly with claws an eyes that stuck out on sticks fron their head. I had a cow for a pet an a chicken. They use ta run aroun in a town all over. No one could tell who they belong ta. They were stupid those people. They neva put a tag on a chicken so they could tell who own it. They jus start ta do that when I left P.R."

Connie was becoming less certain that Manuel had diffi-culty expressing himself. Then, as Manuel continued talking, she realized it was more than just a language problem. He loved the mountains, he told her. When he lived in Puerto Rico his uncle had taken him into the mountains at night and left him there. His uncle said that he would be back. However, when he didn't come back, Manuel found a cow which led him down through the mountains. It was the scar-iest thing that had ever happened to him. He wouldn't go back into those mountains at dark even if somebody paid him. Old people who didn't have any money hung them-selves from branches in the mountains. He used to go with his uncle to cut the people down.

That didn't make sense to Connie.

"Weren't you too small to cut them down from the branches?" she asked.

"No! The boy who live with my granma make me cline the tree and cut the string they hung on," Manuel answered, contorting his face into a look of fear. "Lo's a people kill thenself in P.R. They haf ugly face, ugly face. I never forget the ugly face."

Connie knew Manuel couldn't have climbed up the trees, yet from his face it all seemed true. She tried to convince herself that he really didn't believe it. But she had to admit to herself that he did.

Manuel changed the topic, to her relief.

"I like P.R. more than New York," he told her. "Man, when I firs got here I froze ta deat. Man, P.R. was a good place. I din go ta school there. They try ta make me go ta school . . ."

Connie was tempted to ask him why since he was too young, but she didn't. She was already as uncomfortable as she wanted to be.

"But I din. I knew I woul'n like it. New York schools a

cheap. I hate school. I play hookey—sonetine for a month."

Then, perhaps nervous about what he had told Connie, Manuel added he liked our school and didn't think he would play hookey, at least not very often.

"HIGH" TALK

Don had played good boy for two days. It was time for him to begin to reveal himself. It happened in the art studio where he and Willie were listening to the radio as Willie was working.

"Man, it's a groove. I'm still high. The music's way-out when you're high," he told Willie.

Willie nodded in agreement.

"I smoked three joints last night."

"Yeah? Where?"

"Home—alone—I don't go for crowds. That's the way you get into trouble with the cops."

Bill, who was standing nearby, felt uneasy because he didn't know how to react to the conversation. He decided to keep quiet and moved closer. The conversation continued as the boys talked about different kinds of highs. Don said he sniffed glue.

"Not me—that stuff can mess you up inside. It'll eat up your brain," Willie told him as he looked at Bill for confirmation. Bill nodded his agreement. It was two against one. Bill and Willie against Don. Don joined them. Pot and pills were one thing he said, shooting heroin, that was another. Willie agreed. So did Bill, but he knew Don was lying for his benefit.

OLD-TIMERS

As we became more involved with the new boys, Harold became more jealous and unhappy about the attention they were receiving from us, and he continued his attempts to reassure himself that we still cared for him. He made himself at home in Henry's office by transferring his belongings from his locker to Henry's desk. Then he told him about his difficulties at home, his loneliness, and his lack of success with girls. When sadness overcame him, he shook himself out of it by littering the office with newspaper that he had shredded into confetti. Later, when Bill tried to console him, he told Bill to leave him alone or else. He put his hands around Bill's throat and squeezed.

"Control yourself," Bill told himself. "Don't let Harold know you're angry. Don't give him what he wants. Maybe he'll stop." Then, in as calm a voice as he could maintain, Bill managed to force out, "I'm not leaving," through the hands Harold had clenched around his throat. Harold picked up a chair and held it threateningly over Bill's head. Again Bill maintained his cool. Harold shook the chair menacingly as if he were about to bring it down on Bill's head. Still Bill maintained his calm front. Harold wanted another reaction, something like the irritated look Connie gave him or the angry face Norm and Herb gave him. When he realized that he could not shake Bill up, when Bill showed no sign of fear, Harold tossed the chair over the desk, walked out, and joined Manuel in Marilyn's music room.

The only sour note during the day was the call we received from the Vocational Institute about Stanley.

The intake worker hinted that we might spare Stanley some disappointment if we withdrew the referral because she doubted he would be accepted. She was concerned about Stanley's problems and skeptical about the progress we said he had made in our school. We assured her that we were convinced Stanley could make it in their program. We listed the various obstacles Stanley had overcome, which led us to think that he was ready, and implied that we wouldn't withdraw the referral. Finally she agreed to an intake interview. Stanley and Herb would go to her office together. First she would interview Stanley privately, then Herb would sit in with the two of them.

PLANS

Before we left, we discussed our plans for the following week and the Christmas vacation. We decided to have another three-day week before the vacation, a recreational trip during the vacation, one more three-day week following the vacation, and then a regular five-day school week to include four days of classes. The fifth day would consist of unscheduled activities in the school during the morning and an afternoon trip or a full day-trip.

We also set up a definite schedule for each boy. Since we had not found someone we all wanted to hire for the social studies position, we didn't have social studies courses except for Connie's work with Manuel. Harold was scheduled for biology, algebra with Bill, English with Connie, and art with Bill. Don would have biology, English, art, and shop. Manuel was assigned to Connie for two periods of English and social studies, and one period of art and shop. Willie's program consisted of biology, two periods of shop with Norm, and one period of art with Bill. He, Don, and Harold were also scheduled for music with Marilyn.

Monday, December 19, through Friday, December 23

PRODUCTIVE CLASSES

The first week of scheduled classes went better than expected. Don, Willie, and Harold went regularly to biology, and before the end of the week Norm knew the kinds of difficulty he would have with each of them. Norm had started discussing one-celled animals, hoping to move rapidly into

a course in human biology. Don, however, was already involved in human biology. He told everyone that a parame-
cium reminded him of a "hairy twitching twat" and the
amoeba was "cool" because it could "blow his own
pseudopod." Harold followed Norm's lectures closely but
pressured him to write more on the blackboard and talk less
because it was difficult to take notes. Willie, on the other
hand, took too many notes, almost burying his head and his
mind in his notebook in order to avoid the challenge and
frustration of learning. Getting something down on paper
was Willie's goal. Whether he understood it or not wasn't
important. He was acting like a student and that was what
counted.

Norm was on to the boys. He was tempted to do
something about them, especially Don who broke up the
class with his remarks. However, Norm kept quiet because
he knew it was more important for us to learn about the
boys than for them to learn about biology.

The rest of the day Norm's room was used as the shop.
That suited Willie who turned out to be an excellent wood-
worker. He was busy working on a bookcase, while Don,
who had wanted to make a tomahawk, was making a
"throwing hammer." Harold didn't do much in shop. He
wandered in from time to time to smear paint and rap with
Norm. Manuel kept busy making monoprints and glass col-
lages, scowling and talking angrily to himself in Spanish. Or
so Norm thought, until he made a point of listening to what
Manuel was saying. Then he discovered that Manuel wasn't
speaking Spanish or English, but nonsense.

Bill's art studio was also open most of the day. Manuel
spent most of his time in the studio painting . . . concentrating on his work, not really talking to, or even noticing
the other boys. Toward the end of the week he began
painting a series of *fincas,* Puerto Rican farmhouses, on a

mountain with smoke coming from their chimneys and surrounded by plants and flowers. It reminded Bill of the peaceful life in Puerto Rico Manuel had been telling Connie about. Harold mushed clay, played with the new potter's wheel, and sang along with the radio, switching from station to station to find a song he liked without considering whether anyone else was listening. Willie and Don "rapped" about "highs."

The music program was popular. Willie spent most of his free time practicing "Yesterday," a Beatle song Marilyn had taught him to play on the piano. Don took music lessons but had no interest in practicing. He had a natural feel for the guitar, he told Marilyn. He already had a rock and roll group. He only wanted to pick up some more chords. He was talented, Marilyn observed, but as undisciplined a musician as he was a student. Harold and even Manuel took music lessons. Harold practiced singing along with the radio, but Manuel just flirted with the piano.

The rec room wasn't as busy as we expected, perhaps because the boys were going to all of their classes. Norm and Bill played basketball with Harold and Willie. Willie played delicately, as if he was afraid that he might have to fight if he bumped into someone. Harold, making up for Willie, barreled into everyone. Bill started a tumbling and exercise group in order to get Manuel and Don involved in gym. Although it tempted Don and Manuel into partial participation, they both preferred playing Ping-Pong with Connie.

PRETTY ROUTINE STUFF

Outside of class the boys kept to themselves. Willie spent almost all of his time in the shop and music room. Even Harold toned down his provocative behavior. Don was an exception. During the week he became involved with Henry much faster than we expected. The involvement began when he told Henry that he had stayed out all night during the weekend. As soon as Henry picked him up on it, he changed his mind.

"No, man, I was just jiving. I was home."

Henry remembered the other times Don had run away from home. He told Don he couldn't just let it drop. Don insisted he hadn't done anything wrong. He rejected society's norms, he claimed. He was liberating himself from "conventional middle-class morality," just like his friends in the Village. He was into other things, Buddhism, mysticism, self-exploration. He was trying to find his real self and the true pleasure and meaning of life.

[Don's spiel was familiar. Straight T. Leary head-culture talk, but in Don's case it was clearly rationalization.]

As the week progressed, Don sought Henry out to talk about Buddhism and his self-induced trances, during which, he claimed, he could conquer any problem. He was especially interested in Nietzsche's concept of the superman (not that he had ever read it). He told Henry that Hitler must have been a "pretty smart guy" if he could conquer so much territory and kill so many people before he was finally defeated, and he kiddingly spoke of what it would be like if Eichmann were the President of the United States. As Don spoke, Henry could sense his tremendous concern about his partial Jewishness and a thinly veiled anti-Semitism which Don dared not voice.

Momentarily Henry's thoughts wandered back to his own childhood in Germany. He remembered that men like Eichmann had wiped out his family. Then he thought about Don whose anti-Semitism seemed pathetic. Originally Don had chosen his mother's religion. He had even pressured his mother and stepfather to allow him to study for his bar mitzvah. Their refusal had devastated him. "Perhaps,"

Henry thought, "Don believed it was his stepfather who objected. Perhaps Don felt that he and his mother had something in common that Mr. Russo didn't share. . . . They were both Jewish. If Don denied his own Jewishness, he could place distance between himself and his mother and feel less sexually interested in her."

Henry changed the topic of the conversation to Don's situation at home. Don spoke in vague terms about how he got along much better with his mother than his stepfather. That was the opening Henry had been waiting for.

"You and your mother really swing close," he commented, hoping to get Don to talk about his interest in his mother.

"Yeah!" Don answered, trying to be cool, yet obviously involved. "You wanna make it with my mother?"

"You know what I mean, Don. . . . You and your mother playing tiddlywinks."

Don gave Henry a sheepish smile which seemed to Henry to imply, "I know what you mean. But that's something no one talks about and I better not either."

From that point on "tiddlywinks" became Don and Henry's code word for Don's sexual interest in his mother.

Wednesday, December 28

A CHRISTMAS PRESENT

During the Christmas vacation we acquired another student, Carlos Rivera, who was in Youth House waiting to be sent to a state training school. Carlos was an extremely short sixteen-year-old Puerto Rican who looked more like fourteen. He was called "Chino" because of his protruding buckteeth and barely opened, squinted, slightly crossed weak eyes which were dwarfed by his large horn-rimmed glasses. But he had the kind of appealing quality that made you disregard his unappetizing appearance when you got to know him.

When Henry visited him in Youth House, Carlos seemed frightened but wouldn't admit it, even to himself. Henry told him about the school, then asked him if he wanted to attend. Carlos claimed he didn't need us because he wasn't in any real trouble. There was no reason why he couldn't go to the school in his neighborhood, he insisted. Henry thought Carlos might want to attend once he got over his initial defensiveness. So he made arrangements to have Carlos released to visit the school after the Christmas vacation.

Henry also visited Carlos's parents in their apartment. When he arrived, only their daughter was home. She told Henry that Carlos was the family problem. When Mr. Rivera arrived, he said the same thing, using his daughter as an interpreter. He told Henry that his wife was a very sick woman. She worried so much about Carlos. If only Carlos would stop being such a bad boy his wife wouldn't be so sick. Later, when Mrs. Rivera arrived, Henry asked her about her health, but Mr. Rivera interrupted him by offering to show him the rest of the apartment. He led, Henry followed, Mrs. Rivera wasn't too far behind. As soon as she dropped back far enough so she couldn't hear them, Mr. Rivera whispered quickly, "Wife— cancer." Then, when they returned to the living room, he continued to make sure that they discussed his son's "badness" rather than his wife's illness. Henry wondered whether Mr. Rivera was trying to keep the fact that his wife had cancer from her and the other members of the family. Perhaps, Henry thought, one of the ways of keeping her from learning that she had cancer was to blame her illness on Carlos.

When we received Carlos's probation report, we learned

that he had been in court four times for such things as drunkenness, delinquent behavior in subways, possession of a zip gun during a gang fight, extorting money from younger children, shoplifting from stores, beating up his sister, and threatening to kill his family. Carlos had been enrolled in a special school for disruptive students, but he was truanting regularly. According to the results of the intelligence test he took in Youth House, Carlos was slightly retarded. He couldn't spell simple three-letter words at first-grade level, and he only recognized a few letters of the alphabet.

Tuesday, January 3

FRUSTRATION

Since the boys were not scheduled to return from Christmas vacation until Wednesday, we had Tuesday to ourselves to talk about the students and the program. Connie wanted to talk about Harold.

"Harold refuses to use his class time productively," she told us. "He seldom spends as much as twenty minutes of any period working."

"What does he do instead?" we asked her.

"He claims that he can't concentrate. He will walk out of the room and spend five, ten, or even fifteen minutes in the bathroom or recreation room until *he* decides to return."

Connie believed that Harold was unwilling to conform when he was actually unable to do so. She was also trying to hide her frustration and anger from us and perhaps from herself, but we could sense it in her voice. Although she wouldn't admit it to herself, the waiting for Harold was particularly annoying to her. She was acting as if Harold was trying to provoke her by staying out of class when he was really trying to avoid tension. We advised her not to take his behavior personally, if possible, and to find something else to do while he was out of the room.

DON SPLITS

Henry told us that the Russos were coming to see him around eleven o'clock. Mrs. Russo had called him Sunday because she hadn't seen or heard from Don for five days. Why had Don run away, we asked each other. Did it have something to do with us? His conversation about sex, pills, pot, and Zen Buddhism was increasing rapidly. Maybe he was opening up too fast? Maybe we weren't handling him right? Were we putting him down? Henry and Herb asked if some of us, especially Norm, were telling Don indirectly that he was just a boy trying to play big man. Norm said he wasn't cutting Don. He was supporting him. Don was worried about a lot of things, especially sex, especially about being "blown" by some women in the Village. Sometimes he even imagined women in the subways wanted to "blow" him. He didn't know what to do. He wanted to try it, he told Norm, but he was afraid it was perverted. He asked Norm about it. Norm explained that different kinds of sex weren't good or bad, only different. It was up to the people concerned. Norm thought that his answers were supportive, especially for a fifteen-year-old kid who was confused about a lot of things, who messed around mostly with women his mother's age, who talked about Oedipal complexes as if he knew where he was at with his mother.

Maybe we weren't confronting Don. Maybe he was spilling his guts too fast. Was Henry letting Don spew out all his weird fantasies too rapidly? Wasn't Don moving too fast? Was he anxious about all the ugly stuff coming out of his mouth? Yes, he was, Henry agreed. However Henry wasn't encouraging Don. Don was doing it by himself.

We didn't know why Don had taken off, so we weren't sure what to do. Still, we thought it would be better not to confront him about his "big man" behavior and to discourage him from spilling his guts if possible.

Around eleven, two long-haired hippie-looking friends of Don's came to the school asking for him.

"Don isn't here," Herb answered. "He ran away the other day. Where is he?"

"We ain't seen him. We figured he'd be here. He told us to come down today to transfer to this here school."

"When was the last time you saw him?"

"Friday night, he was going to a party in the Village."

"Are you sure you haven't seen him since then?"

"Yeah."

"How come you showed up today, coincidence?"

"Yeah."

"How do you know Don?"

"We're in the same group."

"What do you do?"

"I play drums and he plays bass."

"Listen, you know where he is. He must have sent you here for a reason. But you can come up for a while and look around." So Herb showed them around. As they were leaving, Mr. and Mrs. Russo walked through the door. Mr. Russo stared at the boys contemptuously and demanded: "What the hell are you bums doing here? Did Don send you?"

"No, we were just looking for him," they answered.

"If you see him, tell him to get the hell home."

They went upstairs to Henry's office and met Norm who was fixing the door. Mrs. Russo smiled at him.

"You must be Normie baby," she said, fluttering her eyelashes.

Norm felt embarrassed; although the kids called him "Normie baby," it didn't seem right to him for her to say it.

Mr. Russo also felt uncomfortable. Rocking from leg to leg and obviously feeling put down by the way his wife had greeted Norm, he mumbled a hello. After a silent pause, during which Norm wondered how he might set Mr. Russo at ease, Henry walked in and took over.

The Russos told Henry that they were very concerned about Don, not only because he hadn't contacted them but because he hadn't contacted his girl friend Lisa either. They couldn't think of any reason why Don ran away. Things weren't any better or any worse or any different from the way they had been. Henry got no clues from them. After they had talked a while they all promised to keep each other informed and to work together. Then the Russos left.

ILLITERATE VIRGIN

Meanwhile Herb and Connie were having a supervisory session. As Connie described her work with Manuel, Herb felt she found it difficult to view Manuel objectively. Connie still wouldn't admit to herself that Manuel believed the stories he had told her about Puerto Rico.

"But he does so well in his school work," she protested when Herb described the ways in which Manuel's thinking was distorted.

"Look closely and you'll see where he isn't doing as well as you think," Herb replied.

Herb also thought that Connie was overly optimistic about Manuel's reading ability. Although Connie assumed that Manuel could recognize the consonant blends and vowel combinations he read in the words Connie gave him, Herb wasn't convinced. He told her to see whether Manuel could sound out the consonant blends, suffixes, prefixes, and vowel combinations that appeared in the words which he had been studying without using the rest of the word as a clue.

When Connie mentioned in passing that Manuel was

very good-looking and would probably be quite a lover when he grew older, with his creamy skin, bedroom eyes, long eyelashes, and gentle manner, Herb replied that we couldn't be sure that he wasn't already a lover. Connie said she was certain that Manuel was a virgin because he was so shy and only fourteen. Herb disagreed. He wasn't so ready to assume that Manuel was as shy outside of school as he was with us. Herb had grown up only a few blocks from where Manuel lived. Connie was from the Midwest.

DAREDEVIL DELINQUENT

After lunch Henry and Herb had an initial intake interview with another prospective student, Larry Keating, and his mother. Henry and Herb had somewhat different impressions of him. To Henry, Larry seemed like a good-looking, fairly tall, physically mature and athletic fifteen-year-old white teen-ager. Herb thought he was chubby, long-haired, and somewhat effeminate. Larry's mother, they agreed, was an obese, sloppy-looking middle-aged woman who smiled an inappropriate silly grin and complained in a singsong voice.

"I hope you can help this boy," she said. "He is so much trouble. I try to talk to him, but he won't listen. He stays out late at night drinking and getting drunk. He invites boys up to the apartment for drinking parties when he knows the building police told them not to come into the building. He won't go to school and he climbs onto the roofs of elevators and lets them go up to the top floor. I don't see how anyone can help this boy. He won't come to this school, will he? I've tried everything, he just won't listen."

Larry disagreed.

"She's always complaining about me and my friends," he said, defending himself. "I'm not a baby any more."

Mrs. Keating didn't appreciate that. "Oh Larry, how

could you say that in front of them?" she asked. "You know that's not true."

As the interview progressed, the conflict and tension between Larry and his mother increased. She nagged him constantly and he resisted by going in the opposite direction, whatever it happened to be. As Mrs. Keating spoke about Larry, Henry and Herb realized that he had been involved in some pretty unusual behavior even for our kids. Besides riding on the roofs of elevators, he did gymnastics on fire escapes, walked between roofs on a wooden plank, and swung from buildings by means of grappling hooks and ropes.

At the end of the interview, Larry agreed to try our school. However, he and his mother both implied that he might not be able to come because of his truancy and "weak will."

According to his probation report, Larry was first arrested when he was thirteen, almost two years before. While he was at home awaiting a hearing, his father, who was still alive at the time, called the police and had him placed in Youth House because he had threatened to kill his mother and his maternal grandmother. At the hearing, Mrs. Keating asked the court to place Larry in an institution because he came home drunk, called her "a prostitute and a fucking whore," threatened to kill her, and had wild drinking parties, during which he often locked her and her husband out of their apartment. He was paroled pending "a more complete investigation" of his case.

A few weeks later Mrs. Keating asked the court to return Larry to Youth House because he had gotten worse; because of him she was about to be evicted from her new apartment in the housing development. The court yielded to her pressure.

After a few more weeks, Mrs. Keating went to court to say she thought that Larry's stay in Youth House had taught him a lesson and she wanted him home. Larry's parole officer believed Larry's earlier threats about what he would do if the court forced him to stay home and he wanted Larry to remain in Youth House until his hearing. However, Larry was paroled once again in September, pending his investigation. A week and a half later Larry broke his hip when he fell from a tree while he was performing for some friends. So, when he and his mother reported to his parole officer for their regular appointment, Larry was sporting a cast. Mrs. Keating wanted Larry to stay home because his behavior had improved. Larry wanted out of the house so he claimed he was only temporarily out of commission because of his cast. In the fall, after he had enrolled in a Catholic school, started therapy in a private agency, and asked for another chance, the judge placed him on probation instead of sending him to a training school.

Larry made a successful adjustment in Catholic school during the fall, despite the death of his father which he seemed to take surprisingly well. However, he was getting high on pills regularly. At the end of January he was found unconscious in the street from an overdose of pills and had to have his stomach pumped.

During the spring, Mrs. Keating changed her mind again. She complained that Larry did as he pleased at home, truanted, and failed all of his subjects in school. As a result, Larry was returned to Youth House where he was beaten and raped by a group of black youngsters because he had insulted their Muslim religion. In order to avoid further problems in Youth House, Larry was released prematurely into his mother's custody.

Larry was referred to four residential treatment centers during the summer and early fall but rejected by all of them. While he was waiting to be sent to a training school, Larry developed a close relationship with a young nurse who had taken care of him while he had been hospitalized for his hip injury. She and her mother asked the court to allow them to care for Larry as his foster family. However, Mrs. Keating told the judge that she would rather see him institutionalized than living with them.

Larry was hospitalized again around Thanksgiving after he had cracked up a speeding car. In January he was still truanting, still failing in school, still having difficulty at home, and still awaiting placement in a state training school. He was also still alive and able to come to our school instead.

OVERDUE INTERVIEW

After the Keatings left, Herb took Stanley to the Vocational Institute for his overdue intake interview. Stanley went in first to find out he wasn't eligible for IBM training. Herb joined him about twenty minutes later to do what he could to help Stanley accept the facts. However Stanley wasn't ready to compromise.

"Well, what do you think, Stanley? Are you still interested in applying now that you know we may not place you in the IBM section because you do not have a high school diploma?" the worker asked.

"I don't know," Stanley answered, looking at Herb with the same dopey expression he had on his face that first day Herb had met him.

The worker told Stanley that he would have to decide within the next day or so. If he was interested he should telephone her and she would set up some additional interviews for him.

After the interview Herb took Stanley for something to eat, then asked him: "Do you want to go out and work without being trained, or will you at least look to see what the possibilities are? Do you want to have some more interviews to see what kind of a program they come up with, or do you just want to do nothing?"

Stanley was too disappointed about IBM to think about another program. He felt like doing nothing, but he had come too far to settle for that. So he said that he wanted to think about it some more.

Herb was frustrated because he felt sure Stanley could make it if he tried. We had finally gotten the Institute to think about giving Stanley a chance, but Stanley was acting as if he might not accept it. All Herb could do was to wait until Wednesday to see how much effect the previous twenty months would have on Stanley.

Wednesday, January 4

ABSENTEES AND PRESENTEES

The morning after the vacation began anxiously. Don didn't come to school. Since he hadn't been home for seven days, we were half expecting him not to show. Larry Keating didn't come. That was different . . . a poor way for a new student to begin. We'd have to check that out. And Manuel didn't show either. We wondered about him.

The absences kind of got to us. Our minds wandered. It had been a long vacation—perhaps too long. "Maybe the boys had gotten too much of a taste of freedom before they were hooked on us," we thought. "Maybe they had gotten into trouble. Maybe they had quit us." Maybe! Maybe! Maybe! We were worrying because we were insecure. But we knew enough to be calm. We'd just wait and see.

IMPORTANT ISN'T ALWAYS IMPORTANT

With three students out, Harold got some extra attention in his class. Connie asked him to pronounce a group of words from a list. He started off trying to pronounce them correctly, but he began guessing as soon as he made his first mistake. Connie made him go back each time he guessed, but he merely guessed again. Seething with frustration, Connie tried to convince him that it was important to go back and get it right but that approach didn't work either. Harold already knew it was important. He still couldn't do it because he was too tense. When Connie reminded Harold of what he was losing by not going back she made him more, not less anxious. Then Connie tried coaxing him and got a fairly good response for a short while. However, after about ten minutes he became tense; he began to pace around the room, went out for a drink, came back, said he was going to leave, and finally left.

Connie wouldn't have felt so defeated if she had known that Harold wasn't doing too much better in geometry. He was learning the method but messing up on the computations and becoming nervous and fidgety. Recognizing the early signs of impending explosion, Bill asked, "What's wrong, Harold?"

"I got the number all runnin around in my head. I don't know which ith which."

Bill asked him what he meant. Harold told him that he was aware of all the numbers involved in the different steps of the calculation and was unable to select the figures which he needed for the particular step. Bill told him to take a break, to work on his pottery for a while, to relax. They would find a way to solve his difficulty. Bill wasn't sure why Harold couldn't keep his numbers straight. He remembered the minimum brain damage Harold supposedly had sustained. Was that it, Bill wondered. If so, it didn't suggest any educational techniques for teaching him geometry.

HOORAY! SHIT!

Stanley came to school to talk to Herb about the Institute. He had decided that he wanted to go. Hooray! Herb thought. But he didn't want to call the intake worker.

"Shit!" Herb mumbled as he sensed that Stanley didn't want to surrender his independence.

"How do I let her know?" Stanley asked.

Herb didn't reply.

"She'll call the school." Herb still said nothing. Stanley knew what he had to do. He hesitated for a minute as he wrestled with his conflict, then called her. He told her he was interested in going, but only to the print shop. That could make it difficult for him to be accepted, she replied. Stanley told her he realized that, but he still only wanted printing.

[Stanley had made all the compromises he could. We would have to await the results of their evaluation with our fingers crossed.]

Thursday, January 5

Thursday was a better day. We had a full house except for Larry. Although we wondered about him, we didn't call his house. The boys stuffed themselves during the warm-up, all except Manuel. Manuel was eating lunch, but he still wouldn't eat anything for breakfast. While the others ate, he told Connie that he had been to court Wednesday for a parole hearing which the court had neglected to inform us about. After the hearing, he had gone back to his old school to see some of his friends and teachers.

"Oh, did you like your teachers in the other school?" Connie asked.

"No! They too cheap. I wen back anyway. The guidance teacher saw me and chase me roun the hall cause I had no pass, and he's always cheap bout a pass. I run fasta then hin, so I scape. I always scape fron hin when I play hookey. You know, once I play hookey for three whole month. In the winter I use ta sneak in school and get warm. Once a teacher grab me but I knock hin down and ran. So they suspen me."

"Did you see your friends in school?" Connie asked, keeping the conversation going.

"Yeah I saw then but they woun believe I go ta this school every day. They think I still play hookey. I coun even tell then I could read cause they woun believe I'n comin here now."

I NEVA READ IN A BOOK

It was time for class. Willie and Harold headed for biology. Manuel went with Connie. They began the session doing geography and ended by sounding out, spelling, pronouncing, and reading some of the words which they had discussed before the vacation—such as earth, globe, equator, North Pole, day and night. Manuel was amazed that he remembered the words. He was doing so well Connie felt he might be able to read a few easy sentences in the geography book. He read them and almost flipped because it was the first time he had read anything from a book. Then Connie wrote out sentences of her own in script which he couldn't read until she printed the words for him. Toward the end of the class, she told Manuel, "You've really made a lot of progress today, Manuel."

He smiled, nodded, and said, "But it ain all so easy."

"No, it isn't," she agreed, "but once you get started you can continue to progress faster and faster."

"Yeah," he answered, grinning and very pleased with himself. "Man, I neva read in a book. I neva knew i's so easy. I's a pushover."

MUSICAL FREE STORE

Willie also had a good day. He took pages of notes in biology, worked on his bookcase in shop, and spent two periods in music with Marilyn. The music room was like a "free store," full of candy, and Willie was like a little kid who hadn't had any. Although he was just beginning to get acquainted with the piano, he was already able to pick out tunes without music. Marilyn helped him find a few notes for another Beatle ballad, promised to buy a book of Beatle songs for him, and wrote the melody out for him so that he could practice it in the meantime. Marilyn didn't want him to practice exercises. She wanted him to experiment on his own.

DON'S LISA

Don's day was good too. When he came to school he went straight to his English class with Connie without stopping to say anything to anyone. Connie gave him vocabulary work to do because he had said it was what he liked. Taken in by Don's intellectual front, she gave Don the most advanced book in the series, which was too difficult for him. Correcting herself, she started Don in a book at his level. However he was unwilling to look up the words he didn't know. Don wanted *her* to tell him what the answers were. When he discovered that Connie wasn't going to do so, he looked up a few of the words for appearance sake, then guessed at the rest, including quite a few obviously easy ones which he could have gotten correctly if he had tried. "Perhaps he's frustrated by being confronted with work he doesn't know," Connie thought to herself.

Connie was about to coax him when they were interrupted by a call that Henry, Lisa, and one of her girl friends were waiting for Don in front of the building. When she told him his girl was downstairs, Don said he had to call his mother, then added, "I better go clean up, I need a shave," and left.

Since it was almost time for lunch when Don joined them, Henry offered to take the three of them out to eat. At first Don said he wasn't hungry, but after the girls said they wanted to go and Henry coaxed him, he agreed. They made small talk in the restaurant as Don wolfed down his food like he hadn't eaten in days. Then the girls left, and Don and Henry returned to school.

After lunch Don went to his music "session," which was a better word for it than "lesson." He toyed with the piano and guitar, rapped to Marilyn about the record his rock group was supposed to cut and avoided her attempts to teach him anything. Marilyn knew Don was only "rapping" about the record. He bragged a lot, even though everyone around him understood that he was "bull-shitting." The boys had an agreement about letting each other "bull-shit." So she let Don play the game with her even though she would have preferred to teach him a few things on the guitar or piano.

WE'RE ALL BLACKBOARDS

Harold continued to have difficulty in geometry. Bill had thought about Harold's difficulty since their last class and was prepared to help him.

"Harold," he said to him, "when you start doing a problem, you're okay in the beginning, but when you remember how you did the previous part of the problem, the figures stick with you, so you can't forget them. You don't erase them."

"That's it," Harold agreed, pleased that Bill understood the problem. "But I'm not a blackboard."

"Well, to some extent we're all blackboards," Bill answered. "We remember things."

"Yeah! That it. I can't get them out of my mine."

"Well then, what you ought to try is to write down things on paper as you do them, then forget them."

"No! No! That no help," Harold insisted, unwilling to write anything that he didn't absolutely have to.

"If you write down each step in order, in advance, you

should be able to forget about them because you won't need to remember them," Bill explained, acting as if Harold hadn't disagreed with him. "You have to learn to narrow your attention to what's under consideration at the particular moment and block out the information that preceded it and what may follow it. In this way, you won't be aware of too large a span of information at one time."

Bill must have done something right because Harold was able to stay the full period and then some. When Connie came down to call for Harold, she was surprised to see Harold still engrossed in his work. The contrast between what she saw Harold doing with Bill and what she expected him to be doing with her crushed her. She admitted to Bill that Harold still wasn't able to work for more than fifteen minutes in her class. Sensing Connie's concern, Bill reassured her that we all had our good and bad times with Harold. If she was having bad times, he told her, good times were on their way. Connie thanked Bill for his comments as she realized that she was beginning to look forward to the support he gave her.

Connie had good times with Harold that very day. At the start of his class with Connie, Harold seemed restless and unwilling to conform to anything except what he wanted to do. After a few breaks and fifteen or so minutes of work, he slammed his book shut, threw his pencil on the floor, and complained:

"What good i thith anyway if I not gettin a nacademic diploma?"

Connie tried to reassure Harold that she was teaching him the kind of English he needed, regardless of the kind of diploma he would earn. That didn't reassure him. Harold wanted his diploma; he wanted his college.

A few short minutes later Connie was again trying to get Harold to pronounce a word he had repeatedly mispronounced. Suddenly erupting in an outburst of frustration and anger, he threw his book down, grabbed her around the neck, and growled at her through clenched teeth, "I'm gonna kill ya. I'm gonna choke ya. You neva theen me when I'm really angry."

Harold was holding her, squeezing her, but still controlling himself. Connie had been growing accustomed to Harold. She was beginning to realize that he wouldn't hurt anyone, despite his threats. So she didn't feel afraid. And when she recognized that she had finally learned how to handle her feelings with Harold, she felt almost relaxed.

Harold stood there waiting for her to react as she always had. His grip tightened around her neck. As he became more and more aggravated by her lack of concern, he threatened in an almost pleading-for-her-to-be-afraid voice.

"You dunno how throng I am. You dunno how dangerouth I am."

Connie smiled. Harold's anger turned to tenderness and he let go. Noticing that the room was cold, Harold gently placed his jacket over Connie's shoulders, insisted she should wear it for the rest of the afternoon to keep warm, and went back to work for the rest of the period. Connie felt they had established a new kind of relationship—at least for today, she thought, correcting herself. Connie appreciated the good times. She was also beginning to be more accepting of the bad times that were bound to follow.

Friday, January 6

HAIR POWER

Friday was an especially good day. We had classes in the morning and a trip after lunch. First thing in the morning the intake worker at the institute called to tell us she had set up a number of intake appointments for Stanley and his parents. His parents? Herb knew they wouldn't cooperate. He told the worker so and explained why their cooperation wouldn't be necessary.

The worker was still concerned that Stanley might drop out of the program even if he were accepted. Nevertheless, she said, she was willing to continue the intake proceedings because Stanley had done much better in the interview than they had expected. Great, Herb thought to himself. But maybe it was really because Stanley had his hair cut the day before the interview.

PREACH ISN'T PEACH

Since it was Friday, we expected to have a recreation morning, but most of the boys chose to go to class. Connie continued working with Harold on spelling. He made a lot of mistakes because his responses were impulsive. Connie tried very hard to get Harold to take a deep breath or to pause before he answered, in the hope that he would correct the initial errors himself. Why should he? He was able to convince himself that his mistakes were correct by seeing the word he pronounced rather than the word he wrote. When Connie asked him to write the word "preach," he wrote "peach." When she asked him to read what he had written, he looked at the word and read "preach, preach, preach," almost as though he was unable to remove it. At other times, when she called his attention to the "s's" he had omitted, he told her that Herbie said he did not hear the ends of words, meaning she shouldn't expect him to be able to do it correctly. Connie noticed that if she got him to stand at the other end of the room and call out the sentences, he tended to pronounce the endings much more correctly than he did when he was just leaning over a book and mumbling into it.

Marilyn had also observed that he pronounced words much better when he sang out, which surprised her.

CHICKEN LEGS

Connie also had a class with Manuel before the usual Friday afternoon trip. They reviewed some of the sounds he had learned in his previous classes, then worked on double vowel sounds—"ea," "ee," and "ei." He read "weak" and "week" and looked puzzled that they could both sound the same until he realized that the second vowel was canceled out and the first one made the sound.

While they were studying the word "steak," he started talking about different kinds of meat and parts of meat he would eat—"chicken maybe, but no leg of a lamb." He had never heard of leg of lamb and he wouldn't eat a leg of anything. That was a funny idea, Connie thought to herself.

"Well, I'm sure you've eaten chicken legs before," she said.

"No," Manuel insisted. Sure his family ate chickens at home but not the leg. They threw that away. He often went to the market with his mother and saw the butcher cut off the chicken's head and watched the headless thing run around. It was ugly. He couldn't stand it, but he liked to watch anyway. After a while Connie realized that Manuel thought that the chicken leg was the chicken's feet, even though he had seen them often. Connie remembered that the cook was fixing chicken for dinner for the boys who used the building during the evening. She marched Manuel downstairs for a chicken anatomy lesson. It took fifteen minutes to explain to him where the chicken's knee joint was, that the part that he objected to, the feet, was no longer on the chicken, and what he had eaten was really a chicken leg.

WOUNDED DAREDEVIL

Before we left for the trip, we called the Keating home to ask why Larry hadn't been in school since his initial interview. Mrs. Keating told us that Larry had fallen and had broken his jaw. He wouldn't be in for at least a week or so, until his jaw was repaired and he was able to take care of himself. But maybe not that soon either, she hinted.

"Now that the boy has hurt himself, he really won't be coming to school. Now that he has this excuse, it will be impossible to get him to come. Won't it?" she asked.

"No it won't," we declared, realizing that we would have to work at least as hard with the Keatings as we had with the Russos to get and keep Larry.

3 Learnin Bout Them

Monday, January 9, through Friday, January 13

AIN YA GONNA SEARCH ME?

Carlos Rivera was discharged from Youth House during the weekend so he could start with us on Monday. When he came into the building Herb introduced himself to Carlos and walked him toward the warm-up.

Assuming a tough-guy stance, which just didn't fit his five-foot-two- or three-inch frame, Carlos asked, as if to show that he knew the score, "Ain you gonna search me?"

"Search you? What do you mean?" Herb answered.

"Don you search kids here? They always do in my ol school."

"What for?"

"Knives and things and cigarettes."

"We're different," Herb explained. "Didn't Henry tell you our school's different? We don't search kids. You can have all the cigarettes and knives you want."

Carlos gave him a you're-puttin-me-on look. Herb answered it.

"Really! You look like you don't believe me. You'll see—"

Carlos just didn't look tough. Underneath his false front, Herb could sense that he was terrified about what might happen to him. Herb asked him what he had been doing in school before he had been sent to Youth House.

"Nothin. I jus hung aroun! Sometimes I didn go."

"When was the last time you went to school every day?"

"A long time ago when I was little, maybe ten, eleven years ol."

As they talked, it became clear that Carlos was too nervous just being at the school to be ready for real academic work. Herb gave him the "he-could-hang-around-the-first-floor-in-whichever-rooms-he-liked-and-they-would-talk-later" message and dropped him off in the rec room where he spent most of the day hardly talking to anyone. During the afternoon he joined the staff-student basketball game and outplayed all the other boys although they towered over him.

After he had some time to adjust to the school, Herb gave him some informal achievement tests. The results were discouraging. Carlos had difficulty with comprehension and basic vocabulary even when Herb read to him.

His functioning in arithmetic was hardly better. We immediately realized the extreme handicap Carlos had been facing as a sixteen-year-old boy supposedly ready for eleventh-grade work.

During our staff meeting we talked about Carlos's educational difficulties. Henry thought that his difficulties were too severe to be explained by the language and cultural differences he faced coming from Puerto Rico. We agreed with Henry that they were probably caused by the same personality problems that kept Carlos at a very infantile level. He would need an individual tutorial program for reading and arithmetic if we wanted him to work on these subjects. We hoped that Natalie, one of Herb's gradu-

ate fellowship students at Hofstra, would be able to work
with Carlos one period a day, two or three times a week
during January, and then on a regular basis starting in February when she would be working half-time in the program
regularly as an educational intern.

Natalie would be a good teacher for Carlos. She had
taught for six years in a ghetto school and was studying
full-time for a graduate degree in special education. So she
would be able to deal with both his remedial and special
problems. Even before the school had reopened, Herb had
been encouraging Natalie to do her internship with us because he felt she would be perfect for our infantile boys.
Her experience in the ghetto schools of New York City had
taught her to be extremely patient with the boys' educational difficulties and sympathetic to their personal problems. Even more important, she had a soft spot in her heart
for poor kids and she enjoyed being nice to them.

Natalie would provide the same kind of alternative to
Connie's approach to the boys that Bill offered to Norm's
approach. Natalie would work well with the educationally
retarded boys, especially those who attacked and disrupted
in order to relieve their internal pressures. Connie, on the
other hand, worked well with the better functioning students, especially those who turned their anger on themselves
and suffered internally.

Natalie read Carlos's record Wednesday morning, then
took him to her office for his first lesson.

"He *is* small for his age," she thought to herself. "But he
carries himself very well. He's probably a good athlete. His
eyes aren't weak and his teeth don't protrude as much as
Herb seems to think. Henry's description was much more
realistic. Why do the others think they do? Are they prejudiced against him?" she wondered, already coming to Carlos's defense.

Carlos was too nervous to say anything. Natalie broke the uncomfortable silence.

"I guess we're both new in the school, Carlos," she said, trying to put him at ease.

"Not me," he answered. "I bin here three days aready."

"Oh! I see. Have you gotten used to everything yet? I guess this kind of school is strange. It's strange for me."

"No."

"I haven't either. Do you want to do some work now?"

"Sure."

"Which would you rather work on, math or reading? It's up to you."

"Then les do math."

They began working. As he did, Carlos told her that his friends called him Chino because he looked Chinese. She asked if he liked the name. "No," he answered. "You call me Carlos." Natalie asked him if his old school was good. "I's a special school," he answered, looking surprised at her question. Did he have any teachers he liked? "No." Were the teachers rough with the kids? "Yeah, they hit us a lot." He seemed to be losing interest, so Natalie ended the lesson and took him to the gym.

During the week, Carlos established himself with the other boys because of his basketball ability and involved himself in other parts of the program. He flirted with sculpture in the studio and flitted in and out of the music room, staying just long enough to ask Marilyn if she could give him piano lessons.

We noticed a startling difference in Carlos's behavior. In the gym, he was energetic, spontaneous, and relaxed. In Natalie's room, he was cooperative but unenthusiastic and subdued. Carlos was putting on an act for us. He was pretending to be a well-behaved, highly motivated student. We expected an about-face in his behavior once he realized that nothing bad would happen to him if he acted up, probably within the next few days.

THE "BOY" STAYS HOME

Our other new student, Larry Keating, stayed out all week. Since we suspected that his mother was probably encouraging him to stay away, Henry called Mrs. Keating to ask when Larry would be starting school.

"Oh! I couldn't let the boy go back to school yet," she told Henry. "He still has rubber bands in his mouth you know. What if one of the boys hit his jaw? Oh! I don't think the doctor would allow me to send him to school yet. Do you?"

"That would be up to the doctor," Henry answered. "But if it's all right with him, we would make sure Larry wouldn't be involved in any activities that he could get hurt in."

"But he can't eat or talk the way he is," she countered. "What would he do in school?"

"We could get him special liquid foods. We're a special school. We can make special arrangements for our students."

"Well, I really don't know."

The conversation lasted a while longer. Finally when Henry offered to consult with Larry's doctor, Mrs. Keating gave in. With no excuses to fall back on, she agreed to send Larry to school the following week, if the doctor agreed.

FAMILY THERAPY

Henry also spoke to Mrs. Russo. When she visited the school Monday, she said she wanted to speak about Don, but she actually wanted to talk to Henry about her relationship with her husband and men in general. Although Mrs. Russo blamed her husband for her problems at home,

Henry sensed that underneath she felt that there was something wrong with her. Taking advantage of the opening, he said to her, "You know, Mrs. Russo, when a grown woman like yourself can't quite make it with men, she sometimes finds it easier to get along with her son."

Henry had tried to approach the sexualized relationship between Don and Mrs. Russo, but she wouldn't bite. Instead she said, "If Don could get along with my husband everything would be all right. Help me with that."

Henry felt he had to go along with Mrs. Russo. So he spoke about how she could improve the relationship between Don and her husband.

Don was coming to school regularly, but late. He spent most of his time in the gym and shop and as little time as possible in academic classes. He wasn't ready for any kind of formal academic work except math. He seldom paid attention in biology unless they discussed sex or some other topic which he brought up. He had almost no frustration tolerance in English, and he didn't do very much in shop except on rare occasions when he worked on his "throwing hammer." Even that simple project was taking him ages to complete.

Although Don wasn't engaged in much work, he was constantly involved with Henry. He joked about his sex life and the many girls he had "screwed." He told Henry that girls who let him get into them were "sluts," while his girl friend was pure, untouchable, and wonderful.

"Just like your mother," Henry commented.

"There you go with that tiddlywinks stuff," Don responded.

Henry thought that Don would be a good candidate for a more traditional insightful psychotherapeutic approach. Don's wish for his mother, his substitution of Lisa for his mother, his division of women into the "bad"—the sexually available—and the "good"—the sexually unavailable, his wish to escape from his mother and yet at the same time to be with her were already coming to the surface. Henry believed that Don could be helped to understand these things in a reasonably short time. Some of us were still concerned that Henry was moving too fast with Don. However, Henry felt that the more often he saw Don and handled things with him, the less likely it would be that Don would raise topics with the teaching staff which they couldn't handle as well as Henry. With that in mind, Don was given a regular daily appointment with Henry for psychotherapy sessions.

MANUEL'S FIRST BOOK

Manuel started his week by picking a book—the first book he would ever read completely—a Dr. Seuss children's book, a fantasy. As he held it, thumbed through it, read a page, and triumphantly turned to the next one, he told Connie: "I neva thought I kin read a book. I neva knew wha's in a book."

After a few pages he noticed a picture of two animals fighting and said, "Hey! That's what I like ta do."

"Fight?" Connie asked anxiously.

"Sure—in my neighborhood you gotta fight," he answered. Connie gave Manuel a disapproving look, so Manuel explained that he had to fight with his friends . . . he had to. Other guys tried to use their park. He didn't like to be beaten up. He couldn't let them run over him. He had to fight.

Connie didn't agree.

"Here you are learning how to read and you are just going to get all banged up in a fight," she told him, still concerned that he might be hurt.

"No, no," he answered. "I ain gonna get banged up. I jus hafta protect myself."

WHAT A THOSE THINGS?

Connie learned some other things about Manuel when he asked her, next time, what a question mark was. She told him and thought nothing more about it. A few minutes later, he pointed to a period and asked her what it was. After she answered him, he admitted he had thought it was just a little dot, like the dot over the "i," that happened to be in the wrong place—"maybe it fell down or somethin." He also thought that quotation marks were "66's" and apostrophes were misplaced commas. In other sessions, Manuel confused "b" and "d" when he printed on the board. Although it was the first time Manuel had made reversals in Connie's class, he had been having difficulty distinguishing between "E" and "F" and "C" and "G" in music. These reversals were a real problem for him.

Connie was still reluctant to look at Manuel's difficulties objectively. So she found it difficult to believe that he really didn't know what periods and question marks were. She hoped and had half-convinced herself that he was playing dumb for some reason.

Since Connie accepted her own reassuring explanations for Manuel's educational difficulties, the sessions seemed relatively uneventful to her. However, when we heard about them, we became even more aware of the extent of Manuel's lack of basic information, his unquestioning attitude about the things he perceived, and his tendency to create nonsensical explanations for things that he didn't understand.

YOU'RE NOT THAT CRAZY

Connie was in fact shaken up enough by Manuel's misperceptions so that she asked us during the next staff meeting to advise her on how to react to his revelations. She told us that she had been following her immediate impulse, which was to tell him, in effect, "I know you're not crazy. You're not that kind of a bad boy. You wouldn't do such things." However, she was beginning to wonder whether that was the correct thing to do. And Connie was right. Certainly she felt better when she thought that she had reassured Manuel about his doubts and when she reassured herself that he could not be that crazy or that bad. However, Herb and Henry weren't sure Manuel felt better.

They didn't think Connie should communicate things like: "Manuel, I know you're too nice a boy to use a knife in a gang fight," when he told her he carried a knife in case he had to defend himself. They were concerned that Manuel might interpret her statements to mean "Don't tell me about such things. I can't believe them. They're too much for me to handle. They upset me." That could make Manuel clam up and cut off the kind of communication which Henry and Herb felt was essential to Manuel's progress.

They told Connie to continue to react to Manuel's statements with spontaneity and interest, but without concern or anxiety. Herb would continue to meet regularly with her to discuss Manuel's revelations. Hopefully Manuel would gradually begin to talk to Herb who was in a better position to handle the information.

Connie had a chance to put into practice what Henry and Herb had preached during her last session of the week with Manuel when he talked about his lousy teachers and the lousy schools he was forced to attend. Connie reminded him that he didn't have to come to our school.

"Whadaya mean! Ya don hafta cone ta school," he answered. "Of course ya gotta cone ta school. Henry tol me the firs day if I din cone ta school, he would get me outa bed."

Connie explained that Henry had meant he would help

him wake up, not force him to come. Manuel laughed about it, but Connie could tell that he wasn't sure whether someone would come after him if he stayed home.

Toward the end of the period she asked Manuel to draw a big envelope on the board and address a letter to himself. He did not know what "Mr." stood for and he did not know how to write "New York" although he did know his name and his address. When she asked him for his zip code he wrote down eight irrelevant numbers. He said he knew how to write letters because he used to send bad letters to his enemies. Then he told Connie a rambling story about a dirty letter he had sent to his neighbor. The neighbor had come to the school, looked at everyone's handwriting, and had recognized Manuel's. Manuel had been called into the office. Manuel said that he had not done it when the man had accused him. However, he had been caught because the man had seen him outside of his house copying down the address.

Connie remembered the advice we had given her. But she still felt troubled by what Manuel had said. She just couldn't understand how Manuel could believe such a story, or why he would want her to believe it if he knew he was lying.

Manuel worried Connie a little, but he worried Norm a lot. Messing up in English was one thing—messing up with the power tools in shop was another. When Manuel had first stared at the whirling tools and made comments to Norm like, "Boy, that kin cut right through ya. Look how it cut that wood. How it feel cuttin me?" Norm had been nervous about having him in the shop. Then, as Manuel became used to the tools and seemed less interested in them, Norm relaxed. Tuesday Manuel started staring at the power saw again. He moved closer and closer to it . . . timidly . . . yet resolutely . . . like a fish deciding to take the bait or a bather preparing to take the plunge into the cold ocean. Suddenly when he was almost close enough to reach out and touch it, his face froze in a look of terror and his whole body began shaking as if he expected the saw to attack him. Norm called Herb into the shop to get his opinion about what should be done. Together, they watched as Manuel stared terror-stricken at the revolving blade which he imagined was moving toward him. Finally he lowered his eyes, turned, and walked away. It was a morbid yet fascinating scene, one which committed Norm and Herb to intense but unnecessary concern about Manuel's movements in the shop.

During the week, Manuel gradually overcame his fear of the saw. As he did, he started making a stool for the school . . . a stool which would take a long time before it was completed because Manuel needed as much individual attention in the shop as he did in his academic classes.

Manuel also drew closer to Bill. He started to spend most of the free afternoon periods either working in Bill's studio or playing Ping-Pong with him in the gym. He was definitely not one of "Normie's boys," even though he spent time in Norm's shop. We guessed that Manuel was probably attracted to Bill because of the quiet, relaxed manner in which Bill related to the boys. Norm was already actively attempting to involve the students, while Bill tended to stay back and wait for them to approach him.

FIFTY DOLLARS FOR A DAMN JACKET

Herb had his chance with Manuel on Friday. Manuel had been telling us that he needed a leather jacket but he hadn't asked us to buy one for him. On Friday he did. Herb said that he would buy Manuel a jacket during the following week because the school didn't have enough cash on hand. Manuel looked as if he thought he was getting the run-around. Herb noticed Manuel's look of disappointment and suspicion. He didn't want to miss his first opportunity to get involved with Manuel. So he offered to leave a deposit on a jacket and pay the rest on Monday. Manuel smiled happily, then said he wanted a leather jacket with a zip-in lining because leather was the only thing that could protect him from the wind. Leather would keep him warm like the cows in Puerto Rico.

After lunch, they went to one of the big department stores nearby. Herb sneaked a look at the prices on the leather jackets and felt sick. The cheapest cost sixty dollars. "Fortunately," thought Herb, "none of the jackets will fit Manuel."

"Let's look at some other jackets, Manuel," he suggested. Manuel didn't want another jacket.

"They cheap," he insisted.

"No they aren't," Herb thought, "but they're a hell of a lot less expensive than leather jackets."

They left the department store—Manuel looking for a leather jacket and Herb almost hoping that they wouldn't find one. Then Herb realized that Manuel would be as unwilling to buy another kind of jacket as he had been to eat anything but roast beef for lunch. If that was the case, Herb thought, it would be worth the extra money to convince Manuel that we respected his wishes and would try to satisfy them. Financial problems could be taken care of later.

They walked into another store. Fortunately for Manuel there were two leather jackets, one of which fit him. Fortunately for Herb the jacket had been reduced for clearance to fifty dollars.

Herb bought the damn jacket. Damn jacket, because Herb was uneasy about having to spend so much of the school's money on a jacket—damn jacket, because he had never spent that much money on a jacket for himself—

damn jacket, because he felt pressured into it by Manuel's difficulties. When Herb returned to the school he was anxious about the fifty dollars. He had never spent money that way and he wasn't sure he had done the right thing.

"Shit," Norm told him, "no one else's gonna treat the kid nice. If you have the chance, go ahead and do it. This is an experimental program, right? If you think you should try it, then try it."

Herb was relieved by Norm's response. He was especially reassured because Norm was usually critical of the permissive way Herb and Henry wanted to give money to the boys.

MAYBE HE DON'T BELONG

Although Manuel was becoming more involved with us, Willie was still lying low. He was still out to please us, still doing what he thought we wanted. Occasionally he let something slip, as he did when Norm commented that the bookcase Willie was building would look good at home. Willie said he wasn't making it for his home. He wanted to hang it in the shop for the biology books. At first Norm was puzzled because Willie didn't seem that attached to us. Then he remembered how badly Willie had been treated at home and he understood why Willie did not want to make anything for the apartment.

We were moving slowly with Willie. He was observing us and we were watching him. No one was ready to make the first move. When it came right down to it, we weren't sure that Willie had big emotional problems, that he needed our help, or that he really belonged in our school.

ENCOURAGING BUT SAD NEWS

Toward the end of the week we received encouraging news about Stanley. The intake worker called to tell us that Stanley had visited the Institute and impressed her very much.

Not only was he there on time at nine in the morning to meet her, but he had been there half an hour early because he wanted to make sure that he was on time in case he had gotten lost. If that was the kind of motivation Stanley had, she said, she was more optimistic about accepting him.

At first she had been a little worried that Stanley wouldn't want to attend when he had criticized the place because there "were too many Negroes and the girls were ugly." But she felt better when he added that he would go because he liked the printing shop.

Herb was pleased to hear the encouraging developments. At the same time he was hurt by Stanley's statement about "Negroes." Herb thought of Stanley's many black friends in the school. He wondered how much of that friendship had been real, then felt sad.

MASTURBATION

Harold, our other old-timer, also made progress but on another front. He spent a lot of time talking to Henry about masturbation. He had begun to masturbate, but he was feeling queer about it. So it was difficult for him to admit it to Henry. "Thure I jerk off," he admitted. "All teen-ager jerk off." Then he took it back. "I don't haf to jerk off. I got a lotta girl. . . . Only crazy people jerk off. . . . I bet you jerk off, Henry. You don't have a lotta girl. I bet that why you think I do."

Henry agreed that most teen-agers masturbated. Although Harold had said so first, it was hard for him to believe it until Henry cleared up some of Harold's misunderstandings about masturbation. After Harold had made his first confession, he found it easier to talk to Henry about his difficulties with girls. It was a rough week for Harold and therefore for us. However, we knew it would be worth it in the long run.

Monday, January 16, through Friday, January 20

BITTERSWEET ENCOUNTER

We started the following week with an administrative day. Most of the morning was taken up by a gripe session. Connie complained that Herb interfered when she handled disruptive students.

"You always come to my rescue when I don't need help," she explained resentfully.

Herb was hurt and fought back with a question.

"Are you sure that's why you're angry? Or is it that I criticize you in front of the kids? Is that what bothers you?"

"Well truthfully," Connie answered as she found the courage to speak bluntly, "you act as if I can't handle disruptive boys. You don't exactly interfere. You're overprotective because I'm a woman."

"Overprotective? I don't overprotect women," Herb insisted. "I don't overprotect Marilyn or Natalie. Ask Natalie. Do I, Natalie?"

Before Natalie could respond, the other men joined in. Henry and Norm told Connie that they had often seen her signaling for help from them as if she were overwhelmed by the situation. Perhaps Herb was especially ready to respond to her signals, Henry suggested, because he was the person with the most responsibility for the school. Bill had a different comment to make. It was critical but also supportive. He thought Connie had been acting as if she needed help in order to appear to be a modest beginner in the school even though she was better able to cope with the students than she herself realized.

Herb was convinced that Connie was uncomfortable with disruptive kids. He also felt certain that Connie had asked him for help and when he had given it, damn it, he thought to himself, he had gotten his face slapped. He didn't believe that Connie was all that competent despite what Bill had said, and he was almost angry enough to say so.

It was Herb's turn to gripe. He had something to get off *his* chest. He was aggravated that Bill and Norm had been playing Ping-Pong together while the boys were watching idly. Norm, who Herb thought was the major offender, said the boys liked to watch him and Bill play so they could learn from them. Herb disagreed. He said he knew that the real reason Norm played was to enjoy himself. Connie told Norm she felt he was too competitive with the boys. He played to win, not to help the boys, she insisted. Herb reminded Norm that he had voluntarily barred himself from the old pool table we had during the pilot project for just that reason. Norm didn't buy Herb's complaint that he and Bill monopolized the Ping-Pong table, but he agreed that he was too competitive. He said he would cool it. Bill agreed to do the same.

Norm's reaction changed our criticalness to sympathy. We quickly rushed to make "nice nice" to him. Henry told him that his competitive spirit often got the boys involved in basketball and other games. During the team games Norm and the rest held ourselves back and let the boys do most of the playing and scoring. It was the one-to-one situation which somehow aroused the competitive nature of almost all of us, not only Norm.

Natalie was next. Herb told her that she was being fooled by Carlos's cooperative facade. Herb couldn't believe that Carlos's anxiety about school, his fear of authority, and his delinquent front had miraculously vanished because he had become one of our students. He advised Natalie to avoid feeding into Carlos's facade by not teaching him anything new for a while.

"Play games with Carlos, take him shopping, and allow

him to decide what to do," Herb suggested. "Develop a relaxed and informal relationship with him. If he asks to do academic work, make sure it's below his level so he will definitely succeed. Above all don't be sucked into trying to teach him anything new."

Natalie disagreed, but didn't say anything. She had just begun to work in the school. Besides Herb was her professor and supervisor. It would be a while before she would be able to express her disagreements.

OUR FIRST PREGNANCY

Stanley came to school just before we all left.

"My girl's pregnant," he told Herb.

"How do you know?"

"Because I came in er."

"So, how do you know she's pregnant?"

"It was just the right time, fourteen days after er period. That's——"

"That doesn't mean she's pregnant," Herb interrupted. "Did she take any precautions?"

"No. I wanted er ta take some pills but she wouldn't."

"You look very upset," Herb commented, changing the nature of the conversation from confrontation to support.

"Yeah, I think about it all the time," Stanley answered. "I think maybe we should run away to Maryland and get married. You don't hafta have a blood test or proof a age there. Right? But if I get caught? She's jail bait. They'll get me fa kidnappin cross state lines. I'd get married here, but she gotta ask her father and he could get me fa statutry rape. I'm gonna run away to California. They'll neva find me there."

"I thought you wanted to marry her?"

"If she's pregnant so I wouldn get in trouble."

"And if she's not pregnant?"

"Then I don't wanna get married. Why should I?"

"Maybe she's not pregnant. How many times did you do it?"

"Once. It was the first time. She was a virgin. But there's somethin I don get. There wasn't no blood on the bed."

"Nothing at all?"

No answer.

"Nothing at all?" Herb asked again.

"Some pink spots," Stanley unwillingly admitted. "But they weren't blood."

"But they were reddish, weren't they?" Herb insisted without being able to shake Stanley's conviction that there had been no blood.

"Why is he so worried that she wasn't a virgin?" Herb asked himself. "Does he believe he can only get into whores? Is that it?" Herb marked the question in his mind for the future, then returned to Stanley's immediate problem. He told Stanley that he could understand why he was so upset, but he explained it was extremely unlikely that his girl was pregnant. They had taken only one chance. It was the first time and he had hardly penetrated her. Besides, Herb reminded him, he had no information that she was pregnant. He told Stanley to talk to Norm about conception so he could understand it better and asked Norm to explain why it was unlikely that Stanley's girl had conceived.

Tuesday, January 17

LONG-AWAITED ARRIVAL

When the boys returned from their three-day weekend Larry returned with them. He had lost so much weight that Herb wouldn't have recognized him except for his wired jaw. Once he saw that, Larry's English face and dark wavy hair fit into place. Larry told Herb he wanted to take a regular academic program. Herb asked him to take some informal achievement tests first so we could get a rough idea of where he was at. Larry refused. He read as well as any high school student, he insisted. So there was no reason for him to take tests. Herb asked him to take them anyway. Larry resisted, but then finally agreed to take them with Connie.

When Connie met with him, he said he liked to write.

"They say I can be a writer," he told her.

"Who are they?"

"Oh, my teachers."

"What do *you* want to be?" Connie asked, emphasizing the "you."

"A doctor or a nurse, whichever comes easier," he answered.

Larry decided that he wanted to spend the period writing, but he wanted to choose his own topic—a short story about flying from ledge to ledge on a roof in the development where he lived. He wrote:

Intrigue in the Night

When the days shine with a welcoming flow and the trees are swaying to and fro, you can get an idea of what the night will be like and then your bones feel the yearning for the cool breeze of a dark alley. You look forward to the gentle carefree swaying of your body through the air which rushes up from the ground to meet you and a thrilling embrace. Every muscle moves with graceful ease, a ease that you have acquired thru careful learning. The rope which you clutch tightens in your grip as you sail downward a forward then upward to the next building. When you reach your peak, let go and outstretched hands paw for the ledge of a nearby casement. You look back at what you have accomplished and remembered all its glee then you sail back with a mighty jump and reach for the rope that you love so dearly.

The jolt is trememdous reminding you that you are like a free flying eagle enjoying your natural way to fly.

SICK LITTLE BOY

As soon as Carlos came to school, he looked for Henry.

"Man, I'm sick," he complained to Henry. "I got a high fever. You got a thermometer in this school? No! This school ain got no thermometer."

"Maybe Phyllis has a thermometer," Henry answered. "If not, we can buy one."

"Man, I'm gonna die. Me an my mother . . . both gonna die. I ain gonna make it for even five years."

"Five years?" Henry thought to himself. "That sounds like the length of time doctors often give people with terminal cancer. Perhaps Carlos knows unconsciously that his mother has cancer. Perhaps——"

But Carlos interrupted Henry's thoughts with a whined, "Oo I don feel so good."

Carlos's whine reminded Henry of a little boy who feels sorry for himself and wants some special attention from his mother. So Henry tenderly took his temperature, which was normal, and told Carlos anytime Carlos felt sick, he would take his temperature. Then Carlos had an art period—just him and Bill. When Bill asked him what he would like to do, he tried the same maneuver he had used with Natalie.

"Whadaya wan me ta do?" he demanded.

"Whatever you want to do," Bill answered permissively.

"What should I do?" Carlos insisted.

"Whatever you want to do," Bill answered calmly.

They repeated themselves, back and forth, back and forth. Finally Carlos yielded.

"I wanna make a head."

Bill gave him some clay, but he wasn't satisfied.

"Thas no good for a head."

"What's wrong with it," Bill asked in a voice which indicated that something must have been wrong if Carlos thought so.

"I wanna make a real head—the same size, a real head."

Bill understood. He gave him a lot of clay, more than he needed. Carlos still wasn't satisfied. He wanted something else from Bill. He wanted Bill to be his model. Bill agreed.

Next period Carlos walked into Natalie's room yawning and looking pooped. She asked him, "Didn't you sleep well last night, Carlos?"

"Wha?"

"I asked how you slept last night."

"Okay."

"You look tired."

"Wha?"

"You look tired. Didn't you hear me?"

"Yeah, I got tire in Bill's room."

"Are you too tired to work with me?"

"I kin do work."

"What would you like to do?"

"Whadaya wan me ta do?"

"Whatever you want to do."

"Like wha?"

"Well, we can read or do arithmetic or just talk, whichever you wish."

"Okay."

"Okay, which one, Carlos?"

"Any one."

"It's up to you, Carlos, you know it's your choice."

"Then les read."

Natalie handed Carlos a reader, but without opening it he said, "It's too hard. I can read a Big Book."

Natalie asked him to open the book before he decided he couldn't read it. He opened the book to the first story and read it with little difficulty.

"Do you want to read some more?" she asked when he finished.

"No."

"Do you want to do math?"

"Wha?"

Natalie repeated the question, this time using the word "arithmetic."

"Oh no. Kin we play Ping-Pong?"

"Sure."

They went to the gym to play. When Natalie looked at the clock to check the time, Carlos told her he had pawned his watch because he needed money.

"What for?" she asked.

"Ta get high."

"How do *you* get high? Do you drink? Do you smoke?" she asked, hip to the different ways in which kids like Carlos got high.

"No," he answered, changing his mind.

"How?" Natalie asked again, without realizing that Carlos didn't want to say more.

"I was jus kiddin. I din pawn my watch. I got money . . . and I don steal," he added.

"Then what did you mean?" Natalie asked, pressing him to continue.

Carlos blushed, said he was only kidding, and looked away, unable to look her in the eyes.

Just before lunch Carlos went into the music room while Natalie went upstairs to get her coat. When she returned she asked him to think of some things he might like to do with her the following Tuesday.

Carlos laughed and said: "I don wanna be with you."

Natalie was surprised and hurt. She could take aggression much better than rejection. She responded immediately, and a little defensively.

"It's all right if you feel that way, Carlos. You don't have to stay with me, but you'll have to talk to Herb about it."

"Good," Carlos answered, still teasing her. "You remine me Tuesday ta tell im."

"If it's important enough you'll remember yourself."

Carlos smiled, pleased that Natalie had risen to his bait. Satisfied, he changed the topic.

"They're broken," he said, pointing to two depressed piano keys. "No one kin blame me. I din do it . . . I don care if they blame me anyway," he continued angrily.

Natalie reassured him: "You don't have to worry, Carlos. If you didn't do it, no one will blame you."

"Good. You know I was jus foolin about Tuesday. I be with you."

During the afternoon Carlos asked Henry to buy him a leather jacket like Manuel's. Henry explained that Carlos didn't need one because he already had a leather jacket. Carlos didn't like that. He shouted that Henry was cheap and cheating him. Henry said he understood that Carlos could be angry about not getting a jacket like Manuel's but he asked him to try to understand why. That worked. Carlos reduced his demands. He began whining that his jacket lining was ripped and two buttons were missing. Henry heard the compromise that Carlos had in mind and offered to have the jacket repaired at the school's expense. Carlos accepted happily.

Carlos's shell was starting to crack, as we expected. The real Carlos had come out. First he was peeping through to see if it was safe. He was asking us, "Can I show you what I'm like? How will you react if I show you that I'm really a little boy? What if I tell you I'm sick? What if I ask for a lot? What if I ask you to be my model? Will you treat me nice or hit me? Natalie, can I tell you I don't like you? Can I tell you I'm bad? Will you yell at me for breaking the piano? Natalie, Bill, and Henry on the wall, who do you like the bestest of all?"

A PIANO GETS BROKE

Carlos also forced Willie to move out a little. After lunch Willie walked up to Herb in the rec room and inconspicuously led him out into the hall. When he was sure none of the other students could see, he half-whispered, "Carlos broke the piano."

"How do you know he did it?"

"I heard him bangin on it this morning and when he came out two keys were broke. Why should he bang on it, if he's not taking lessons?"

"I'm sorry it's broken," Herb told him, "but it doesn't matter. It wasn't any good. That's why it broke so easily. We're returning it tomorrow. We're getting a new one this week."

Willie looked angry. He still wasn't satisfied. Herb was pleased that Willie was expressing his anger. However, he didn't want any trouble between the two boys.

"I don't blame you for being annoyed," he said to Willie. "But are you sure Carlos did it? Did you see him?"

"I didn't exactly see him, but I heard him bang on it like he was breakin it."

"Well, don't worry, the new one won't break so easily."

INEXPERIENCED ABORTIONIST

Stanley came to school for another session about his girl's "condition." He started off on the same tack until he said, "I bin thinkin about gettin some pills or some'in to kill the kid."

"Is that what she wants?" Herb asked.

"Ah! She's crazy. She don't wanna take nothin. She's afraid."

"Then you're the one who wants her to take the pills?"

"Yeah! She ain't even worried about havin a kid."

"Do you mean she wants one or she doesn't think she'll have one?"

"That's it. She don think she's pregnant."

"Then you're more worried than her?"

Herb was trying to reassure Stanley by pointing out that his girl wasn't worried, but Stanley wasn't listening. His mind was on the pills.

"Why can't she take pills. It ain't dangerous . . . is it?"

Herb told Stanley that he couldn't give him any information about abortions because he didn't really know much about them. Even if he did, Herb explained, he wasn't a medical doctor so he wouldn't be able to advise him. Herb did advise him not to push the panic button before it was necessary. He reminded Stanley that his girl was expecting her period in a few days and told him to wait at least until then before doing anything.

Wednesday, January 18

I BIN THINKIN

Stanley returned to school to talk about his girl friend. He was even more anxious than he had been the first time he had spoken to Herb about his girl.

"Maybe you think it's nutty," he started. "I bin thinkin I could kill the baby by stabbin it if I jammed my penis all the way in."

Herb didn't answer—Stanley continued.

"If she won't take pills, I gotta do some'in. Could I poison it by shootin in er again?" Stanley answered his own question. "I guess it's nutty . . . I gotta do some'in."

"You sound desperate . . . I guess you still can't relax.

Look you can't kill a baby that way. Remember your bio classes. Anyway she probably isn't even pregnant. Hold on a few more days," he advised Stanley. "Then you'll kick yourself for being so nervous for nothing."

MORE BOY-GIRL DIFFICULTIES

Lisa, Don's girl friend, came to see Henry after she had called to ask him if he would help straighten out a problem between her and Don. Although it was Lisa's second visit to the school, she was still too shy to go inside. So Henry spoke to her and Don in the street in front of the building. Lisa seemed comfortable, but Don was uneasy and embarrassed about the whole thing.

Lisa complained that Don was too possessive. She told Henry that Don wanted her to go steady with him or else he would break off with her. Her parents, who knew what was going on, wanted her to stop seeing Don . . . not because they didn't like him, but because they didn't want her to get serious when she was only fifteen. She liked Don very much. She didn't want to lose him, but she also wanted to go out with other boys. She felt intimidated by Don's pressure and she wanted Henry to get Don to let her go out with someone else once in a while.

Henry felt that he was caught in a bind. He realized that Don desperately needed Lisa. However he also sensed that Lisa was a much more adequate and mature person. Lisa was very good for Don, but Don wasn't the best boy friend for her. Henry felt a little guilty about having to sacrifice Lisa's best interests to help Don. Nevertheless, he told Lisa that although he understood her predicament, Don needed her a great deal. Perhaps, Henry suggested, she and Don could reach a compromise.

Don changed the subject before they could discuss a compromise. He hinted to Lisa that he had funny ideas about his mother, approached closer and closer to spelling them out, joked about them, then backed off. All the while Lisa reacted in an almost maternal manner to Don's discomfort.

"Isn't it strange," Henry thought to himself, "Don sees his mother who's in her thirties as a girl friend, and his girl friend who's fifteen as a mother."

DRINKING, SNIFFING, BUT NO SHOOTING-UP

Like most of the other boys, Manuel wanted to talk rather than study when he started class.

"I like ta drink," he told Connie. "It burns ya throat and make ya feel good, reeal good, reeal high. Man, I sweat when I get high. Every Friday night I get high . . ."

Connie wanted to respond but, remembering our advice, she remained silent.

"I use ta sniff . . . not coke . . . glue. You know the stuff you get fa airplane models, but I stop cause it give me a stiff neck over here. My cousin, he still does it."

Connie was following him, except for coke. She thought coke was Coca-Cola, not cocaine. She was just beginning to learn about the kids' culture.

Manuel continued, "Ya know those cigarettes?"

"Pot?" Connie asked.

"Yeah. I neva try then, but I ain fraid. I don carry a gun a knife like that crazy kid. My cousin, he got a twenty-two automatic. I kin get it anytime I wan it."

That unnerved Connie. Nevertheless, instead of lecturing him she turned her face away to hide her concern.

"You know," Manuel continued, "my father gay me my firs drink, a screwdriver, in the seben grade. I like it."

Manuel stopped talking and read a story about a birthday party for a while. Connie asked him when his birthday was.

"I forgot," he answered.

"You forgot?"

"No, May twenty-one. I forget so I be surprise if I get a presen an I don be disappointed if I don. I preten to forget. . . . My cousin he want to cone ta school with me cause he see my leather jacket. But I'n afraid ta ask if he could. I don like askin fa things, I got too much a'ready. I don think I bring him anyway, he's crazy. Sonetime he break things in the basemen. My whole family's crazy."

When Manuel had finished talking, Connie asked him to write some of the words from the story. He reversed "g's," "p's," "q's," "b's," and "d's." She tried to point out his mistakes but he said,

"No, thas wrong, thas not the way it goes." Then he added nervously, "I know thas the way, but I like ta write then THIS way. I like to write things backward."

Connie was about to continue the discussion, but Herb, who had been watching the lesson, signaled her not to get into an argument because he felt that Manuel was extremely threatened by the realization that he sometimes wrote backwards without knowing it. So Connie suggested that they walk to the post office. On the way, he said he was going to practice writing at home.

TWO UNHAPPY BOYS

Carlos and Harold were both unhappy when they came to school. Carlos was still worried that he was sick. He told Henry he thought he had heart disease and wondered if his mother had given it to him, but added characteristically, "I was only kiddin." Henry reassured him that we would take good care of him, took his temperature which turned out to be normal, and gave him some aspirin anyway.

Carlos then went in the music room, interrupting Willie who was playing a tune for Herb which he had figured out by himself. While he was playing, Carlos began to hit some of the keys. Willie continued playing as if nothing was happening. Amazed at Willie's controlled acceptance of Carlos's interference (especially when Willie had accused Carlos of breaking the keys the previous day), Herb waited in vain for Willie to say something, then made Carlos stop.

Harold was also unhappy. However, he was too unhappy to talk about whatever it was that was bothering him. Instead he spent most of the morning making clay ashtrays and taking out his hostility on Bill by dirtying up the studio and keeping himself clean by wiping his clay-soaked hands on Bill's work clothes. Instead of reacting angrily, Bill tried to convince himself that it was Harold's way of relating—of demonstrating the friendships and warm feelings which he couldn't show without disguising them in some aggressive cloak. Bill reminded himself of the times during the early months of the pilot program when he had eaten himself up inside because Harold's provocation had gotten to him and he told himself he didn't want to go through that again. And when all that failed, Bill consoled himself with the thought that he could have been wearing his good clothes rather than his work clothes.

Harold was still too upset to do any academic work when he went to Connie's class. After a few minutes he slammed his book shut, told her he couldn't take any more, and walked out. She followed him into the hall where they sat on the stairs. He said his mind was too mixed up in the afternoon for English and asked her if he could have English during the morning when he could concentrate better. Trying to be as noncommittal as possible, Connie told him to talk to Herb about it.

Thursday, January 19

The next morning Connie told us about Larry's statement that he wanted to be a "doctor or a nurse, whichever came easier." She took it literally and thought he meant that he was not sure whether he could get through medical school or would have to settle for less training. Norm felt that it represented his questioning of his general ability. Herb interpreted it to mean that he was not sure whether he wanted to be a man or woman, perhaps sexually or perhaps in terms of traditional male-female role differences.

Connie also told us that Harold had asked her to change his English class to the morning. Since Harold was able to work in other academic classes in the afternoon, we doubted that changing the time of his class would make any difference. Norm and Henry thought that Harold might be so sexually aroused in Connie's class that he could not work with her. They asked Herb to explore the possibility with Harold. In the meantime, Connie was told not to exert any pressure on Harold to come to class or to stay in class.

After warm-up Herb talked to Harold about his English class. Harold claimed that he couldn't concentrate during the afternoon, so Herb reminded him that he was able to concentrate on his other academic subjects during the afternoon.

"They're diffrint sujet," Harold answered.

"Do you think you're having trouble because of Connie, not the subject? Maybe instead of switching the period, you could change teachers."

"No, no!" Harold insisted, "it . . . the time, Connie okay."

Since his probes hadn't uncovered anything, Herb explained that it would be impossible to make the switch immediately because of the schedule, but he would look into it.

NERVOUS TENSION

Don was agitated all day. At first he prowled around the school and quietly paced up and down the halls like a caged tiger. However he was sitting on more tension than he could hold back without some more violent activity. He went into the gym where he began jumping up and down, scratching his sides, and making monkey noises as he changed from teen-age boy into teen-age gorilla. That still wasn't enough. He snarled at Herb, assumed a judo stance, and faked a judo chop, a drop kick, then screamed as loud as he could. Herb offered to wrestle Don on the mats, but he refused. As Herb watched, Don began kicking and punching one of the gym lockers. Larry heard the racket and joined in. They incited each other to a higher and higher pitch, until finally bam! bam! They both gave two good kicks, mashed in one of the locker doors, and reached their climax.

Don looked at Herb, obviously concerned about what might happen.

"It's okay," Herb told him. "If you're upset, you're upset. Better a locker than a person."

Things quieted down. Larry went off to English class and Don went to shop instead of English, which he had not attended for over a week anyway. In English, Connie asked Larry to rewrite his composition. He complained that he hated to rewrite anything but did so. He wrote:

The swing coolness that can either scare or give courage is the intrigue of adventure. Buildings quickly rushing past and a casement coming closer is a thrill that can only be experienced by one who had the nerve to try swinging on a rope attached to a

3¼ lb. grappling hook on a windowsill or over the ledge of a building.

The night in which all the intrigue takes place is welcomed by a clear hot day in which I feel the yearning to be free away from a crowded street.

"My friends call me the daredevil," Larry told Connie as he worked on his composition. "Because I'm not afraid of nothing. The other guys in the neighborhood just want to sit around. They never want to take any risks. I love to take risks. Man, the two coolest profession's got to be a body-guard or a cat burglar. Man, there's tremendous risk in both."

After Larry finished rewriting his composition he gave Connie a detailed description of how he rode elevators and climbed buildings while she listened openmouthed. Connie had learned not to worry too much about Manuel's wild stories because they were mostly fantasies. Larry's adventures frightened her because he did them all.

After English Larry went to music where he played the base guitar which he had brought to school. Don heard the music, wandered into the room, and quickly joined in on his lead guitar. Marilyn got Willie out of shop. Willie's piano made it a trio until Don drifted out of class, leaving Larry and Willie playing together.

After class Larry told Herb that Marilyn thought we ought to buy a base guitar and a set of drums for the school so the boys could have a band.

"Are you sure that it's Marilyn who wants the instruments?" Herb asked.

"Yeah," Larry answered. "She told me just before when she heard me play my guitar. Stanley plays the drums. Man, we could have a groove. Me and Don on guitar, Willie on piano, and Stanley on drums."

Herb thought Larry was trying to put the con on him and

he didn't like it, but didn't say so. Instead he told Larry that it was Marilyn's program and Marilyn's decision.

"Then you can talk to her about it later, you'll see," Larry replied.

Herb liked that even less. He was particularly sensitive about being told to do anything when it concerned his wife.

"We'll see," he answered.

AIN'T THAT SOME SHIT

Nat Stevens and his mother visited the school. Nat was a tall, thin, but well-built fourteen-year-old black youngster whose twinkling alert eyes and quick movements contrasted with his dopey expression and quiet withdrawal. Mrs. Stevens seemed like a woman who was too worn out by her struggle to raise eight children to be able to give Nat the time and energy he needed to succeed in the well-ordered, demanding world of school. She and her eight children were crammed into a six-room slum apartment in an extremely deteriorated building. Nat and his three brothers slept four in a double bed, the girls had a little more room. Depending almost completely on welfare payments to survive, the family had little furniture and even less clothing. There was no heat in the apartment and the water had just been turned off. Mrs. Stevens was concerned about Nat, but as tired as she was, she was extremely glad that we were about to assume some responsibility for him. Mrs. Stevens left after the interview, but Nat stayed for the day.

After Nat had wandered through the school for a while, Herb asked him what he would like to do. Nat said that he liked gym and would also like to do a little shop work. He wasn't too interested in reading and arithmetic, but he might do a little bit in reading. Herb told him that we had a nice woman in school, meaning Natalie, who might work with him alone for part of the day. His program would be two periods of gym, a period of shop, a period of art, and a period of academic work with Natalie.

Since Nat had never traveled into Manhattan by himself, Herb took him over the route he would take home. He walked with Nat to the corner, rode on the bus with him, walked him to the subway, then down to where he would buy the tokens, and showed him which side to go to get his train. He asked Nat to read a few signs in the subway. Nat couldn't. He was illiterate, except for a few words which he had learned to recognize.

We had received Nat's probation report a few days earlier. According to the report, Nat had been in court a number of times during the preceding three years. He was first arrested when he was eleven years old after being caught in the streets with several cartons of cigarettes which he had stolen from a neighborhood supermarket. About a year later he was caught vandalizing the neighborhood school. His third arrest occurred a year and a half later when he and a friend were caught driving a stolen car. Finally, he was brought to court when he was fourteen by his mother because she couldn't handle him. She complained that he stayed out until the early hours of the morning, came home drunk, threatened to jump out of a window if she did anything to him, and refused to attend school. The court recommended placement in a state training school, but he was referred to our school instead.

Nat's school record was terrible. He had never attended regularly, and he had been a terror in school when he had attended. He fought with the other students, cursed his teachers and threw things at them. He had been transferred to special classes and special schools and hadn't been in school during the preceding year.

There were numerous explanations in his probation report for his delinquent and disruptive behavior. The court psychiatrist thought Nat was almost "completely lacking in insight and judgment." The court psychologist felt that Nat's 69 IQ score indicated that he was mentally retarded. The probation officer believed that Nat had spent "so much time living with relatives and friends in the South as well as the North that his upbringing was inconsistent and his relationships transitory." During his previous court appearances, Nat's behavior had been attributed to brain damage, psychosis, and mental retardation. Poverty had never been suggested as a factor. "Ain't that some shit?"

Friday, January 20

TIDDLYWINKS

Friday started off on a high pitch because Connie and Herb were taking the boys skiing in the Bronx. As more and more of the boys arrived in school the level of excitement increased. By ten thirty everyone but Willie had arrived. The boys were in Connie's room waiting for her to bring up the milk and cake. Herb was in the next room trying to get Willie on the phone to check if he had left.

"Where's Herbie?" Harold asked.

Don, who was sitting on his usual chair, bent back against the wall, with his feet up, answered, "He's playing tiddlywinks with Connie . . . why the fuck shouldn't he play tiddlywinks with her. Henry says I'm playing tiddlywinks with my mother."

Don had meant it as a joke at Herb's expense, but it hadn't come out that way. When he realized what he actually had said, he jumped to his feet, slammed his fist down on the window ledge, and shouted, "That's bull shit. That's insane."

The boys looked at Don but said nothing, perhaps because they could see that he was very serious.

Don was losing control. He stood there staring out of the

window for a few moments. Suddenly, without warning, his fist was being rammed through the windowpane. The impact returned him to his senses. He spun around, shaking all over.

"Somebody else did it! What's gonna happen?" he asked in a panic. He thought for a few seconds, then headed for the door shouting, "Tell Herb someone threw a brick."

As he reached the door he bumped into Herb who was coming in from the hall.

"What's all the shouting about?" Herb demanded. "What the hell's going on?"

Herb could see that Don was upset, but he wasn't sure if it was because of what Don had done to the window or what he had said about himself and his mother. He guessed that Don was frightened about losing control of himself and tried to reassure him by telling him that he wasn't the first kid to get upset and smash his fist through a window—and he wouldn't be the last one either. It was like smashing the locker—no big deal. Don calmed down and went back in.

[Don's tension had been building up all week. He had been able to let some of it out in his gorillalike antics, but finally it became too much for him and he had exploded. His "secret" was out in the open and he was dealing with it—explosively at first but then in other ways. That was our expectation at least.]

SKIING

Finally Willie arrived, so we left. Our first stop was the corner dry goods store. Everyone needed gloves for the rope tows and knitted caps for the cold. Fifty-nine cents for a pair of gloves and eighty-nine cents for a hat. Willie didn't want a knit cap. Herb and Connie wondered why. They found out five minutes later when they passed a nearby store. Willie wanted a hat like the one in the window. Nat wanted one also . . . just like a jealous brother—whatever he gets, I want. But Nat had already gotten a hat and Willie hadn't. So they bought one hat and continued on to the subway.

Since the train was fairly empty, the boys spread out in groups: Manuel and Connie; Carlos and Nat; Willie, Harold, and Herb; Larry and Don. After a few stops a drunk sat down next to Connie and started talking to her. Willie and Harold started grumbling that they were going to get the guy. Herb tried to joke them out of it, but he was worried they might still cause a scene. Fortunately Connie got up and changed her seat.

The first thing the boys did when they got to the ski area was to eat. Then they joined a group lesson, everyone but Larry who couldn't ski because of his broken jaw and Connie who sat out the skiing to keep him company.

Herb watched the boys during their lesson. Everyone except Carlos paid attention and tried to get the hang of it. Carlos just stood around, seemingly lost in his own thoughts. Nat was unable to follow the instructor. As the skiing was about to start, Herb got nervous. "Someone's going to break a leg," he thought to himself. "Carlos probably or Nat or Harold . . . someone."

Fortunately he was wrong. No one was hurt except for Herb himself who needed some stitches for a cut he received over his right eye when he and his ski pole collided. After the boys finally learned how to go up the rope tow, they all did well, especially Carlos who skied down the slopes like the natural athlete he was.

By late afternoon most of the boys were pooped. Connie and Herb led Larry, Willie, Manuel, Nat, and Don back to the subway. Carlos and Harold stayed for the night skiing.

4 Niggers, Spics, Jews, and Bastard Babies

Monday, January 23, and Tuesday, January 24

Monday and Tuesday were fairly routine. During the morning coffee the boys talked about their skiing trip. Harold claimed he had picked up a girl after the others had left. The one "I were talkin to at the food stand," he told us, as if to prove his claim. Don tried to put him down with a look of disgusted disbelief, but the others seemed at least a little convinced. The conversation continued until class time. Larry, Don, Harold, and Willie went to Norm's for biology. Willie was still wearing the hat we had bought him Friday. Carlos went with Bill to work on his clay head. Manuel went with Connie, and Herb took Nat for some informal math and reading assessment.

TELEPHONES AND TOOLS ARE FOR TOYS
Nat tuned Herb out as soon as Herb asked him to read. He picked up a phone and dialed some numbers. Herb didn't interfere because he wanted to see what Nat would do. Someone at the other end answered.

"It's me. In school. A man wonta talk to you," Nat said, as he handed the phone to Herb. Caught by surprise with a phone in his hand, Herb sat immobilized.

"Who's on the phone?" he asked.

112

"My father," Nat answered.

Herb began talking. Not knowing what to say, but having to say something, he said that Nat had just started school and was doing well. Nat's father, or whoever was at the other end of the phone, seemed as lost for words as Herb. After a short silence Herb said good-bye and hung up.

"What the hell was that all about," he thought to himself, puzzled and uncomfortable. "What a weird thing. Was that really his father? Why did Nat call him?"

Herb asked Nat to read and found out what he had already known—Nat couldn't read. He was even less literate than Carlos. His math was almost as bad as his reading except that he had learned to do some very simple addition and subtraction on his fingers.

During the next period Norm kept Nat occupied in the shop. Intuitively he showed Nat the electric hand drills and hand sander. With pistol grips, they looked like toy guns and Nat used them exactly that way. Carlos came in but he didn't feel like working on the wooden table he had started. So Norm kept him in the shop by working on it for him.

[Norm got right down to the boys' level—toys for Nat and "ADC" (Aid to Dependent Children) for Carlos. It hit the spot.]

Herb asked Marilyn to work with Nat during the third period. Marilyn thought he was kidding. Nat needed toys not instruments, she argued. Marilyn was right. All Nat wanted to do was bang on the piano and make noise. Her nice new piano—she wasn't ready for that.

Tuesday Nat discovered the telephone intercom system while he was alone in the gym. People had said Nat was retarded. Yet he learned the numbers of most of the offices and classes in a matter of one period (and he never forgot them). Since Herb was the person with unscheduled time, Nat kept calling him to ask him to come down to the gym.

When this didn't get him the attention he wanted, he went into Phyllis's office. Phyllis ignored him, so he started playing with her electric typewriter. Since that got him what he wanted—a short, attention-getting argument—he left.

CONVERSES

Carlos spent most of his time thinking about Converse brand sneakers (the Cadillac in the sneaker field). We had bought Converse sneakers for the other boys before Carlos joined the school so naturally he didn't want to settle for less. But Converse sneakers weren't sold in the neighborhood. Monday just before lunch, he cornered Herb and asked him when he could get his Converse sneakers. Herb told Carlos that he could take him across the street for regular sneakers, but if he wanted Converse, he would have to wait until Tuesday when Natalie could take him out of the neighborhood. Carlos pouted and whined, like a little kid rather than a sixteen-year-old, that all the other boys had gotten sneakers from the school so why couldn't he. Herb explained why, but Carlos wouldn't believe that the local stores didn't carry Converse sneakers. When Herb took him across to the shoe store and Carlos found out that they really didn't sell Converse sneakers, he scowled at the owner, told him it was "a fuckin store," and asked Herb to take him out of the neighborhood for a pair of Converse. Herb laughed and said, "Come on, Carlos. We both know you're just teasing so let's forget about the sneakers for today."

Tuesday Natalie took Carlos from store to store without finding Converse sneakers. Carlos became more angry and more frustrated, calling the storekeepers "stupid" rather than "fuckin," probably because he was with Natalie not Herb, and belligerently bumping into people in the street. When Carlos bumped into an old man and cursed him out,

Natalie had enough. She could be patient about the sneakers but not about the scene in the street.

"Let's go, Carlos," she insisted.

"I din do nothing. He bump me," Carlos protested.

"That's not true," Natalie replied, trying unsuccessfully to control her anger. Natalie could accept aggression in the school. The public streets were something else. "There are things you can do in school that people on the streets won't tolerate," she told Carlos.

"It's his fault, not mine," Carlos claimed. "Tha old man's a stupid fool."

"Then it's all the more reason for you not to act like one," Natalie contended.

"Okay, get a taxi. We go to Klein."

"We don't need a taxi, Carlos. It's only nine blocks away and it's a nice day for a walk."

Carlos tried again.

"All women a cheap. Bill always take a taxi."

That didn't work either. Natalie could handle that "rap."

They arrived at the store. Carlos did some window-shopping before they went inside.

"Gemme a suit," he demanded as he looked hopefully for Natalie's reaction. "That one an the blue knit an the hat . . . an don forget my sneakers."

"You know why we came here, Carlos," Natalie answered. "We're only going to buy sneakers."

Another round lost for Carlos. Still the battle wasn't over. They went inside. Carlos knew his way around. He obviously had been there many times before.

"See," he said, pointing to the red T-shirt he was wearing. "I lifted this from here."

The way he knew every corner of the store, Natalie believed he had "shopped" there often.

They went to the shoe department. Again no Converse

sneakers. Carlos wanted to go to another store, but they had to return to the school for lunch. Since it was late, they took that cab Carlos had been pressuring for. At least that was a minor victory for Carlos.

On the way into the dining hall, he asked Natalie to stay with him in the afternoon. She said she couldn't.

"Oh, you wanna get rid a me," he whined.

"Of course not, Carlos. You know that I don't stay a whole day, but I'll return tomorrow."

"Will ya take me ta my otha school tomorra aftanoon?"

"Carlos!" she raged, angry that he wouldn't take no for an answer, "I just told you I didn't work in the afternoons. Anyway, I have an appointment to go to the beauty parlor."

Carlos still wouldn't let her off the hook.

"Lemme go with ya?" he asked, changing his approach. "I won cause trouble. I promise."

Wanting to say no, but feeling bad about doing so, she said, "We'll have to wait and see what happens tomorrow."

That was another minor victory for Carlos.

IT'S OKAY TO SAY NO

While the boys were eating lunch, Natalie asked Herb what she should do about her beauty parlor appointment. She enjoyed working with Carlos, she told Herb, but at the same time she felt he was making more and more demands on her. Herb told her she couldn't possibly do everything that Carlos wanted her to do for him. Besides, even if she did things that she really didn't want to do, she would communicate her anger and resentment to him. Natalie agreed, and thought of an excuse she could comfortably give him.

CRAZY BOUT HORSES

Manuel couldn't concentrate in class because he was preoccupied about the visit he had to make to his probation officer later in the week. He began to read, but he didn't seem ready to work. Connie asked him if he wanted to stop reading.

"No," he answered as he put his hand over his face with his thumb and his middle finger on either side of the top of his nose and rocked his head back and forth and up and down.

"Manuel, what are you doing?" Connie asked.

"Concentratin," he replied, but he really couldn't concentrate. Instead, he talked about the ski trip which he had liked so much that he was going to go again as soon as his parents gave him an allowance.

"My brother, he a'ready got allowance," he added. "He's the oldes so he got allowance. He don drink, he don smoke, and he goes ta school. Tha's why he ge's allowance."

"Did you ever ask for an allowance?" Connie asked.

"I don wanna ax. I'n not allow ta smoke in my house. I'n the crin'nal, but I'n use ta it. Once my ol man, he took my lighta away, but he gabe me it back when I make a sad face. Sonetine I sneak cigarettes inta my house in my shoes cause my ol lady break em up when she fine em. . . . She goes ta the church where they don let you wear listick or smoke, not even drink or dance. Not me," he protested, "I don go ta tha church no more. Even my ol man ge's stone sonetine like on New Year Seve."

After lunch, and after Manuel had thrown up three sandwiches, Connie took him to a nearby auction gallery where he stood rooted in front of a painting of a wild horse, saying, "I'n crazy bout horses, specially white one. Wish I could run fas like a wile horse. I ride one if I could. Once I try but I fell off too many tines."

On the way back to school Manuel mimicked his father who angrily called him a crazy kid and hit him when he couldn't remember a word.

"My father's nervous," he explained as if he were trying to excuse him. "He has that . . . ya know, asthma," pointing to his stomach. "He can stop hinself when he ge's mad so my mother has ta get hin offa me. I'n neva gonna let hin know I kin read cause he might gimme too hard a word to read an hit me."

The next morning Manuel arrived late. He told Connie that he had ridden past his stop because he had been day-dreaming about something "private" on the subway. Connie took out a piece of strawberry shortcake she had brought to school hoping to tempt Manuel to eat something in the morning. He grinned, said: "Strawberry shortcake! Howdya know thas my fav'rite?" and ate the cake and some milk without getting sick. But he still wasn't ready to read. He began racing, skipping, and substituting words.

Connie asked him if he was guessing.

"Yeah," he answered. "There's nothin in there," pointing to his head, "jus plain water, thas why I drink so much water. I got water in a brain."

Manuel was too moody, too preoccupied, and too restless to work, so Connie suggested that they do something else. He wanted to draw on the board. Automatically, as if he had done so a thousand times before, he drew a roundish rectangular shape with a square above it with a "D" written inside of the square.

"Guess what it is," Manuel asked.

When she couldn't, he told her, "I's a grabe with a tune stone. The 'D' says dead."

He replaced the tombstone with other drawings until he completed a picture of a man dressed like a woman. When Connie couldn't guess what it was, he snickered and said, "Ax Don if he knows. He won. He stupid . . . there was one on Fif Avenue by Forty-seben Street. Me and my frien ax hin, 'Hey mister, you got the tine,' cause we know he was no woman."

HIGH AND RESTLESS IN ENGLISH

We assigned Don and Larry to English together. Connie had each of them sit on opposite sides of a bookcase which served as a partial room-divider in the hope that they wouldn't distract each other. Don didn't need any distraction. As soon as Connie tried to get him started, he put on a confused, dazed look and told her he was high. Paying no attention to his message, she gave him his programmed English text to work on. Don flipped the pages for a while as if he were shopping for something interesting, put the book down, picked up a short-story book, and started reading. Connie felt better . . . prematurely. As Don read he moaned, "It's a shitty story, it's a shitty story" until he could no longer sit there, then walked out.

After leaving Connie, Don found Henry in his office and spoke to him about his problems with Lisa and his ambition to become a pop singer with his own group. Henry thought Don was using his fantasy about becoming a pop singer to excuse his inability to function in class. So he told Don that while it was a goal to strive for, it was an extremely difficult accomplishment and nothing he could really count on. When Don agreed that he ought to put his eggs in more than one basket, Henry was able to involve him in a discussion of his work in school.

Meanwhile Connie gave Larry a vocabulary book which he correctly claimed was too easy for him. She gave him another one which was too difficult for him. Then just like "Goldilocks and the Three Bears," she found one that was just right. Larry glanced at the words and said, "I'm always restless, I don't know why."

Blocking out his message about not wanting to work, Connie asked him to get started. But he was too impatient with any word that he didn't already know to continue very long. After a few minutes he announced, "I'll go crazy with one more word, if I have to look up one more word," and looked at Connie to see if she believed him. When Connie registered nothing, he told her more directly, "You don't know how close I am," just as Phyllis called out that lunch was ready.

During lunch Larry took Herb into the music room to hear him play the bass guitar and amplifier Larry had brought to school. Soon he was telling Herb that the amplifier wasn't any good because it was for a lead guitar, not a bass. Then he told Herb that he knew of one the school could buy cheaply. Herb didn't bite. Larry offered to leave his guitar in school for the other boys. Herb thanked him but told him we could buy one if we needed one. That was all Larry needed to hear. He was off and running about the different instruments the school should buy and where they could be bought cheaply. Herb thought he had heard that story before.

"It's up to Marilyn," he reminded Larry, feeling even more irritated than the first time Larry had asked him about the instruments.

During the afternoon Don and Larry got together again. They hung around playing music and talking to Bill and Norm about how they often smoked pot and how it helped them play better music.

STANLEY'S WHORE

Stanley's girl wasn't pregnant . . . but he wasn't smiling . . . something was wrong. He had broken up with his girl because she was a whore.

"What do you mean?" Herb asked.

"There wasn't any blood on the bed."

"What about the pink spots?"

"Maybe that's where she came," Stanley answered.

Stanley told Herb that after his girl had her period, he became very suspicious, called her a lying whore, cursed her, pushed her, and hit her—a little. How did he feel about that? Herb asked. Well, he couldn't get it out of his mind. Suddenly he had seen red and the next minute it was all over and he had hit her. That wasn't what Herb had asked. He wanted Stanley to say something about what he had done. He asked again. Stanley seemed sorry but unable to admit it. The best he could do was to hint that there was some slight possibility that he might have been wrong. But, he added, she didn't prove that she was a virgin.

"How could she prove it?" Herb asked.

Stanley didn't know, but that didn't make any difference.

Herb tried to get Stanley to talk about how he thought his girl might have felt, but Stanley seemed completely unconcerned about her feelings. Herb warned Stanley to take precautions if he did anything again or else he would have the same problems in a few weeks. Then he let the conversation end.

Wednesday, January 25

I DON'T CARE IF THEY DON'T LOVE ME

Willie was the first one in for the morning warm-up served by Henry. Taking advantage of the privacy of his situation, Willie asked if the school could buy him a winter coat. Henry said we probably would. Then Willie's conversation turned to how badly he had been treated at home. His voice dropped, his hands fell limp at his sides, and the depth of his sadness showed on his face. But Willie couldn't allow himself to feel sad. He had to deny the hurt he felt.

"I don care if they don love me," he added, touching the hat we had bought him. "Just as long as they don't bother me."

Henry was about to respond when their privacy was interrupted, first by Carlos, then by Nat. Perhaps annoyed by

Carlos's interruption or still angry about the piano, Willie began ranking Carlos who, in turn, passed it down to Nat in a low-key, good-natured but nevertheless clear pattern.

TELEPHONE CALLS HOME

It was time for class. Manuel, Don, Larry, and Harold were "no-shows." Manuel had to go to court. The others we didn't know about. Henry waited until eleven o'clock, then called their homes. Harold answered his call, said he was sick, and produced an unconvincing cough. He had been coming to school, he told Henry, even though he had been sick, until he finally became too ill to attend.

Larry also answered his call. He said he was too weak to come to school. In fact, he claimed, his doctor thought that he might need intravenous feeding because he was weak from lack of solid foods. Henry thought Larry was either lying or exaggerating with his mother's support. However, he didn't challenge Larry directly. Instead he tried to convince him to come to school Thursday.

Mrs. Russo answered Henry's call. She told Henry that Don had left for school and she didn't know where he was. Henry offered to call her if he learned anything. Mrs. Russo nervously asked what time he would call because she was afraid her husband would find out that Don hadn't been in school. Henry felt Mrs. Russo should be confronted with what she was doing. Keeping the truth from her husband wasn't helping anyone including Don, he answered. Mrs. Russo half agreed, but felt that Henry didn't know how violently her husband would react. Henry suggested that her husband should be helped to accept Don's behavior instead of being kept in the dark.

"You don't know what my husband is like," Mrs. Russo protested. "Don's been good. Still my husband acts nasty. He's just looking for Don to do something wrong to get him out of the house."

Henry told her that it would be best if she and her husband came to see him. She agreed at first, then changed her mind and said she wanted to discuss it with her husband before making it definite. Henry wasn't sure why Mrs. Russo was hesitant. Was she afraid of her husband? he wondered. Did she want to keep him in the dark, or did she want to maintain the situation as it was for her own reasons?

When Don came to school, he told Henry that he couldn't come earlier because he didn't have carfare. He claimed that he had spent the allowance and carfare money we had given him so he had had to borrow money from a friend. His friend wouldn't lend him any money, so he had to sneak into the subway and that's why he was late.

More concerned about Don's problems at home than his phony excuse, Henry called Mrs. Russo again and learned that Don and his stepfather were arguing constantly. After his conversation with Mrs. Russo, Henry asked Don about what his mother had said. Don opened up to Henry about his contempt for his stepfather, the "bastard," who treated his mother so badly that he had to protect her. As Don spoke, Henry could hear how attached he was to his mother, how both of them had teamed up against his father, and how, with his mother's encouragement, Don was deliberately ignoring his stepfather and antagonizing him.

Henry told Don what he thought was happening between Don and his parents. He explained why it was bad for Don, his mother, and his stepfather, and why Don would be better off giving up the role of his mother's protector. If his mother needed protection and help, Henry told him, we could help her.

CHEAP JEW

Natalie had promised to take Carlos for sneakers, but when he reminded her she realized she was committed to too many other things to make the trip uptown and back. Instead, she offered to take him in the neighborhood to have his jacket repaired. Carlos asked her to take Nat with them.

No sooner had they left the school than Carlos started in on her with: "Les go uptown ta get sneakers."

Natalie countered with: "Carlos, you know we're going to have your jacket repaired. That's what I said we were going to do and that's what we're going to do."

Switching from simple asking to whining, Carlos hit her with: "You tol me yesaday we could get sneakers—you promise me."

Carlos had her. Natalie agreed that it was her error, but she insisted on going to the tailor anyway.

Natalie was learning how to say no. But Carlos had already learned how to deal with people who said no. He had lost the skirmish, but he made her pay for her victory by bumping into people, making passes at girls, and walking in the street closer, closer, very much closer to the oncoming traffic. Finally they arrived at the tailor shop . . . safe and sound.

Carlos asked the tailor what it would cost to fix the jacket.

"Five dollars."

"Five dollar?" Carlos asked, surprised. Then, acting like he wanted Natalie to spend more money on him, he told the man: "Clean the jacket too. Charge more money."

Natalie intervened immediately. "How much extra would it cost to clean the jacket?"

"For a leather jacket like this, seven dollars," the tailor answered.

That was more than it cost to repair the jacket . . . too much more.

"Never mind—just repair it," Natalie told him.

"Cheap, all women a cheap," Carlos shouted. "Whada *you* care? Spend the money. I's not yours."

But Natalie was learning to set limits with Carlos, so she was able to ward him off with: "It doesn't matter whose money it is. We came here to get your jacket fixed, not cleaned."

Carlos gave it one more try, but Natalie ended the battle with a firm "No! Now let's go back to the school."

As they walked, Carlos told Nat, who had kept out of the battle, that Natalie was Jewish, and asked her to speak her "race." Natalie told him she couldn't speak her race, and again explained the difference between race, religion, and language, as she had done the day before.

"Ya know," Carlos continued, "a man kill a million Jews, then found out he was Jew too." Thinking of Jewish and killing reminded Carlos of something he had heard.

"Did you kill God?" he asked her only half-seriously.

"Of course not," Natalie answered somewhat more seriously than Carlos had been.

"Well, other Jews did," he contended.

"No, they didn't," she answered, a little too personally involved. "Even the Pope said that the Jewish people did not kill God."

Carlos didn't believe her. He continued talking about Natalie's Jewishness and insisted in an increasingly demanding tone of voice that she speak her language . . . and when she didn't, began insulting Jews. Each time Carlos stopped harassing Natalie to take a breath, Nat irritated her with a question about her personal life. The more uncomfortable she felt about being caught between Carlos's anti-Semitic remarks about cheap Jews and Nat's continuous questions about her social life, the further away the school seemed to be. She tried to ignore Carlos's remarks and to answer Nat's questions matter-of-factly, but it didn't work too well. Her relief came only when she saw the school ahead.

They all went upstairs to the gym. Letting Natalie off the hook, the boys played Ping-Pong and insulted each other's background, making good-natured but continuous comments about niggers and spics. Then Natalie played a game with Carlos. When it was Nat's turn to play, Carlos interrupted them until Nat finally told him to shut up. Changing his attention-getting tactics, Carlos began calling people on the intercom. Natalie asked him not to, then tried to grab the receiver from him. As she did, Carlos pulled it back. Norm walked in. Natalie let go and walked away, relieved to be rescued, but concerned about the rivalry she thought she was creating between the two boys.

Thursday, January 26

WHERE WE STAND—SUPPOSEDLY

During the morning meeting, Bill asked how he should handle the fairly continuous discussions about drugs in the studio. Bill didn't want to lecture the boys, but he was becoming anxious being just a listening bystander. He wanted a way of involving himself in a more active approach. Although Henry and Herb said that Bill was already doing the right thing, Bill was concerned that the boys might interpret his silence as approval. Henry didn't believe so. He and Herb thought the boys had already decided, although inaccurately, what position each of us took about their delinquencies. We guessed that the boys probably assumed that Henry, Bill, Herb, and Connie were on the side of the law, that Norm was sympathetic to some of their delinquent hip behavior, and that Marilyn was an easy touch who would give in to them as long as their inclinations weren't clearly illegal. There seemed no reason for us to spell out our attitudes for them, except for Norm. We didn't want the boys to be fooled by his appearance.

Instead of saying anything to the boys, each of us would

attempt to maintain a neutral position compatible with his own style, in order to get as much "information" as possible.

SEX EDUCATION

Then Norm told us that he had been spending most of the time in his biology class on sex education since Stanley had asked him how he could tell if his girl had been a virgin. The boys were interested in birth control, conception, and the anatomy of the vagina. They were especially eager to discuss why infants could be born with congenital syphilis or drug addiction. Attendance had been great.

MORE ON THE JEWISH QUESTION

After the meeting, Manuel picked up with Connie where Carlos had left off with Natalie—the Jewish question. While he was reading, he came to a picture of two children on the way to school wearing little black beanies and asked, "A these kids Jew?"

"Why?" Connie asked.

Manuel pointed to the black beanies.

"Look."

"No," she answered. "That was probably the style, you know, a little cap that kids wore."

We were obviously dealing with the Jewish question in the school . . . Don, Carlos, and Nat, now Manuel.

[What were Larry and Willie thinking? Were they different or just keeping quiet? Stanley and Harold we knew about. They were Jewish. Nat and Carlos were also going through a black-Puerto Rican thing. We would have more of that from time to time.]

Nat interrupted the class. Manuel got angry and tried to slam the door in Nat's face but Connie intervened.

After class Connie took Manuel to buy some things for

the school. As they walked, he talked about his "crummy" neighborhood. He asked her to visit him there. Then he changed his mind because he knew some "real nasty guys" would be nasty to her.

"I'n gonna buy me a knife," he told her. "Ya never kin tell when some guy's gonna pull a razor on ya. I's a tough neighborhood here."

"Has anyone ever bothered you in this neighborhood?" Connie asked, trying to reassure Manuel that he didn't need a knife.

"No, but ya never kin tell when it kin happen, everybody gotta die sonetine," he explained. "I got ratted on two tines —once by a frien the police beat hin up and once by sone guy I din know. I even got blane fa things I din do wrong. Even my own mother rats on me. She sign the paper fa me ta go ta Youth House. She don like me. She put me away. Yeah, she don like me."

When Connie and Manuel returned, Nat was in front of the school waiting for them.

"Where you been?" he demanded. "You always goin way with Manuel. Ah neva gets to go nowhere. When do ah go on a trip? When do ah be with you?"

[Nat wanted Connie's attention. He wanted her for "his person" too. But he had Natalie and he would have to be satisfied with one person.]

I'N STUPID

Manuel was still depressed during his afternoon reading session. "I'n not a genius, I'n stupid," he told Connie. "My mother says I'n stupid cause I like this school cause you gimme baby stuff. I follow my uncle. He stupid too . . . there's nothin wrong with my brain, there's sonethin wrong with me. I should a wen ta school. I don know what I'n doin . . . I tol the psychiatrist I hear things but I neva do.

I jus wanna goof on hin. I gabe hin a sad face and said I hear things . . . I only like myself when I'n drunk. I laugh ina mirror and say, 'dope!' . . . When do I go back ta see a psychiatrist? When I go back I'n gonna have me sone laugh."

Nat interrupted them again. Connie got rid of him, then Manuel told her, "Na's crazy. I'n crazy too . . . my life stupid. Nothin happens ta me thas fun. Stan on a corner is all I do. I din wanna cone ta school today. If I stay home, I gotta stay in my room."

"Why do you have to stay in your room?" Connie asked.

"I'n the last one ta bed so I gotta turn off the lights then go in my room in the dark," Manuel answered, too occupied with his own thoughts to think about Connie's question.

"Ya neva get weak fron not sleepin. If you don sleep, ya not weak, ya kin use any sleep. I eat slop at home. She don know how ta cook, only meat she cook good, nothin else good. She can even read. She only wen ta sick grade. My old man, he almos finish high school. He stupid ta quit but I'n gonna quit when I'n sickteen cause I got more ta go than hin. He wish he din marry my ol lady . . . I don believe in love, I don love no one. I jus wanna be free. I don wanna be boss around. Live on a island then I won be boss around . . . just fish and not get tire. . . . People a made diff'ren. I'n neva gonna be happy. Thas my way."

Manuel had talked himself into a depression. Connie wanted to say something to cheer him up, but she was too sad herself.

MUSIC MAKERS

Don, Larry, and Willie spent most of the morning with Marilyn. Willie was absorbed in his lessor s. Larry only wanted to talk about shopping for musical instruments and forming a rock 'n' roll group in school.

Don had the last lesson. The previous week Marilyn had shown Don how to play the chords to the latest Beatle hit, "Eleanor Rigby," even though he had been sure that he couldn't play them. So she expected a good carryover. But Don didn't even want to play the guitar. He wanted to fool around with the piano. It was like he wanted to prove to himself he could play everything, but he couldn't work at anything . . . just enough to convince himself that he could be great if he set his mind to it . . . if he really tried.

Don wanted to experiment by himself. He wanted Marilyn to be available to help him, accompany him, or just keep him company, but she wasn't supposed to place demands on him or expect him to learn. Marilyn felt frustrated watching Don flit from one instrument to the next, never following through on his potential. He was good—he picked out tunes—had a good ear—he could sing. Music seemed like something he should want to do. He certainly wanted to, but he was restless and fidgety. He had the shortest attention span of anyone Marilyn had worked with. It was almost too frustrating for her to bear.

After lunch Marilyn took Larry, Don, Harold, and Willie shopping for musical instruments. They were all excited, jabbering about starting their own rock 'n' roll group. Don would be lead guitarist and vocalist, Larry would play bass guitar, Willie would play the organ, Stanley the drums, and Harold—well, no one said anything about him. Anyway, Harold was holding back. Although he had been taking guitar and singing lessons with Marilyn for almost two years, he was still a loner about certain things.

When they returned from shopping they were even more excited. They had gotten two electric guitars, a good amplifier, and a complete set of drums, all on sale. They were ready for business. The instruments would be delivered the next day. Drums? They had never been mentioned before. Herb asked Marilyn about them after the boys had left. Larry had felt they needed the drums for the band and she had gone along reluctantly.

BAD NIGGER

During the evening Henry visited our ninth student, George Jackson, and his parents. George was a wiry, light-skinned but nappy-haired, good-looking, extremely bright four-teen-and-a-half-year-old black youngster. Although George was small he had a kind of electric charge to him that said: danger—high voltage—don't touch. And when he gave you a bad-eyed stare, it took a little courage to keep looking him in the eye. Like most of our boys, George was awaiting placement in a state training school. He had been referred to the court for extorting money from other children, little white children, one little white girl espe-cially, by placing an open knife at their throats and threatening to kill them if they didn't give him their money.

George had been in trouble even in elementary school because he provoked fights with students, argued with his teachers, and disrupted his classes. He was kept back at the end of eighth grade but that hadn't helped. The next semes-ter he was caught stealing from the principal's office and finally suspended from school. A few months later he was caught extorting money from children and sent to Youth House.

In interviews with George's probation officer, Mrs. Jack-son said that she had had a happy common-law relationship with her husband for ten years. He worked regularly, was a good provider, and never gambled. After they married, he was extremely jealous, always questioned her about things, never really enjoyed the three children, and constantly said that they were all going to be delinquents who should be institutionalized. She said he had an explosive temper and hit her and the children without reason. Once he was so mad about the way George kept his room that he ripped the door down so that George couldn't close the door to hide the mess.

Mrs. Jackson admitted she had been having difficulty with George for several years because he was disruptive in school, picked on children, and stole. However, she blamed George's problems on the unfair treatment he received as a black in a world full of hate and prejudice. She told the probation officer that George had admitted that he shook down youngsters, but then she said that he needed the knife for protection against some white boys who had jumped a group of blacks. She claimed George had only threatened the white girl, he would never hurt her. Yes, she felt George was a disturbed boy, but it wasn't her fault. She had been sending him to a psychiatric clinic, but she stopped because the doctor told her that George refused to talk, had no interest in therapy, and used to fall alseep during the sessions. She said that she was afraid to take George home from Youth House, because he would get into more trouble and she didn't want her neighbors to blame her.

George told his probation officer a similar story. He claimed he was carrying the knife because some white boys had jumped him a couple of weeks before. He denied that he put the knife to the girl's neck or anyplace else. He just waved the knife and took the money from her. He suddenly got the urge to jump the girl and take her money. He didn't need the money. He just got the urge to jump her. Although he admitted that he didn't know why he did it, he felt he didn't need any help, especially from a psychiatrist. "All my psychiatrist did," George told his probation officer, "was ask how's school and how are you doing. So I fell asleep."

George scored 104 on an IQ test in Youth House, which

was thirty points below the 134 he had scored a few years before. His reading and math scores were above grade level, but he had failed all of his academic subjects.

When Henry visited the Jackson's home he was impressed by the contrast between their middle-class dress and speech and their lower-class neighborhood. The home they rented and planned to buy was especially neat and well furnished for the neighborhood. After Henry had talked to them for a while, although it was really much too early to tell, he had a hunch that the conflict between George and his parents was due primarily to the contrast between George's "bad nigger" delinquency and his parents desire to attain middle-class acceptability. They seemed to be pressuring George unsuccessfully to act in ways acceptable to the white community, so they were intensely angry that he behaved in just the delinquent ghetto way that they were trying to escape.

Friday, January 27

MYSTERIOUS RUNAWAYS SOLVED
Friday morning during the pre-warm-up meeting, Henry told us that Mrs. Russo had called him in the middle of the night because Don had gone out for a walk at one o'clock in the morning. Torn between anger that Don had left and anxiety that he might have run away, she wanted Henry to do something to control Don. Henry told her that he would do what he could and he reminded her of his warning to expect some difficult behavior from Don because of his involvement with us.

When Don came to school he tried to convince Henry that he had only felt like going for a walk. When that didn't work he admitted that he left the house after his mother had told him she was ready to go to bed while his father was still out working on snow removal duty. In fact, he added, he had been regularly avoiding sleeping home whenever his father was on the night shift.

After they had talked for a while, Henry called Mrs. Russo to tell her that Don was in school. Mrs. Russo was relieved yet still angry about the trouble Don's disappearance could cause between her and her husband.

"You don't know what he would do if he found out Don stayed out last night," she told Henry. "I'm running out of lies to tell him, I don't know how to cover up for him anymore."

It was time for Henry to see the Russos again . . . as soon as possible.

CRAZY BASTARD BABIES

There were no academic classes during the morning. The boys hung around the shops, rec room, or music room until lunch. After lunch Herb took Nat, Larry, Carlos, and Don to the movies. As they walked down the street, Don began ranking Nat and Carlos. Larry quickly added his support. Soon Nat and Carlos had stepped up their pace and were walking ahead of the others. Don asked Herb why he and Larry had to go to the movies with those "two crazy bastard babies." Herb answered that they had all chosen the same movie and all had the same rights. "Besides," he added angrily, "they don't seem particularly eager to go with you either." Herb began to walk faster and positioned himself between the two groups in order not to appear to choose one or the other.

Don started shouting toward Nat and Carlos: "Why the fuck do you babies have to come with us? Can't you do anythin on your own? Do you have to follow us, you crazy bastards?"

Carlos handled himself well. Returning insult for insult, he gave Don a "Ya the crazy one. Ya the one playin aroun with ya mother."

As they passed a nearby movie theater, Larry excitedly suggested they skip the other movie and go to the closest one. Everyone was convinced, perhaps because it was raining and the other movie was still quite a few blocks away. At the last second, Larry, then Don, both recalled that they had seen the movie and said that Nat and Carlos ought to go without them—an obvious attempt to get rid of them.

Herb was in a difficult position. He didn't want the boys to think he supported Larry and Don, but he didn't want to act as if he felt Nat and Carlos were so weak that they needed his protection. Trying to avoid both alternatives, he told both groups that he was sad that they couldn't get along together and had to rank each other out.

By that time Nat and Carlos were feeling the effects of Larry's manipulation and Don's verbal barrage and decided that they didn't want to go to any movie. Carlos had other plans, or so he claimed.

"Ya go ta the movie ina pourin rain. Me, I'm gonna get my jacket outta the tailor fa the weekend."

"Me too," Nat added.

Herb didn't want Don and Larry to win.

"Tell you what," he answered, ducking out of the rain into a doorway, "you two go to the tailor, it's only two blocks away, and we'll wait here for you. Then we'll all go."

"No! I's rainin too hard. Man, I got things ta do. I jus get my jacket and go home. Me an Nat both."

"Yeah, ah'm goin too," Nat agreed.

Herb saw he was losing the battle, but he kept trying. Perhaps, he thought, if I choose to go with them rather than Larry and Don they might reconsider.

"Look," he said, "I'll drop Larry and Don off at the

movie down the block while you guys get the jacket. I'll meet you in front of this movie in ten minutes and we'll go together."

But the damage had been done and they refused his offer. Herb asked how much it would cost to get the jacket out of the shop. Carlos said five dollars and showed him the ticket. Herb gave him the five dollars. Carlos gave Herb a puzzled look, took the money, and walked away with Nat. Herb, still feeling bad, went after them, made his offer again, was turned down again, and started toward the movie with Don and Larry. After they had walked a block or so, Don asked Herb why he had to go with them. Didn't he trust them? Couldn't he give them the money and let them go by themselves? Herb, figuring Don was trying to con the school out of the money, gave him his usual pat answer and kept walking. Don changed his tactics. He claimed he wanted to go, but had to meet Lisa in the park first.

Herb replied, "Fine! Let's all go meet her."

"No," Don answered. He would feel like a kid who had to be accompanied by his teacher. He asked Herb to give him the money for his ticket. He would meet Lisa, pay for her, and meet them in the movies. No, Herb and Larry would wait for them outside the movie and then he would buy Don a ticket. The discussion continued until they reached the park where Don was supposed to meet his girl. At that point Don told Herb that he had been kidding. He wasn't meeting Lisa and he couldn't go to the movie. He was meeting his uncle for supper and then they were going out.

"Then why did you make up all those other stories?" Herb asked angrily.

"To get the money for the movie ticket. It was for me. Right? Why shouldn't I get it just because I couldn't go?"

"You mean you pulled that shit on Nat and Carlos even though you weren't going to the movie?" Herb asked.

"You handed out all that stuff about not wanting to go with them when you weren't going anyway? That stinks. Next time be a man and ask for your money straight out instead of trying to con for it and making other people suffer."

"Would I have gotten it?" Don asked.

"Hell no," Herb answered, "but at least you would have been straight."

[Herb knew that self-righteous anger seldom helped, but he said what he did anyway . . . not because it was helpful to Don, not because Don had hurt Nat and Carlos, but because Don had made Herb feel guilty, impotent, and manipulated. Had Herb been less involved personally, he would have realized that putting people down was one of Don's problems and blaming him for it wasn't any way to solve it.]

Don asked Larry if he wanted to hang around the Village with him for an hour or so until he met his uncle. Larry looked at Herb, then said he still wanted to see the movie. Herb and Larry left for the movie, while Don walked into the park.

TOGETHERNESS

The number of boys in the program had reached a "critical mass." We had now brought together enough boys so that the forces which influence relationships between groups of people in the real world were beginning to emerge in the world we had created. Jealousy, rivalry, differences in color, national origin, religion, and sophistication were coming into play. Individuals were combining into groups based on personality factors, color, and creed. We could see it in the way they clustered around teachers, in the way they spent their free time in school, in the way they walked in the street, and in the way they sat in the subway.

Don and Larry were one group—bright, sophisticated, and pseudo-intellectual . . . into drugs, mysticism, and hippyism. They floated in and out of various activities as their moods and inclinations dictated, while pretending to others and probably to themselves that they were academic students. They were seldom disruptive and adjusted well to the nonacademic aspects of the school, especially fiddling around in the music room and engaging the staff in conversations about their fantasies. They both spent a lot of time rapping with Norm because his hip manner appealed to them. In the gym they avoided basketball and other group activities and preferred to talk with staff, play Ping-Pong or music, or rap with each other. Willie was attached to but not a regular part of their inner circle, perhaps because he kept within his own shell, perhaps because of his cooperative facade, perhaps because he was less hip, and perhaps because he was black.

Nat and Carlos made up a second group—the school disrupters. Infantile, impulsive, illiterate, threatened by school and almost any kind of demands, they were the ones some of us had not wanted to take into the school. They required a very special kind of program—a great many physical activities, lots of individual attention, short periods of different activities, a great deal of space in which to play, and "toys" to play with. They forced the staff to give them their attention, turned the classrooms and offices into play areas, and made tools and equipment into "toys." They were attracted to Natalie, food, and active sports like basketball.

Nat and Carlos's presence in the program threatened Don and Larry's self concept, and led them to attack the other two . . . an attack that created a pecking order in the school. Don, the chief instigator, was at the top. Larry and Willie were under him. Carlos and Nat were at the bottom.

Harold and Manuel belonged to neither group. Loners in their own ways, they kept to themselves without forming any alliances. When necessary, they would join in the ranking, more to defend and protect themselves against Don's and Larry's attacks than to put down Nat and Carlos. Manuel was afraid to rank. Harold had other more effective techniques. With Willie they formed a third educational group occupied for most of the day in various classes. Their programs seemed well suited to them and except for an occasional outburst from Harold, they seldom made a ripple in the daily flow of events. A modified school program was appropriate for them.

Stanley was his own group. He was an eighteen-year-old old-timer who acted like he had been through it and knew what it was all about. Since he had overcome many of his problems, he wanted no part of the other boys' fun and games. Harold usually went along with Stanley when he was around.

The boys were also attracted to some teachers more than others. Don and Larry were drawn to Norm, Larry perhaps more than Don. Larry even wanted to go up to Norm's apartment or studio to paint. He rapped to Norm about being a member of the Black Devil Society, told him that his mother and grandmother had asked a priest to drive out the devil in him, and finally convinced Norm to let him paint one of the rooms in his apartment. Norm was also receptive to Willie's tentative advances. Manuel and Harold were comfortable with him and he with them, but they didn't spend as much time with him as with the others.

Nat and Carlos were a different story. Norm didn't like taking care of "infants." He didn't like them turning his tools into toys and he didn't care much for the kind of baby talk and teasing they enjoyed. Besides he liked the boys to accomplish things in his shop, and Nat and Carlos couldn't accomplish much of anything except on the basketball court.

Nat and Carlos felt more comfortable with Bill and Natalie. Bill wasn't nearly as interested in a finished product as he was in encouraging the boys to express themselves—by experimenting in different media. The boys puttered in Bill's studio and produced in Norm's shop. Bill often sat on the sidelines while the boys did their thing, talked to each other, or listened to the radio. Norm was much more likely to engage them or at least actively attempt to do so. Perhaps that was the appeal Bill's studio had for Manuel.

Connie related best to Willie and Manuel. Her personality seemed to fit their passivity and complacency. Nat and Carlos got under her skin—as much as they got to Norm, but she didn't realize it. That was probably because it would have been too threatening to her to admit it to herself. Instead of disengaging herself from Nat and Carlos when she felt annoyed, Connie encouraged their attention. Connie got along better with Don and Larry. They seemed to feel comfortable around her . . . everywhere but in the classroom. In the classroom she got into difficulty because she didn't accept the fact that they couldn't really function academically. She encouraged and coaxed them, but succeeded only in creating friction and tension.

Marilyn liked kids she could talk to—kids who would sit still, not bouncers and hitters. So she worked well with most of the boys except for the "infants," Carlos and Nat. Carlos wanted to play the piano alone which made Marilyn feel useless because he didn't want her to teach him anything. So she preferred to have him use the piano on the days she wasn't in school. Nat? Nat just wanted to bang on the piano. He was fun, but not in class.

Harold, Willie, Stanley, and Larry were all serious about their music, and Marilyn appreciated that. She especially liked Willie, Stanley, and Larry. Willie was sensitive, talented, interested, and dependable. Stanley learned a lot, and he had changed from a dirty repulsive kid to a regular person with clean fingernails. Larry was Marilyn's favorite. She felt afraid for him, tender toward him, protective of him. She thought he desperately needed a father and hoped Herb would fill in.

Harold was all right. Marilyn liked him but not when he demanded things from her. It wasn't so much the rides home after school he nagged her into giving him as it was the sexy things he did on the way . . . like lighting two cigarettes in his mouth and giving her one. Marilyn felt uncomfortable about Harold's sexiness, but she knew he needed female approval. So each time he politely asked her if she wanted him to light her cigarette or something, she thought, "Oh what the hell, it's better than hurting his feelings," and said yes.

Then there was Don. Don was a frustration—a pleasure, a pain, a potential promise.

5 We Complete the Family

SCHEDULE CHANGES

The week started off very promising as two more joined the team. Ed, a special education graduate student from Columbia University, would be interning in our school three and a half days a week until mid-May. He was going to supervise the rec room and work individually with Nat and Carlos. Jack, a new teacher we had all agreed on, was joining us full-time. He had just completed an internship in the ghetto schools in Washington, D. C. Although Jack was inexperienced as a teacher and somewhat naïve about our boys, we felt he had the personality and dedication we wanted. Jack would teach social studies half time and do other things the rest of the time. Jack wanted to know what the "other things" would be, but we told him he would have to wait and see. We advised him and Ed to spend time observing what went on. After a while they would be fitted into a program.

Our Monday morning staff meeting was taken up with various scheduling problems. We established a new class schedule which included Ed and Jack. It provided for an additional structured period from two to two forty-five for those boys who might be able to use it plus more meeting time—Monday nine to ten and two fifteen to four thirty, Tuesday nine to ten, Wednesday eight thirty to ten, Thursday nine to ten, Friday nine to ten.

NUMBER THREE MAN

We also had to decide who would be in charge of the school when Henry and Herb left together after lunch on Tuesdays. Whoever it was, he would have to supervise the disruptive kids, handle the emergencies, and make the spot decisions that had to be made. Bill, ruling himself out, said that Norm should be the one. Norm didn't want the job either. Bill and Norm both wanted to run their own shows and rely on Henry or Herb to handle the crises. However, with Henry and Herb gone, they didn't have that option. Who was it going to be? Herb was ready to appoint Norm if he had to make the decision. Then Connie said that Norm had been the one she and Natalie had turned to in Herb's and Henry's absence if they needed help with a disruptive kid, so Norm should be the one to fill in for them. Bill smiled quietly to himself. Herb felt relieved. Even Norm felt good about what Connie had said.

Norm agreed to take the job if he could handle things his own way because he didn't think he could be a Henry or a Herb. He wasn't a clinician and besides he had his own style. Herb wanted Norm to do it Herb's way, but he realized that Norm was right. Norm could only be himself.

It was time for warm-up, then for class. Manuel went with Connie; Nat went into the gym with Ed, although he was supposed to be with Natalie; George went looking for Henry because the boys had told him to ask for an allowance; and the others went to biology with Norm.

NORMAN ON BIOLOGY

The biology class was moving ahead. Norm had just begun using a technique for keeping the kids interested in class. Bearing in mind their interests he assigned each boy a bodily function. Willie was sensation, Harold, locomotion, Larry, digestion, and Don, sex. They were all part of the same animal and they each had to explain how and when their function was carried out. Willie would see something, Harold would get it, Larry would digest it, and Don would do other things.

The technique kept the boys' attention focused on the topic, but it didn't solve their academic problems. Willie still didn't understand the work and took notes instead of listening. Harold still pressured Norm to write everything on the board and Don still disrupted the classes with such sexual associations as "Puerto Ricans dick goats up the ass or tie girls down and let goats screw them."

CON

The other boys were also busy. George was talking to Henry about his allowance. Unlike the other boys, George couldn't come right out and ask for something. It had to be a "con." He began by telling Henry how much he liked the school and how hard he would try—not like he used to. Henry realized George was telling him what George thought he wanted to hear, but Henry didn't say anything.

"How much do you need?" Henry asked.

"A hundred dollars."

"What?"

"A hundred dollars."

"Really?"

"Okay, five dollars."

That was less than the seven dollars many of the boys

were getting. Just like most deprived kids, George didn't expect much. He had big eyes and the "gimmies," but he was willing to settle for less than he should.

Henry told George his allowance would be the difference between what he got at home and the seven dollars we guaranteed all the boys.

With the allowance out of the way, George asked Henry to make sure no one told his father about the school. Henry asked why. Because, George answered, his father never let him have a good time and he might not let him come anymore if he found out he was having a good time in school. He might even be punished if he had a good time in school.

RESOLUTE SCHOLAR

Downstairs Natalie was looking for Nat who was avoiding her. When she found him he told her defiantly, "I wont ta stay here. I don wont ta go with you," but he soon went anyway. Natalie gave him some very elementary addition flash cards which he could only do by counting on his fingers, despite his claim that "they's easy." Remembering our advice not to teach Nat anything or give him anything difficult to do, Natalie started him on a second-grade workbook which was just right. Toward the end of the period, when Nat looked like he had about had it, she suggested that he stop. Stop? He wanted to make an impression . . . on both of them.

"No," he told her, "ah do two moe pages." Then he looked through the book, was shocked at the many pages left for him to do compared to the six he had completed, and asked hopefully: "Do ah gotta finish it today?"

"No, of course not," Natalie answered.

Still not satisfied with his achievement, he looked back at the six pages he had completed, shook his head proudly, announced, "Oo, ah did a lot" and went back to work. After

another ten minutes he really looked pooped. Natalie interrupted him.

"Nat, would you like to stop now?"

Nat wanted to, but he didn't want to.

"No, ah wont ta keep doin it," he answered.

Natalie insisted, "Now, Nat, I wouldn't like you to think
that I work you too hard," she teased. "You won't want to
come to me again."

Nat laughed.

"Oh no, ah come. Okay, les stop."

"Good, what would you like to do?"

"Whatchoo wont ta do?"

"We could talk or go downstairs and play basketball or
Ping-Pong."

"Okay, play Ping-Pong. Ah bet ah beats ya."

"We're not allowed to bet in school."

"Okay, let's play anyway."

THE INTERRUPTER

In second period the boys switched classes. Natalie stopped
playing with Nat and started working with Carlos.
George stopped working on Henry and went to class with
Connie. Don went for his regular therapy session with
Henry, Larry and Don had math, Willie went to shop with
Norm, and Nat busied himself with the phone in the gym.
As Nat called the second-floor extensions Ed watched pas-
sively, not knowing if he should interfere.

"Nat, get off my phone—come on, Nat, you know
you're not supposed to use the intercom."

"Herbie wont you in his office."

"God damn it, get off the phone." Then, "Get the fuck off
the phone, Nat, before I come into the gym."

Victory for the second floor. Nat escalated the battle to
the floor above.

"This Norm. Ah needs you in the gym."

"It's not Norm. It's you, Nat. Leave the phone alone."

"It ain't Nat, it's Norm."

"I'm hanging up. Good-bye."

Nat dialed another third-floor number—Connie's room where George was having his first English class. Connie had given him a reading achievement test which she thought would require most of the period. But George had raced through it without any unusual difficulty. She had then asked him to write a composition on any topic. She thought it would take up the rest of the period. Again he finished it in a few minutes. He wrote:

Basket Ball if my favoirate sport. To me this is very fast and exciting game and is very fun to particapate in. I enjoy this sport.

Connie had just switched George to grammar when Nat phoned.

"Phyllis tol me lunch's ready."

"I told you not to use the phone, Nat. Phyllis will call me when lunch is ready. I'm busy now. Please hang up the phone."

Connie went back to George, who was very edgy about grammar, while Nat called Herb.

"Phyllis say it's lunchtime."

"Christ, Nat, get off the phone. Who's in the gym with you? Nobody? Where's Ed? Put him on. Ed, don't let him use the phone. He's tying it up with calls to everyone. Put him back on. I'm really getting annoyed, Nat. You can't keep calling everyone. I've got work to do, calls to make. Leave me and the telephone alone. Henry's busy too. Play with Jack or go into Bill's room. That's it! I mean it."

Nat kept phoning until he interrupted Henry who was having a therapy session with Don. Don was trying to convince Henry that he needed a larger allowance so he could take Lisa out in style. After he disengaged Nat from the phone, Henry, as he had done before, suggested that Don and his girl could go Dutch treat when his money ran out. Don couldn't see it.

"A man has to treat his girl, he can't let her pay. That's for creeps," he contended.

Henry suggested that he ought to ask some of us what we thought. He brought Don to Connie, Phyllis, Bill, and Norm, and asked them what they thought about Dutch treat dates. They all said they had done it a lot, even when they had been older than Don. However, Don remained unconvinced.

While they were in the shop talking to Norm, Henry received a call from the intake worker at the Vocational Institute. She told him that Stanley's mother had refused to see her, although Mrs. Burns worked only four blocks from the Institute office. If she wouldn't even walk four blocks to get Stanley into the program, the worker asked, how could they count on her once Stanley was accepted.

Henry had explained Stanley's home situation to the worker before. So had Herb. Evidently she had forgotten. So he did so again and reassured her that although Stanley's mother wouldn't cooperate, we would substitute for her as much as possible.

HAROLD'S ASSASSINATION

Finally Henry was able to see Harold who had been waiting most of the morning. Harold had bottled up his thoughts so long that they exploded in an unintelligible series of vaguely familiar sounds. After Henry calmed him down, Harold told him that someone wanted to kill him. Harold had stopped a friend from killing his friend's mother. His friend had sworn to kill him and Harold thought he was "crazy enough to do it." Harold was so frightened that he wanted Henry to hide him in the residential treatment center he was supposed to go to before coming to the school. Henry calmed him down again, reminded him that every time he had asked to be sent away when he had problems they had always passed, and asked him to wait a while to see what happened.

SEX EJACATION

Stanley came to school a little before lunch still thinking about his girl. "Ya know," he commented as he started his session with Herb, "the school should a had a course in sex ejacation." Herb asked what made him say that. Stanley didn't answer for a minute or two. Then he admitted he was ignorant about sex. Running away from the subject, he told Herb that he realized his girl probably had been a virgin. Returning to what was originally on his mind, he admitted that sex wasn't all that great. Sex once or twice a month was plenty. He didn't want to go overboard. Herb listened silently as Stanley revealed, then denied, his adolescent concerns about sexual inadequacy.

After a while, when he was no longer preoccupied with his virility and his girl friend's virginity, Stanley told Herb that he had been to the Vocational Institute worker's office. He had made appointments with their psychiatrist, social worker, and psychologist, following which, he was told, they would have a meeting to determine whether they would accept him. Herb reassured Stanley that he or Henry would go to the meeting if his mother didn't attend. Stanley told Herb he had bought a burglar alarm to attach to his alarm clock to help him wake up in the morning, and it worked. Herb thought Stanley was ready to begin vocational training in earnest—if the Institute accepted him.

NORM'S GRIPE

The afternoon was short because it was Monday, our long meeting day. The boys hung around or played basketball among themselves for a while. Then Nat, George, and Harold challenged us to a basketball game which we won (although we were on the verge of collapse when it ended). After showers for the staff—the students had not yet accepted the need for cleanliness—the boys left and we got together for our meeting.

Norm started the meeting by telling Herb: "We gotta do something about Nat and the phones."

"Fine! What?" Herb asked, putting the question back to Norm.

"Look, he's a pain in the ass," Norm answered. "As soon as Ed stops him in the gym he runs into my shop and starts playing with my phone. I don't want to be a baby-sitter for him."

"Well, what should I do?" Herb asked again.

"Norm's right," Henry added. "The phones are too tempting. We have to do something. The boys don't have enough self-control. I can't have a session without six or seven interruptions and I certainly can't dictate for the record. The most important thing is that when someone needs help the phones mustn't be busy."

"Fine, tell me what to do," Herb asked again. He had no solution.

"I'm not going to play baby-sitter with him," Norm insisted. "Then Carlos pulls the same thing. I'm losing my temper."

Herb admitted he had no answer.

"What do you want me to do—threaten him . . . punish him? Can he control himself? I think we've been consistent in our demands. It hasn't worked. He's too infantile. I have no solution, Norm. Threats won't work. We have to keep appealing to his identification with us and take the frustrations. I don't see anything else to do. I don't see taking out the big guns over little things."

"He wants a great deal of attention," Henry said. "We can't give it to him so he tries to force us by running into a class or using the phone. Don and Larry need us also. They have to be seen regularly."

"No more time!" Norm agreed. "We got other kids and we can't take as much from the kids as you. You never want to set any limits."

Herb didn't appreciate that.

"Then we'll suffer for a while," he replied. "And if you have to, rip the damn phone out . . . if that's really all we can do. Let's talk about him later." Herb suggested, "I wanna talk about Carlos."

HERB'S TURN

Carlos wasn't in school. Herb was afraid it was his fault. Friday he had mistakenly offered five dollars to Carlos to take his jacket out of the tailor because he didn't know that Phyllis had already given him the five dollars at Henry's request. Herb was anxious that Carlos wasn't in school because he couldn't face coming back after he had taken the extra money. Maybe Carlos felt too guilty. Maybe he was worried that we would punish him. Herb's emotions were racing ahead of his reason. He wanted to send Carlos an all-is-forgiven-hurry-back telegram (Carlos didn't have a phone), and he wanted to do it quickly before Carlos stayed out even longer.

Henry and Connie disagreed. They told Herb that he was pushing the panic button and rushing things because he was feeling guilty. Herb needed reality-testing—like the kind he gave to Stanley and Henry gave to Harold. "Wait another day," Henry suggested. "Don't be panicky. See what happens."

Herb agreed, but only halfheartedly.

Norm had some more advice for Herb. He thought Larry was trying to get close to Herb. He wanted Herb to be Larry's therapist or to at least spend more time with him.

Herb felt that Larry had been seeking him out to manipulate him because he wanted musical instruments, not because he wanted a relationship. Norm said Marilyn didn't think Larry was talking to Herb about her in order to manipulate him as much as to get Herb's attention. She thought Larry was looking to Herb as a substitute for the father he had lost, and she too had been encouraging him to give Larry the attention he wanted.

Herb didn't see it Norm's way. He still felt uncomfortable with Larry. Norm suggested that Herb's discomfort was due to Larry's involvement with his wife. Herb disagreed. It had nothing to do with Marilyn, he insisted. It was just something between him and Larry.

AIN'T THAT SOME SHIT

Norm brought us back to Nat again. We took turns describing how he was using the school as his playground. He had been playing with Phyllis's typewriter and trying to listen to our dictation, despite our attempts to keep him out of her office. Norm had put in a Dutch door so we could keep the bottom half closed. However, Nat had discovered that he could reach in and unlock it.

[Our next move would be to have Norm build a shelf out from the door so Nat could not reach the latch under it, but that didn't work. Nat merely climbed over the door. We would try keeping the door closed with the doorknob off. The secretary would insert the knob from inside if a staff member wanted to come in or go out, but that didn't work. Nat took the knobs off the nearby doors and let himself in. We had to put the knob back on before he had removed the knobs from *all* the doors. We would try keeping the door closed and locked, but that didn't work. Nat learned to hide near the door and rush into the office as soon as the door was opened for a staff member. Gradually we caught on to his hiding places and looked carefully before entering. It seemed that we had won. But no, Nat again kept ahead of us. He took a staff member's key and had a duplicate made so he could let himself in at his convenience. We changed the lock, gave out new keys on a system that could not be duplicated locally, but that didn't work. He learned to take our keys from our key rings without our knowing it. We would even try leaving the door open and allowing him to enter whenever he wanted in the hope that he wouldn't want to keep going in if no one was trying to keep him out. But that would only work for a while. He brought the challenge back into the game by unplugging equipment, taking the dictating belts out of the machine, and walking out of the building with the equipment, if necessary. Some people thought Nat was retarded—now ain't that some shit.]

We continued the description of Nat's disruptions. We recounted the many times he had come into our rooms and disrupted our sessions with the other boys. We all talked about the intercom calls we had received from him—claiming that someone wanted us in the gym, lunch was ready, or other mischievous messages that came into his mind. Yet, although Nat was a pain in the neck, he was likable. We got angry at him, but he only smiled back at us with a twinkle in his eye . . . and he never seemed to feel bad about what he had done. So while we were frustrated, we weren't hostile to him and we weren't ready to take any drastic or punitive action against him. Besides it was time to leave for the day.

EDUCATION FOR COMMUNICATION

During the evening Mr. and Mrs. Russo came to see Henry, who quickly opened up the fact that Mrs. Russo concealed Don's behavior from her husband. Immediately Mr. Russo said he was about to explode because his wife continually hid things from him. Mrs. Russo answered that she had to hide things from him because she was terrified of his temper. Mr. Russo admitted that he couldn't control his temper and was going to be angry no matter what. However, he added, he wasn't really dangerous. No one would get hurt, even if a few pieces of furniture were broken. Henry agreed and tried to help Mrs. Russo see that while he understood that she was afraid of her husband's anger, she was making the situation worse by conspiring with Don to keep information from him. She finally agreed and promised to try to be more open with her husband.

Then Mr. Russo told Henry that their previous therapist had told them directly that Don was sexually attracted to his mother. Henry talked to them about their feelings about what they had been told. Then he offered to see them on a regular basis.

Tuesday, January 31

THEN THROW OUT THE TESTS

Tuesday morning we continued talking about how to handle Nat. First the psychologist who tested our boys told us about the results of his tests. Nat's IQ score was 63, which was approximately the same as when he was tested in Youth House. The psychologist believed that even taking into account Nat's background, his potential intelligence was below average at best. Natalie didn't like that. "Sixty-three is retarded, don't you know IQ tests are unfair to black kids," she declared emotionally. Jack quickly agreed, as Natalie and Norm described the many ways in which Nat functioned at a much higher level than his test scores indicated. The psychologist argued back. She felt that there were indications of brain damage on the tests which might account for Nat's retardation. However, Herb pointed out that the signs she was referring to were far from conclusive.

After we had all had our way, it was clear that regardless of what the testers and interviewers had decided, we believed that Nat wasn't brain-damaged, psychotic, or retarded. He was just infantile and impulsive. If the tests didn't say so, we were ready to throw out the tests.

Since the psychological tests didn't offer us guidance in helping Nat, we based our approach on our understanding of his behavior. Clearly, Nat acted as if he had no commitment to achievement, no ambition, and no long-term goals. He behaved as if he was just interested in momentary and immediate satisfactions, whether it was a telephone that attracted his attention and became a toy or a feeling of nothing to do which he got rid of by running into another room and disrupting the class with a lot of noise. What Nat did, we agreed on. On why he did it, we disagreed.

Natalie and Jack thought Nat's "I-don't-care-bout-nuthin" attitude in school was an act he had learned to put on for white people. Henry and Herb interpreted Nat's attitude as a defensive cover-up for the discomfort and anxiety he would otherwise have felt about his impulsive, infantile behavior. As Nat said to the world, not just whites, "I don't give a damn," he excused his behavior and avoided any need to control it. Connie and Norm agreed with Natalie and Jack. Bill and Ed remained silent. Henry and Herb were in the minority. However they insisted that the issue was a clinical one and asked the teachers to yield to their training and experience. Norm knew that meant the issue was closed. Natalie and Jack, thinking it was still open for discussion, put up a futile argument for a while longer.

Then Henry and Herb suggested an approach to Nat. If they were right, they said, it would be difficult to get Nat to control his own behavior without external control systems, systems which we had not built into our permissive environment. We would have to bring to bear whatever external control we could muster as a temporary measure just to provide everyone with some relief. At the same time we would invest in an approach which might eventually help Nat to develop internal controls of his own.

We had noticed that Natalie was becoming a significant figure for Nat. He liked to spend a lot of time around her, sought her out, and even followed her around the school. We weren't sure if she was becoming a mother figure or a sexual figure for him, but we were sure that she was important to him. We decided to capitalize on their growing relationship, to make it stronger, and then to use it. We would funnel all of Nat's goodies through her. Natalie, rather than Henry, would be the one to buy him clothes, hamburgers, and sodas, give him his allowance and play with him. In this way she would become an even more influential good mother figure and Nat would become even more dependent on her. After their relationship became very strong, and Natalie became a person for whose approval Nat would change his behavior, she would ask him to control himself, to stop making telephone calls, and to stop running into other people's classes.

The clinicians had laid out an approach. Most of the teachers disagreed. But they kept their disagreement to themselves because the problem had been defined as clinical.

Natalie thought: "The approach I have no quarrel with. But, psychodynamics or not, Nat's putting on an attitude for them and they can't see it."

Norm's disagreement was different: "She's no mother figure. He's a street kid. It's sex and not the baby stuff either. Maybe he's even thinking about getting himself a white girl."

Jack had other objections. "I may be new in the program," he admitted to himself, "but I know one thing. They would be better off giving him a strong father figure— especially with no father in the house. There are enough strong black mothers already. He needs a strong father."

Connie objected to the approach. "It's too manipulative for me, even if it works, but it won't work. As soon as we tell him to control himself, he'll feel used and blow up."

That was the unspoken dissent. Being unspoken, it didn't affect our decision.

FOOTSIES

Natalie had a chance to start our approach with Nat first period. After warm-up, Nat asked her, "Do ah be with you?"

"Yes, Nat, if you want to."

"What we goin do?"

"Whatever you wish."

"Okay, let's read."

Nat worked for a few minutes, then asked Natalie for a cigarette. She said she didn't smoke and offered to take him to the store to buy some. He asked if she trusted him to go out into the street alone.

"Caint ah go alone?" he asked.

"Of course. I didn't know you wanted to go alone."

"You come," he answered. "Ah just be foolin."

It was almost the end of the period when they got back to Natalie's office but Nat wanted to read anyway. As he started, his hand became rigid, then trembled slightly. His leg rubbed against hers. Unsure of what to do, she left hers there, for a few moments, then shifted it. His foot found hers again. Feeling Nat's foot against hers, Natalie wondered what Bettelheim would do and left it there, not quite certain if that was what he had meant by "gratifying children's demands." Herb knocked on the door and said

"Ding-a-ling" which meant Natalie was saved by the "bell." She felt relieved to be out of the situation but concerned that she might have done the wrong thing. She remembered the many times Herb had talked about the value of physical affection, but she wondered whether Nat was a little too old for that approach.

Nat continued stalking Natalie during lunch. He got up from his table when she walked into the dining room, and took a chair next to hers. He put his foot next to hers as they ate. Then he took out his lighter and pretended he was going to set her hair on fire. Natalie sensed that Nat was playing and remained calm. Connie wasn't so sure. Feeling anxious, she exchanged worried looks with Nat until he laughed, put the lighter away, and settled for playing footsies with Natalie.

A REAL SICKIE

George looked sick when he came to school. Bill, who was the first person to see him, called Henry.

"You don't look so well," Henry told George.

"I'm okay," George answered as if he didn't want the special attention Henry was giving him.

"Well, let me take your temperature anyway," Henry offered.

"I said I'm fine," George insisted, half as if he meant it.

"You may think you're fine," Henry answered, without confronting George directly, "but you don't look so good. Why don't we make sure?"

George refused again, then finally agreed to have his temperature taken . . . not to see if he was sick but to show Henry that he wasn't.

Henry took George's temperature and showed him that he had a fever.

"Yeah," George commented. "I got a sore throat."

"A sore throat," Henry laughed. "You know it's not that, George baby. It must be something else."

"Nigger! I told you I got a sore throat. Now what you want?" George demanded, as he pretended to scorn Henry's attention.

"I want you to stop acting and admit you're sick," Henry answered, unintimidated by George's tone of voice.

Finally George admitted that his knee had been badly infected for a couple of months. He told Henry that his mother had been treating it with white iodine which wasn't helping. Then why hadn't he gone to a doctor, Henry asked. Because he was afraid to go, George admitted.

The infection seemed to be spreading through George's body. He obviously needed medical attention in a hurry, but his parents didn't seem to be ready to do anything. So Henry decided to make a concrete demonstration of our serious concern about George's condition. He asked Jack to take George home and to tell his parents what we thought. At first George insisted that he wanted to go home himself. Then he agreed to let Jack go with him, and he enjoyed the special attention he was getting.

MISCELLANY

When Don came to school he told Henry that he was tired because he had been out all night. That was true enough, Henry realized, as Mrs. Russo had already called. But Don had been coming to school sleepy-looking so often that Henry suspected there were other reasons as well. So when Don lay down on the mat in the rec room to take a nap Henry said, "You took some stuff again," meaning pills or narcotics.

"You know I wouldn't take anything," Don answered. "But that's not bad stuff ta take. You shrinks think you know about everything."

Taking Don's denial as an admission, Henry told him, "That stuff sure isn't good for you. And that bull shit you pick up in the Village about understanding yourself on drugs is just that, bull shit."

"That's because you square shrinks aren't into stuff like we are," Don answered.

"Me, square?" Henry asked.

"No, you're not square, Henry," Don replied.

Henry thought Don had admitted as much as he could at the time. So he let the conversation end.

Since Don's talk with Henry had kept him awake, Don went to English where he accomplished just about nothing until he told Connie he was upset and couldn't concentrate. Accepting the inevitable, Connie took him down to the rec room and played Ping-Pong.

Instead of going to English with Don, Larry spent extra time in shop where he designed and began building a mystery box, a square box with sixteen drawers . . . eight real, eight false. No one but he would know the formula for determining which were which without trying them. And he could booby-trap it and pull off all kinds of things with it— at least that was his plan.

After this English period spent in the shop, Larry joined Don who had been playing Ping-Pong in the gym with Connie, and the three of them went for a walk to buy a new supply of Larry's favorite soup for his liquid lunch.

After lunch Herb took most of the boys shopping for sweatsuits and gym equipment. So the school was quiet . . . but not for long. When they got back, they discovered that the drums had arrived. Within minutes the drums were assembled, the guitars were plugged into the amplifiers, and the school reverberated to the tutored sounds of Willie on piano, Larry and Don on guitar, and the unspoiled, uncivilized rhythms of Nat and Carlos on drums.

Norm was especially unhappy to see the drums because they were going into the music room next to his shop. He didn't see how he was going to be able to stand the noise. Herb convinced him to give it a try, but Norm didn't expect it to work out.

Wednesday, February 1

BEHAVIORAL SCIENCE APPLIED

Wednesday we devoted most of our morning meeting to talking about developing temporary external controls for Nat. As we saw it, we faced two problems in managing his behavior externally. One problem was that Nat was unable to control himself when temptations were around, especially toy telephones, typewriters, keys, musical instruments, dictating machines, and toy tools.

Bill described how he had been handling Nat. Nat would wander into the studio when he had nothing to do. He might turn on a power saw or something, shove a piece of wood into it, and cut. Or he might drill a few holes or bang a few nails into a piece of wood. Except for a couple of early paintings, Nat's only other accomplishments were broken jigsaw blades. When some of us asked Bill if he was going to stop Nat from playing with the power saws, he responded, "What the heck, how much do blades cost?"

[That's right—how much did a blade cost? Better a blade than an interrupted class or a disruptive telephone call. Bill was beautiful. He had a lot to teach us.]

Then Bill added, "But I don't recommend the approach. I don't care about blades. He can ruin them. I'm afraid he's going to ruin something else . . . like a finger. My studio's really no place for him unless someone is watching him every second."

We had to reconcile ourselves to our inability to make any progress on the temptation front.

The second problem was that, except for gym, we hadn't been able to find any activities that could capture Nat's interest for any length of time. Even in gym, Ed had only been able to contain him for one period. The next period of gym was usually a disaster. We decided to continue to assign Nat to Ed for a second period during the day, but not in gym. Instead Ed would accompany Nat into the art studio, music room, or shop only for as long as Nat's interest was maintained. Ed would work individually with him so Nat wouldn't require more attention from the teacher than he could provide without disregarding the needs of the other boys. By allowing Nat to float from room to room, always accompanied and supervised by Ed, we hoped to provide the one-to-one attention and diversity of activities necessary to keep him quiet.

If Ed's program were successful, that would still make only three well-covered periods out of five—the period with Natalie, the gym period with Ed and the other boys, and an individual period with Ed. Nat's two periods in art and shop were fantasies. So we would still have to find something for Nat to do besides disrupting office routines and classes.

PETTY THEFT

Having made some progress on Nat's difficulties, we turned our attention to Harold who was up to his old tricks—stealing. He had been stealing small things from the shop and art studio, a screwdriver here, a set of leather-cutting knives there . . . openly. By flaunting his thefts out in the open, he was practically forcing Bill and Norm to catch him in the act. But why? We didn't know. What to do about it?

We weren't sure. But we had to do something. Bill and Norm would ignore it for a while and we would see what happened. Henry would mention it indirectly to Harold to see if he would rise to the bait.

[We were too preoccupied with Nat to think through Harold's situation. If we had, we might have put his fear of being murdered, his wish to be sent away into semiprotective custody, and his flagrant stealing together and have come up with a possible explanation.]

Just before our meeting ended, Carlos returned to school. With a big grin on his face, he handed Herb the extra five dollars Herb had given him saying, "This money's yours. Phyllis gay me some a'ready."

Although we were pleased to see Carlos, we wondered what had happened to him. He told us a vague, unconvincing story about helping a cousin, who had just come from P.R., to register with welfare and find a place to live. It didn't seem true, but we didn't make a fuss about it. He was back. That was what counted. The family was together again. School could start.

A KEY PROBLEM
Natalie and Ed spent the morning with their kids, Nat and Carlos. Without realizing it, Natalie started off the period with a toy in her hand—her keys. Nat grabbed them and said he would hold them for her. Although Natalie realized that Nat shouldn't have them, she let him hold them anyway to avoid having to be punitive when she was supposed to be nice to him, or so she told herself. However, she was probably just having difficulty setting limits with the boys.

Natalie started a game of Ping-Pong with Carlos, who cheated as usual, while Ed and Nat watched, laughing each time Carlos made a "mistake." When it was Nat's turn to play with Natalie he couldn't keep the ball on the table. As hard as Natalie tried, there was absolutely no chance to get a volley going. Suddenly Carlos jumped on top of the table and demanded, "Thas all. He can' play. Gimme my turn."

Nat pulled Natalie in his direction. He wasn't going to give her up. Natalie broke away and sat down on the bench, avoiding both of them. Carlos tried again.

"See, Natalie, ya scared a me."

Natalie just looked at him.

"Well, ain ya scared?"

"No, I'm not scared, Carlos," she answered. "But I'm not going to get involved when you and Nat are fooling around."

"Good!" Carlos answered. "I'm goin ta the cleaner. C'mon, Nat, les cut out," he called as the two of them ran right out of the building . . . with Natalie's keys.

Natalie had parked her car near the building. Nat had her keys. "What if he starts fooling around with it?" She thought to herself. "What should I do?" She called Herb on the intercom, described the situation to him and explained that she hadn't followed the boys because she wasn't going to go running after two teen-age boys in the street. Herb agreed. Besides, he reminded her, the boys could leave the building whenever they wanted to anyway. The real problem was that she had let Nat keep her keys. Natalie agreed and resolved not to let it happen again . . . if possible.

The boys came back into the gym just as the second period started. It was time for Nat to be with Natalie. He looked very shamefaced, probably because he had run away —she thought; or because he had messed around with her car—she wondered.

They went into Natalie's office, had a what-would-you-like-to-do conversation and discovered Nat wanted to read.

He read from the Dr. Seuss book for a while, then stopped.

Natalie asked, "What do you want to do now, Nat?"

"Whatchoo wont me to do?"

"Whatever you want to do."

"Make a call?"

"Okay."

Nat called his father's number. A woman answered. He covered the mouthpiece and whispered, "It the stupid lady what lives with my father. Boy, is she dumb.

"Where my father?" he demanded rudely. After speaking with his father for a while he told him, "Ah be there Friday." Then he added, "You clean my coat. Ah lef it there," as if he were used to ordering his father around.

The whole thing seemed odd to Natalie. She didn't think she had ever heard Nat speak like that . . . infantile—yes, but harshly demanding—never. His mother's complaints about him in his probation report were beginning to make sense to her.

Nat began working on math. Carlos opened the door, looked at Nat's work, and told him, "You gotta lotta mistakes."

Nat pouted. Natalie checked his work. It was correct. Nat laughed triumphantly. Carlos retorted, "Oh, they're subtraction stead a'dition."

CONSPIRACY

The period ended. Nat left. Carlos came in. Natalie asked him what he wanted to do and received a straightforward reply: "Gamble."

She responded as straightforwardly: "You know I can't gamble with you, Carlos."

"Why?"

"Because I try not to do anything illegal."

"Don tell me you neva did nothin alegal!"

"Of course I have. Most people do something illegal sometimes."

"Yeah! Then pull down the shade and I get us some dice. We kin shoot dice."

"You can if you want to but don't expect me to."

"Then les break the window."

"Why do you want to do that?"

"Cause! Okay?"

"Well, what do you think?"

"No."

"Good."

"Lemme drive ya car," Carlos continued.

"That would be illegal too. You know you don't have a license."

"So? Nobody'll know."

"Carlos, I would know. That's enough. I control my own actions even if no one else knows."

"Thas stupid. Don ya have no fun?"

Natalie didn't answer—that put an end to the conversation. Breaking the silence, Carlos picked up the phone and dialed a number.

"Who're you calling?" Natalie asked.

"Home."

The phone rang . . . repeatedly. No one answered. Carlos was upset.

"Maybe your mother went shopping."

"My sista suppose to be home an my mother too."

Natalie forgot that Carlos's mother was very sick—probably dying of cancer. Carlos expected her to be home. She was supposedly bedridden. Carlos was worried.

Nat knocked at the door. Natalie opened it. This time *he* wanted to see what Carlos was doing. Natalie told him Carlos was getting along just fine and asked him to go back upstairs to shop where he had been. Nat left. It was almost time for lunch and definitely time for a break.

HOME'S A NOWHERE PLACE

Just before lunch Henry had one of his irregular therapy contacts with Willie in the music room. The music room was less threatening to Willie because it wasn't one of the "therapy offices." So Willie didn't have to admit that he was involved in therapy, even though he was talking to Henry about "therapy things."

Willie showed Henry the ripped jacket which he had promised to bring in, then shyly said the school had bought other boys clothes and he wanted some too. Henry examined the jacket and agreed to buy one for him. Henry asked Willie how things were at home. Bad! His mother did little more for him than cook his supper. The food was good, but supper with his family was so distasteful to him that he almost always ate by himself. After dinner he usually watched television alone because his sisters hardly spoke to him and he hated them anyway.

"Home's food and TV—that's all," he declared with his hand on the hat he always wore in school.

HISTORICAL FIRSTS

That day brought a number of firsts to the program. Jack had his first social studies classes. Following our advice, Jack asked the boys to talk about themselves in order to adapt the curriculum to their interests. However, Jack was too direct in his approach and he found out that the boys weren't going to talk about themselves until they were ready.

With Larry the conversation roamed throughout the broad spectrum of history. Jack was impressed with Larry's

grasp of historical facts and understanding of historical concepts. However, he felt that Larry was putting on an academic show for him which wouldn't last. Jack tried to involve Larry in a discussion of the method of historical
analysis, but he would not bite. By the end of the period,
Larry was arguing that history wasn't useful anyway.

Harold acted pretty much as Jack had expected. He
seemed to be aware of historical facts, somewhat sophisticated about the historical process, but stubborn, argumentative, and provocative. Like Larry, Harold didn't open up
very much. So their conversation drifted to social studies.

Manuel had his first math class with Connie. He had
asked for math. If it worked out, we would assign him to
Jack for a third academic class. The class didn't work out as
well as Connie had expected. Manuel insisted defensively
that he knew all of his math except fractions, although his
actual level of functioning was around third grade. Despite
his protests that he knew the work, Connie insisted that they
go back to simple addition and subtraction. When she asked
Manuel to think out loud so she could follow how he arrived at his answers, she found he was solving most of the
problems but using his own method. He arrived at 9 plus 8
is 17 by adding two 10's are 20, take away 1 for 9 and 2 for
8 is 3, take away 3 from 20 is 17. When Connie tried to
show him more efficient methods of adding and subtracting,
he stubbornly insisted that it wasn't his way.

Manuel's tone of voice reminded Connie of the time she
had tried unsuccessfully to convince him he had been writing "b" and "d" backwards. So she tried to retreat, but too
late. She had annoyed him. He stopped working and talked
instead about the trouble he had with teachers who used to
always tell him, "No, no, you're doing it wrong. Do it this
way." Connie tried to bend over backwards not to push
him.

He sensed her concern, laughed embarrassedly, and said, "I'n stubbin like my ol man. He'sa big success . . . in bed . . . in his dreans. I'n gonna be like hin . . . happy . . . sleepin."

Ed and Nat had their first second-floor class which they spent painting in the studio. When Bill gave Nat the painting equipment, he just sat there looking at the paper, unable to get started. Ed didn't understand what was going on. Harold did. He drew some lines on the paper for Nat, which was what Nat needed. The lines gave him some spaces which he could paint in different colors. But he had to use a different brush for each color.

When he ran out of clean brushes, Ed told him to rinse them off. No, he wanted a different brush for each color. Ed was annoyed, but Bill as usual didn't seem to mind. He gave Nat a batch of clean brushes matter-of-factly, as if Nat's way of painting was the natural way to paint. Nat painted intently, tried carefully to keep each color within the line, and cursed whenever the paint spread over the line. Then he asked Bill to hang up his painting in the display area.

FREE PLAY

After lunch, Herb put on his wrestling clothes and fooled around on the mats with Nat and Harold. Willie went to art, Carlos hung around the gym with Ed, Don and Stanley played the guitars in the music room, and Larry rapped to Norm. After a while Stanley and Don brought the guitars and drums into the rec room. Larry joined them. Herb brought out his conga drum and they had a jam session. Manuel and Connie played Ping-Pong after their math class and Norm organized a basketball game with Ed and the other boys.

In the middle of it all, a visitor walked in and did a double-take. It was his first visit to the "school." No one was in "class." We were all banging on instruments, playing basketball and Ping-Pong, or creating in the art studio.

Thursday, February 2

PERSECUTION OR PROSECUTION

After our morning meeting, Henry called Mrs. Jackson to find out how George was. Mrs. Jackson told him that George had gotten into trouble on Wednesday because he had gone back to the school that had expelled him. The guidance counselor there had called her and accused George of trespassing. Mrs. Jackson felt, however, that the guidance counselor was persecuting George because he was black.

[It was easy for Mrs. Jackson to attribute George's difficulties to racial prejudice, for there was so much around her. However, the facts were that George had repeatedly returned to the school from which he had been suspended and tempted boys there to cut school with him.]

Mrs. Jackson also told Henry that she had taken George to a clinic where his knee and sore throat had been treated. They had found out he had a heart murmur which confirmed what Youth House had found. Although she had not done anything about the heart murmur yet, she planned to take George to the private physician she herself saw. She said that George was feeling better and would attend his parole hearing in court on Friday morning, but she thought he was too sick to go to school after the hearing.

Henry found it difficult to believe that George was too sick to come to our school but not too sick to go to his old school. He also wondered why George attended a clinic even though his mother used a private physician.

PUERTO RICAN JEW

Manuel went to his reading class with Connie wearing a hat, and told her: "I wanna be Jew cause they get days offa school." He talked about "funny-looking" religious Jews he had seen in his neighborhood who wore old-style clothes, beards, and long hair like sideburns, and he asked Connie questions which she couldn't answer since she wasn't Jewish. Then he worked on phonics for the rest of the period.

GOOD SAMARITAN

Carlos came to school around ten thirty, had something to eat, and told Herb he couldn't stay because he was still helping his cousin from Puerto Rico.

"I'm gonna take im ta fine a job cause he don know how ta travel. He can' read or nothin."

"Where is he?"

"Don worry about where he is! I'm gonna pick im up."

"When will you be back?"

"I don know. If he ges a job and starts workin, I come back and get im afta work. If he don get a job, I'm gonna take im home."

"How long can you stay?"

"I gotta cut out now."

Herb didn't know whether to believe Carlos or not. Knowing how suspicious Carlos was, he decided to play along and let him leave without a hassle. True to his word, Carlos "cut out" and didn't return until Friday.

THE JAZZ CROWD

Don also came to school around ten thirty, went directly to the music room, took a record, and started back downstairs. Herb followed him and asked, "Hey, Don! Where ya going? You just got here."

"I got a friend waitin for me, man . . . outside. He plays with the Jazz Crowd. They just got in from England. I told him about this record I wanna lend him."

Herb followed Don into the hall and watched him from a window when he went outside. Down there someone was waiting for Don . . . a rather bloodless, pale, emaciated, effeminate, bizarre-looking kid around twenty with long stringy hair, a skinny beaked nose, and a velvet cape draped over him. Don handed him the record, talked for two or three minutes, then came in.

"You sure that kid plays with the Jazz Crowd?" Herb asked.

"Shit . . . yeah! I'll show ya his picture on the album if you don't believe me."

"He looked kind of effeminate. Is he homosexual?"

Herb was probing, but Don was clamming up. With a "no" shrug of his shoulders which told Herb he wasn't talking anymore, Don walked by him up to the music room. But Don was much more affected by Herb's question than his indifferent shrug had indicated. During the second period he destroyed Connie's English class. Every verb became an active or passive homosexual act. Everything Larry said was queer or stupid. Even Connie was effeminate. When he couldn't get a rise out of Larry, he wrote Lisa's name all over Larry's books. At the end of the period, completely exasperated, Connie asked him if he really felt he belonged in a class.

"Maybe you should have your own individual period," she suggested. That insulted Don.

"Whadaya mean, my own class. You need me here. I'm the best part of this class. Yeah! I'm the only one in this class with a part. You couldn't have this class. It'd be nothing without me."

Don's math class was the same story—homosexuality.

Lunch was another opportunity to talk about homosexuality with Marilyn and Natalie.

"So what if the guy was a homosexual," he told them. "He probably could get any girl he wanted and got tired of girls. He was probably lookin for new kicks."

Marilyn and Natalie disagreed. They told Don they thought that homosexuals didn't become homosexuals because they were tired of women but for other reasons. Don didn't want to hear anything except agreement with his ideas. So he left them and went upstairs where he tried unsuccessfully to convince Bill and Norm that he was right about homosexuality.

MASTURBATION EDUCATION

Then Don went to social studies. It was his first class with Jack because he had been absent on Wednesday. Larry and Harold were ready for class, but Don brought his guitar with him. After he successfully took over the class for a few minutes, Jack tried to involve them in a discussion about the historical method. He put some material on the board and attempted to get them to examine how historians develop and test hypotheses about historical facts. Don quickly turned the discussion to sex and masturbation. Don seemed genuinely worried about masturbation. He had woken up a few nights previously to discover that he had had an ejaculation in his sleep which had seemed weird to him. He wanted to know if he masturbated too much, whether it was a perversion, and what would happen. Larry and Harold were almost as concerned about masturbation as Don. Jack made some reassuring comments that masturbation was almost universal and people's fears about it were mostly superstition.

When the discussion extended into the next period and the boys didn't show up for their next classes, Herb came in to see what was going on. Harold left for the music class, Don and Larry stayed. Don stood on the windowsill, hanging out precariously. Don wasn't in any real danger, but Herb was nervous. A slight slip, he thought, and Don could fall . . . far enough to kill himself.

Hanging out the window, Don asked Herb, "You really think he was queer?" referring to the musician.

"I don't know. I just wondered cause he looked effeminate."

Don dropped the subject but continued leaning out of the window. Herb realized he was nervous about the way Don was leaning out of the window. He knew he was far from being his best when he was anxious. He felt that it would be better to walk out than to create a mess. So Herb asked Don to climb down, then walked out of the room without waiting for him to do so.

About a half hour later Don involved Herb in the same discussion out in the hall. He asked the same question and received the same response. Then he said he had to leave early.

"Why?" Herb asked.

"To look for a job."

"Do you hafta leave now? Can't you look for a job later?" Herb asked.

"I already have the job," Don answered. "I start at three o'clock. Can you get me workin papers?"

"Sure, we've gotten working papers for other kids." That's funny, Herb thought to himself, first he's looking for a job, then he has a job.

"I been leavin early all week," Don continued. "Lisa's got a program change in school. She doesn't get out til four o'clock now."

"So? How can you go to work after school and meet Lisa at four o'clock?" Herb asked as he began to get that I'm-being-manipulated feeling.

Don kept still.

"What kind of job is it?" Herb asked again.

"I'll take any job," Don answered. "I just need some money."

Herb was lost. They weren't really talking to each other. Did Don have a job, was he looking for a job, or just trying to con him? Herb couldn't be sure. Don started leaning over the banister, one leg was already over the side and the other was resting on the railing. He was three flights down. Don didn't seem like he wanted to talk about the job. He just smiled and leaned. He had learned how to get to Herb, who was nervous. He didn't like Don leaning over that way. Herb thought about walking away again, but stayed and, almost pleading, said: "I wish you wouldn't lean over like that. It's dangerous, and it makes me nervous. I can't watch you leaning out windows and over banisters, even if you aren't going to hurt yourself."

Don smiled a long smile, and left for the day with no further mention of the job, the working papers, or Lisa.

Friday, February 3

We spent most of our morning meeting talking about Don. Herb described the incident about the effeminate boy, his conversations with Don at the window and banister, and Don's conversation with Marilyn and Natalie, at least as Marilyn had described it to him. Jack told us about Don's masturbation fears. Connie reported that she had had a similar conversation during English. And Henry told us that Don had been unusually preoccupied with sex most of the week.

After the meeting, Henry looked for Don but he wasn't around. When Don finally arrived, he was still upset about what Herb had said, but wouldn't discuss it.

TIRED

Manuel came late and went directly to Connie's room. He was in a strange mood again, bent over, tired, and filthy. Connie took one look at him and asked, "Manuel, you really look very tired."

"Yeah, I din cone hone till two o'clock ina night and I stay up all night."

"Why? Couldn't you sleep? Were you drunk?"

"No!"

"Is something bothering you, Manuel?"

"Yeah, sonethin . . . I don know. How ya know?"

"I could see it when you walked in, all bent over and tired."

"I don know what. Sonetine I think i's a headache—glasses maybe . . . sonetine a stomachache. Nobody kin help me. They all try . . . teachers, even psychiatrist. Herb couldn't."

"No?"

"I neva been happy. I don even know what it is, sept when I'n drunk. My ol man, he's happy."

"He is?" Connie asked.

"Well, he was sick but they took it out, what made hin sick."

"Is he happy now?"

"I don know, I guess so, sept he got asthma—he coughs when he tries ta laugh, but I'n gonna be jus like hin."

"Do you really want to be?"

"Yeah."

"How come?"

"I don know but if I'n his son, I'n jus like hin."

Nat also looked very tired when he came to school. As Connie had with Manuel, Natalie asked Nat why he looked so tired. "Ah didn go home til morning," he replied, as they started a game of Ping-Pong.

"Were you caught in the blizzard?" Natalie asked.

"Ah was with a girl," he answered sheepishly.

"What did your mother say when you got home?"

"She didn't say nothin. She thought ah be with my father but ah dont stay there cause that dumb woman always be there." Natalie listened silently.

"My mother say, Boy! where you been? So ah tell her ah be with my father, but ah be with a girl."

Their Ping-Pong game continued. As usual, Nat tried to lose by slamming the ball off the table, but Natalie wouldn't let him.

Shouting "No competition, no competition," the victory cry of the students, Nat excitedly challenged George, who had come to school after his court hearing despite his mother's concern about his health. George played like he wanted to win. Nat played like he wanted to lose. They both got their wishes.

Next period was academics for Nat and Natalie. As soon as they entered the office, Nat started his bit.

"What we goin do?"

"What would you like to do?" Natalie asked, already frustrated.

"You the teacher," Nat answered half-passively, half-insistently.

"Nat, you know we can do whatever you want to do."

"Okay, read."

Natalie gave Nat another Dr. Seuss book to read. She told him that it would be more difficult, but she would help him whenever he needed it. He began reading, but the strange names of the characters made it too difficult for him. He stopped and demanded, "Ge me them books there," pointing to two easy readers. After looking them over and choosing one, he declared, "Ah read this one," as if Natalie had no right to disagree with his decision.

Natalie felt Nat's attitude toward her was different, more

demanding. He hadn't asked for anything special. It was just get this and do this—like the way he had spoken to his father over the phone.

A FAT DESPICABLE WOMAN

While Nat was reading with Natalie, Harold was writing with Jack. It was Harold's first class with Jack, his new English teacher. We had switched him from Connie to Jack to see how Harold would react to him. Jack had asked Harold to write a composition. He wrote:

As I was tka taking a train out of New York City the New York Central train out of New York City, There There was a fat despicable woman th taking up to seats two seats and one one lady staen stood standing because becaus of this woman. As the train went though m many little tones tome towns the janitors were clen cleaning the car of old cyarette and perp papers. We pass many trees and sum sum body had a radie rade radio playing the record she loves you. It At my stop which was Chatham there was rats roning aroud around an old a old calendar on the well wall from 1956. As I was about to leve lave leave a cl cop walk up to me and said pi put out that cyarette.

Jack was shocked that a student who seemed as bright as Harold could have so much difficulty spelling. He didn't realize the tremendous improvement the composition represented.

MY 'LOWANCE

After lunch when Henry gave Nat his allowance (Natalie had already left), Nat put it back into Henry's hand saying, "Ah don wont your 'lowance. I ain't goin take it. You keep it."

Before Henry had a chance to reply, Nat demanded: "You gimme back my 'lowance. That *my* 'lowance."

With the allowance safely in his hands once again, Nat

quieted down, only to continue the conversation a few minutes later.

"Ah don need you money," he told Henry. "Ah got anuff for a house."

"Is that true, Nat?" Henry asked.

"No! Ah take all the money ah get," Nat replied.

[Nat was working through his thing about taking money from us. Norm thought he felt a little uncomfortable about being given so much more money than he or the kids in his family had ever received at home. Natalie thought it might have been something racial, a black kid taking things from whites. Henry felt that Nat was uncomfortable because he didn't understand why he was getting money. The other boys knew that we gave them money because we believed the money would help them. Nat, Henry felt, didn't understand that. Getting money from us didn't make sense to him —but he took it anyway.]

Soon it was trip-and-end-of-week time so we all split, or cut out as Carlos would say, for the swimming pool.

6 Drugs, Delusions, and Delinquencies

Monday, February 6, through Friday, February 10

DILEMMA OVER DON

We had decided to make Monday an administrative day. First we heard the results of the tests our psychologist had given Don. Then we had a long discussion about how to help Don handle his sexual problems.

Herb believed Don was being flooded with sexual fantasies and impulses which he couldn't keep out of his conscious awareness. He felt Don's sexual conversations were cries for help to resolve the anxiety his fantasies were arousing in him. He thought they should be handled by Henry through psychotherapeutic techniques rather than through casual conversations and lunchtime debates. When Don tried to involve us in discussions about sex, Herb wanted us to tell him to discuss his sexual concerns with Henry because Henry was the one who could help him with them.

Most of us disagreed. Connie thought she would feel uncomfortable if she had to tell Don to talk to Henry when he started a conversation with her. She said it would be too much like telling him that his thoughts were crazy. Our psychologist also disagreed. She thought that Don was talking about sex in order to learn about it. In her opinion, Don's thinking was so distorted that he needed an unusual amount of worldly education to understand his sexual drives and fantasies. She believed that the best way to handle Don's questions and comments about sex would be to provide him with the facts he was looking for. In contrast to Herb, she favored an educational rather than a psychotherapeutic solution to Don's problem.

Henry believed that Herb and the psychologist were both on the right track. He agreed with Herb that Don was being bombarded with sexual impulses and fantasies which he couldn't handle, but he agreed with the psychologist that Don was attempting to deal with them by finding out what others thought about them. Henry didn't think Don's basic sexual problems could be handled through an educational approach, but he was also very sympathetic toward Connie's discomfort about shutting Don off.

Norm made a suggestion which provided a way out of the dilemma. We would give factual answers to the real questions Don raised and refer him to Henry whenever he attempted to involve us in discussions which weren't primarily questions of facts.

TOO BLACK

After a long coffee break, which we needed, we had another emotional discussion about Nat. Our concern had changed from whether we could contain him long enough to help him to whether we could help him in a program as unstructured and permissive as ours, even if we could contain Nat. Henry and the psychologist felt Nat might need a program which could provide more consistency, limit-setting, and structured education. Henry questioned whether Nat could benefit from a program like ours when he was functioning on such an extremely infantile level. He was far from ready to give up on Nat, but he wanted to air his misgivings. He felt there was no point in ducking the issue until we would have to handle the problem under pressure. Norm and Connie supported Henry's views. Bill and Ed were noncommittal. Natalie, Jack, and Herb disagreed because they didn't think Nat was as infantile as Henry thought he was. Jack suggested angrily and a little self-righteously that the others were prejudiced without knowing it, but he was quickly corrected by Herb and Bill.

The lines were drawn; it was Henry, Connie, and Norm against Natalie, Jack, and Herb, with Bill and Ed in the middle—just about the same groups we formed each time we talked about setting limits.

As the discussion proceeded back and forth and we recounted the difficulties we had been having with Nat, we began to feel less guilty about letting him go if we had to. Finally, we all agreed that we might have to and with that admission out in the open, Connie and Natalie wanted Henry to start looking for another place for Nat. They didn't want him to go to a state training school if we were forced to discharge him. Henry and Herb agreed that the idea was good in principle. Then they took turns explaining to the others that it was a fantasy to believe that Henry would be able to find another good place for Nat. Nat was too old, too infantile, too disruptive, and above all, TOO BLACK.

> If you're white, that's all right. If you're brown, stick around. If you're black, get back, boy, get back.

This news split us into two groups which were pretty much "newcomers" and "old-timers." The "newcomers" angrily asked how we could consider letting Nat go if we didn't have a good place to send him. The "old-timers" explained that they had decided during the pilot project against keeping a student they couldn't help just because there was no place else to send him. They would let him go and accept a boy they could help.

The issue wasn't resolved. Fortunately it didn't have to be. None of us wanted to discharge Nat. We were frustrated and annoyed, but we knew that Nat was attending, relating, and struggling. Besides, we liked him. He was disruptive, not dangerous, so we could afford to keep him for a while. But not too long. If he became too attached to our school, discharging him would be extremely traumatic for him.

JACK'S DISAPPOINTMENT

Next Jack told us about Harold's preoccupation with a fat despicable old lady on her way upstate, whom Henry interpreted to be Harold's mother. He also reported that he wasn't having any difficulty with Harold in English or social studies classes and he asked to continue to work with him in English. Herb and Henry disagreed. They felt that Jack's experience with Harold indicated that Harold had been having difficulty in Connie's English class because he had been reacting to her as if he were reacting to his mother.

They thought it was the time to concentrate on Harold's interpersonal problems rather than his reading and spelling difficulties, because he was ripe and ready for a more insightful approach. They didn't want to miss the opportunity to confront Harold about his problems with Connie and to relate it to that "despicable fat slob" at home.

That didn't make sense to Jack, who couldn't appreciate sacrificing educational goals for psychotherapeutic gains. He submitted to Harold's transfer to Connie, but he didn't agree.

Jack and Herb continued their discussion about Jack's classes after the meeting. Jack wanted to teach Don, Larry, and Harold social studies in a group. He thought they could work together despite their individual problems. He planned to involve them in a unit on the historical method which he thought was appropriate for all of them. He believed he could cover what was relevant in the traditional social studies curriculum through his approach and do a much better job. Herb told Jack that he was pitching his class way above the boys' heads. He was relating to their intellectual ability rather than their inadequate functioning. Herb suggested that studying the historical method and doing history rather than reading about it might be great for normal kids, but our kids would respond better to entertainment, astounding facts, and interesting stories. Besides he didn't think Jack could work with them in a group. He didn't believe that the group could progress at the same pace because Larry, and especially Don, functioned too erratically. Herb was also convinced that Harold's academic problems were very different from Don's and Larry's and thus required a different approach. Don and Larry could think clearly. Their main difficulty was that they couldn't attend or concentrate consistently or for extended periods of time. They needed a class that would entertain them, maintain their interest, and require very little preparation, reading, or written work. Harold, on the other hand, couldn't always think clearly about social studies because he felt very anxious when he was required to interpret facts or arrive at logical conclusions. However, he was able to attend and work consistently. He was ready to prepare for class and complete written assignments. He didn't need to be entertained, just encouraged to overcome his learning disabilities through a tailored and individualized approach.

Despite Herb's warnings, Jack felt optimistic that he could work with the three of them together. So he and Herb compromised. Jack would have a class with all three boys and an individual American history class with Harold. They would watch how things worked out and adjust the boys' classes accordingly.

Jack also received assignments for the rest of the day. He would spend one period in the rec room and he would also work with Don in math for one period so that Bill could spend more time with Larry and Harold.

Then we completed the February class schedule. We gave it to Phyllis to reproduce, wondering how soon it would have to be changed.

GAMES TEEN-AGE PEOPLE PLAY

There was no school on Tuesday because of a blizzard. That made it a four-day weekend and a short school week for the boys. Although it was a short week, it was a week in which the students' self-imposed restraints on their behavior weakened. New behaviors emerged and relationships between students and staff changed.

The boys became more active and argumentative. They complained about the lunch program. They were tired of roast beef, cold cuts, sandwiches, salads, and cold things like that. They wanted hot foods like pizza, heroes, hamburgers, sausages, spaghetti, steaks, and barbecued chicken. What had been great, became "shit," "crummy," "pig's food," and "slop." The boys demanded a change—and they got it. Cold food was out. Hot food was in. One day Italian food, one day hot dogs and hamburgers, another day chicken, one day something else, one day, Friday, eating out.

Nat, Carlos, and George developed a new game to bug us. Lock yourself in the music room and beat on the drums or bang on the piano until someone comes to play with you.

Old games were intensified. Pick up the phone, dial some numbers at random, and curse into it, or say you're the police or the FBI. Nat and Carlos were the champs. Throw a soccer ball against the window and light guards in the gym as hard as you can while yelling "Break, motherfucker." Harold, Larry, and Nat held top honors. Lean out the windows and scream obscenities at people in the street, especially girls. Everyone can play.

[Maybe it was the generation gap. Maybe it was the games our teen-agers played. But they played and we suffered. Maybe we should have done the same thing to them. How would they have liked it? Why couldn't we have fun like that?]

The talk about drugs increased. Larry praised LSD as a religious experience and claimed there was no freedom of religion in the U.S. because hallucinatory mind-expanding drugs were illegal. Willie and Harold denounced the age restrictions on buying liquor. Larry agreed. They all talked about their highs and the relative merits of "ups" versus "downs."

The boys became more physically active. Larry's jaw was unwired so he could fly in school. We soon learned his three favorite methods: hang from the fifth-floor banister rails, out over the first-floor landing, and go down hand over hand; hang from the fifth-floor fire escape rails, out over the back yard, and swing like a trapeze artist; stand on the ledge of the windows without fire escapes, lean out, and say, "I'm a high diver." Fortunately, no one else liked Larry's games. Larry also liked wrestling, so he joined in the wrestling matches. "Let's all try to wrestle Herb down on the mats" was a popular game. Nat and George against Herb—Larry and Harold against Herb—Nat, George, and Larry against Herb—Harold against Larry—Harold against anyone. Herb was getting into shape. All those sweaty bodies, and George was the only one, except for Herb, who took a shower.

Nat started a game with Herb.

"I'll go to class if you carry me piggyback on your back up the stairs." Carlos liked the looks of it and joined in the game. Herb was getting into shape, but tired. So Henry reluctantly became their "horsey."

The boys were all over Henry asking for increased allowances, more clothes, hamburgers, and Cokes. Nat, Carlos, Harold, George, and even Willie all had the "gimmies"— gimme this and gimme that. George wanted more allowance, because his father had stopped giving him his allowance after he falsely accused George of stealing money from him. George got sneakers and hamburgers and milkshakes twice. His extra allowance we would see about. Harold got food and the opportunity to use Henry as a punching bag when he was depressed. Nat and Carlos got food and piggyback rides. Willie got his jacket, actually a topcoat, and an extra five dollars besides.

When Henry offered to take Willie for a jacket, he had already changed his mind. He wanted a topcoat instead, a special one, one that they sold around his block. Didn't they sell one around the school? Henry asked. Didn't he want someone to go along with him? No, and no. Willie wanted the one in his neighborhood. Okay, he could get the coat after school and bring us the receipt.

Fine, he did it. But the tax was for five dollars less than the price which, after close examination, looked like it had been erased . . . by an expert. A call to the store confirmed our suspicions. Willie had "upped" the price five dollars and "pocketed" the difference.

Perhaps we should have expected as much. Didn't Henry tell us even before the school had opened that Willie thought of school as a place where he could get things. We were giving him a lot, including his own music room reserved for him at least one period every day, three music lessons a week, a new piano, and a new coat. Evidently it wasn't enough. Perhaps Willie wanted the feeling of getting his own on his own. Well, it was just an old habit. All the boys had their own problems. Henry and Herb put their heads together. "It was no big deal," as Harold would say. Confront him about it . . . gently. If he admits it, fine . . . if not, don't push it. Just let him know we know, and we know he knows we know, and he knows we know he knows we know.

We admitted we knew, but Willie only admitted we made a mistake. He didn't change anything on the receipt. Oh well, Willie wasn't able to open up yet. "No big deal, Willie baby."

While Willie was starting to act out, Nat was going all out. He grew tired of rubbing legs with Natalie and took up stroking her hair, then kissing her on the cheek in front of the other boys. Nat tried to get next to Connie in the same way, but he got nowhere because it wasn't her style. During the middle of the week Nat locked Marilyn in the music room, took out his knife, and threatened: "Gimme that pocketbook." Marilyn wasn't afraid. She had faced knives before. She thought he was playing around. He was.

At the end of the week Nat got into an argument with Connie. Nat had forgotten that Herb had given him his full allowance earlier in the week so when Connie gave all of the other boys their second installments he complained. Later Herb reminded Nat that he had already received his allowance. Nat wasn't satisfied. While Connie was in Phyllis's office dictating, he burst in to continue the argument. The dictating machine continued recording.

CONNIE: Oh Nat, get out of here, please.
NAT: Fuck you.
CONNIE: I'm not kidding.
NAT: Don come no fuckin closer. Don come . . .

CONNIE: Nat.

NAT: You come any closer ah hit you.

CONNIE: Nat, you've already hurt me once, now listen, I want you out.

Herb came in. Everyone shouted simultaneously.

HERB: Did he get his allowance?

PHYLLIS: He got it yesterday.

NAT: Ah didn' get shit yesterday.

HERB: Okay.

NAT: You betta kiss my ass.

HERB: Forget about it, forget about it.

Nat didn't answer, instead he picked up the dictating machine, started banging it and yelling "Fuck you!"

HERB: Gimme that machine, Nat. You're gonna break it.

CONNIE: Give it back, Nat.

NAT: I won give it back til you gimme my three dollars.

Herb started running after Nat, who was holding the machine out of the window as if he were about to drop it.

NAT: Come on, catch me, don push me. Ah give you a nickel for it, Nigger (laughing). Ah keep it till Monday that's all. You got your 'lowance yesterday, (laughingly mimicking Herb). Hey, look what ah got.

HERB: You got your allowance.

NAT: Today?

HERB: You got your allowance Wednesday.

NAT: Ah'm holdin this thing till ah gets my money.

HERB: How much does she owe you?

NAT: Three dollars.

HERB: You got it.

CONNIE: Give it to him, Nat.

NAT: Yeah (laughing). Ah'm not goin give it to him. You goddam right.

Harold came in, looked at the scene, sized up the situation, and said to Nat:

I know Herbie, you don know Herbie that well, you never fought wi Herbie, I have.

NAT: I wont a dollar, Ah . . . fuck you. Boy, shut up. Herbie . . . ah don't care.

HERB: You got your money already. Let's go outside and talk.

Nat agreed, the two of them left. The incident ended—just like that.

[This led to a new policy. Boys were to sign a dated receipt whenever they received an advance on their allowance. Too many of them had forgotten the money they had been advanced. This system worked out better but not perfectly.]

UNSCHEDULED "TRIP"

We had our first unscheduled "trip" on Thursday. Larry looked high when he came in—maybe on drugs, maybe just flying on his own. But nothing happened until Natalie heard screaming and saw him crouched on the floor in the doorway to Connie's room, hands over his ears, eyes closed, body shaking in terror, screaming, "Save me, save me. The walls, the walls, they're comin in on me, they're squashin me, cavin me." He was on a bad trip, out of contact, in his own delusional world. Natalie didn't know if it was a psychotic episode or a drug trip. Whatever it was, it scared her. Larry continued screaming, "Beasties, beasties." Natalie went for help. The LSD eventually wore off.

ANTS IN THE SUBWAY

Manuel didn't have delusions in school like Larry, but he started to tell us about some of the ones he was having out of school. He began his class with Connie by telling her he had made a down payment on a rifle in a pawnshop. Then he rambled on that he wasn't going to drink anymore because he was afraid he would get drunk and shoot people

. . . if he shot them while he was drunk he wouldn't re-member the incident . . . but the police would put him under the lie detector and find out anyway. He started to read, but he had something to say that he couldn't get out. Finally he admitted, "Ya know, I think stupid things."

Connie waited, but Manuel didn't continue. She asked him what he meant. He hesitated, then blurted out: "I think people on the subway a ants—they look jus like ants. I useta think if I step on a crack I would die. I cure myself. I step on a crack one day and I din die. I got lotsa secret I don tell."

Connie asked why in a voice which tried to disguise her concern.

"If I don say things," he answered, "then I'n not crazy. Only if ya say or do em."

Connie felt uncomfortable about Manuel's delusions in the subway, but she could handle her discomfort. It was the gun that frightened her. Connie was afraid that Manuel might do something terrible with the gun. She wanted some-one to stop him before he did anything dangerous. Herb ad-vised Connie not to worry about the gun. He assured her that most people who talked about their fantasies as if they were real seldom carried them out.

Ed also needed reassurance because Manuel had told him that he smoked pot and sniffed glue. Ed wasn't worried about the pot, but he had heard that glue-sniffing was dan-gerous. Having learned who on the staff to go to for dif-ferent kinds of help, Ed turned to Norm for advice and got it.

ART THERAPY

Don had a terrible week. He came to school disheveled, de-pressed, filthy-faced, wild-haired, and blank-staring, and spent most of the week lying or sleeping on the floors of the gym and hallways. When he was extremely depressed, he spoke to Henry about thinking too much, not being sure who he was, where he was, or even how many he was. When he was less depressed, he told Henry that he couldn't manage on the allowance we gave him because he was used to having a lot of stolen money in his pocket. He had stopped stealing money, he said, but he hadn't stopped wanting money.

Don avoided his classes except for the art studio, where in a burst of creative energy, he worked on an "ear of time" —a sculpture of concentric circles—and collaborated with Larry on a pair of red penises. Don's contribution was the semen dripping down the sides.

We worried all week about Don. We had expected things to get worse with him before they got better. We were seeing the worse. We hoped the better was on its way.

RELUCTANT SCHOLAR

In the middle of the "D's"—drugs, delusions, and delinquencies—George was pushing himself as a well-behaved academic student, but he really wasn't ready. His classes upset him and the "D's" regressed him.

When George walked into his first English class of the week, he looked at his grammar book and said, "I don't want to do this, this stupid grammar book." Getting the message, Connie gave George a vocabulary book two years below his grade level so that he wouldn't have too much difficulty. Unfortunately any difficulty was too much. George knew nine of the twelve words in the section and wrote their definitions. When it was time to look up the other three in the dictionary, he got up, wrote on the blackboard, sat down, looked at the words, got up, went out for a drink, came in, sat down, looked at the dictionary, told Connie that his mother always made him look up words in the dictionary, stood up, went out for a second drink, came in, looked at the three words, opened the dictionary, looked up the word "allowance" instead of the words in the lesson and said, "Sometimes I think this school robs a bank."

So far George reminded Connie of Harold—the way he got up, walked around, avoided work, and talked about his mother.

George looked up two of the three words, then said, "I gotta learn so I can make my mother happy . . . and me too, yeah! I can be a test pilot for the air force. First I'll bomb all the schools. C'mon, let's do some more work."

Then making a complete about-face he said he wanted to go downstairs to look at the new gym equipment that had just arrived. Connie agreed. Then after some pleasant minutes in the gym, George suddenly started screaming at Connie: "I didn't get English. It's your fault. You didn make me." A few moments of silence, then: "Yeah, but I learned two words Willie and Harold don't know."

George was fighting a losing battle to become a student. However he couldn't admit it to himself; his difficulties had to be someone else's responsibility. Connie thought to herself she should have forced him to learn. If he could magnify what he had accomplished that would help too. Even Willie and Harold didn't know the two words he had learned.

The following day George continued working on vocabulary. Connie noticed that he had difficulty finding the words in the dictionary and learned why. Although George could recite the alphabet, he didn't know the order without starting from the beginning.

When he came to the word "impulsive," he said, "I know that word. Impulsive's ugly. Henry says I'm impulsive. Impulsive's mentally disturbed . . . things mixed up in your mind."

"That's not really right," Connie told him. "It doesn't quite mean that. Here, look it up in the diction ry."

"It is," George answered angrily, just as he had gotten angry in the past each time Connie had corrected him.

"Look it up."

"Liar, bitch," he called to her, storming out of the door to get Herb to set Connie straight.

"Connie's a liar. She's cheatin me," he told Herb.

"What happened?" Herb asked.

"What's she doin in this school. She's a liar."

"What'd she do?" Herb asked again, but George wouldn't say anything else until they returned to Connie's room.

Then, when Herb heard what had happened, he explained to George that since he hadn't been there at the time he couldn't say what had happened, who had lied or cheated, or who was right or wrong. But he did know that George was wrong about the word. Zonk! That did it. George had really believed Connie was lying to him. He recovered quickly with an excuse. He was in a bad mood because the doctor had put a needle in his knee and it was Henry who had made him go to the doctor. It was Henry's fault. He ran out of the room, found Henry, and lashed out at him for sending him to the doctor.

George had almost as much difficulty with Ed in his "math" classes. At the start of his first math class, as soon as he and Ed had walked into the room, George said he didn't like math and ran into the gym, returned a few minutes later with the bongos, played them for a while, picked up the telephone, called Herb, said that he was Ed, hung up, and ran into the gym. After about two or three minutes he asked Ed, "Do you know how to play math games?"

"What kind a math games do you want to play?" Ed answered.

"Any kind," George replied.

"I'll play any math game you want," Ed told him.

"Good," George answered as he walked into Norm's shop, then finally back into Ed's room.

Ed gave him a math achievement test. George began working. He completed the first seven problems before coming to one he couldn't do, stopped, and said he didn't want to do anymore. After a short rest and a little coaxing, he started again and worked for a while, stopped again, said he would finish the rest the next day, picked up a piece of loose-leaf paper and played tick-tack-toe, which he called a math problem, until the end of the period.

[George wasn't ready for academic work. We were letting ourselves in for trouble by going along with his fantasy that he could immediately become a good student. He was struggling desperately to control himself, but he was suffering too much in the process. He tried to motivate himself by thinking about how nicely the school had treated him, how happy his mother would be, and what adventurous jobs he would be able to obtain, but it didn't work. It was too much for him. Why? It was too early to tell. At any rate he couldn't do it even though he wanted to.

However, George couldn't assume the responsibility for not being a student. It was too threatening. It made him feel too anxious or perhaps too guilty. So he wanted to act like he was still learning by playing a game which he pretended was learning. He blamed others: Connie, the doctor, Henry, anyone but himself. Finally he exaggerated what he had learned so he would not feel threatened about not completing the work. Why should he feel bad. He had learned two words that Willie and Harold didn't even know.]

HAPPY ENDING

At the end of the week Henry attended the Vocational Institute's admission conference about Stanley. Their psychologist said he was pessimistic about Stanley. Henry started to worry. Their psychiatrist's report was damaging to Stanley's chances for admission. Henry became anxious. Their social worker was concerned about Stanley's parents' negative attitude. And that made Henry angry.

Henry made a passionate plea for Stanley's acceptance. He explained that Stanley's parents no longer had a strong influence over him. He described the tremendous progress Stanley had made. He told them about the burglar alarm Stanley had attached to his alarm clock. He promised that Stanley would continue to be involved and supported at the school and would see Herb regularly. Finally, after a long discussion, Henry was able to change their minds. Stanley was accepted, but only on a trial basis. He could start as soon as there was an opening in the printing shop.

7 From Explosions to Intimacy and Revelations

A TALKY MORNING

After the long weekend anyone would have been able to pick up signs of the impending storm from Harold, George, and Larry. Harold came to school, looking terrible and oozing unhappiness. We could expect something from him. George brought a friend. We could expect something from him. Don hadn't arrived by warm-up. He hadn't slept at home for most of the long Lincoln's Birthday weekend. We could expect something from him if he came to school.

During the warm-up George shot Harold in the face with a paper clip, acting the wise guy for his friend. Harold glared back, flexed his muscles, bulled his neck, and said, "Cut it out or I break your back."

"You couldn't break your way out of a fuckin paper bag," George answered.

"I can break your ath."

"You couldn't break a cherry."

"Yeah"—and Harold was lunging at George, already in a rage, already out of control, as we jumped between them. It was too late to make peace. George had gotten what he

197

wanted and Harold had given it to him. All we could do was protect George from being massacred. Harold found his way blocked. We tried to calm him down, but Harold left cursing and stamping his feet like a mad bull.

Harold took off for the corner candy store while George, his friend Lonnie, and Nat went into the gym with Ed and Natalie. After stuffing himself with peanuts and popcorn—Harold still stuffed himself when frustrated—he went upstairs where he talked to Henry about being mentally retarded, crazy, feeble-minded, and fat. Harold seemed less angry at George than oppressed about his educational problems and the fear that he would never be able to fulfill his goals. Henry tried to give him support and sympathy, but Harold's depression was too deep. Still unhappy after his talk with Henry, Harold went for something else to eat, then to Bill's studio where he mushed clay.

Back in the gym George and Lonnie were planning, purposely loud enough for Ed to hear, to beat up Henry. Ed, thinking he had overheard something he wasn't supposed to hear, called Herb to tell him what George and Lonnie were up to. Herb looked at the boys. They weren't poised to attack anyone. Besides Herb didn't think George would have broadcast his intentions if he had meant them. He told Ed they were probably just trying to worry him for laughs.

Since Don and Harold weren't in class, Norm canceled biology and let Willie and Larry work on their shop projects. Larry was more in the mood for rapping. He told Norm he had stayed out all night driving a beat-up abandoned jalopy he and two friends had "acquired." They had spent the first part of the night stealing parts from parked cars to replace the parts that had been stripped from their abandoned car and the rest of the night driving it around.

Don came to school around ten forty-five, looking as if he hadn't slept for days. He lay down on the couch in the rec room and slept through most of the next period without saying anything to anyone. Before he arrived, Henry had received three anxious calls from his mother. Mrs. Russo had called Henry Sunday to tell him that Don had stayed away Saturday evening, Monday to say Don had returned Sunday evening, and Tuesday to report that Don hadn't been home Monday evening. Henry had a lot to ask Don, but he wanted to give him a chance to nap first.

At eleven o'clock during change of periods, Natalie with Nat, Herb, and Henry all went to move their cars to the other side of the street, while Jack, who didn't have a car, went looking for Harold and George went looking for Henry. Natalie and Nat parked her car, and started back toward the school. Nat asked if her husband had a car. Natalie reminded him that she wasn't married. Nat smiled appreciatively, then asked if she was engaged. She said no. Nat smiled again.

Nat became particularly aware of the white-lady-walking-cozy-like-with-black-boy looks people in the street directed at them. He experienced their stares, tested Natalie's reaction, felt reassured, edged even closer to her, and continued "checking her out." A pretty girl passed. Nat stared at her until he noticed Natalie smiling at the way he was looking her up and down. He laughed embarrassedly but said nothing; neither did Natalie. They were wrapped in a special, very special unspoken warmth—not exactly what we had planned, but "more better," more real, more natural.

While Jack discovered Harold in the art studio, George found Henry and purposely instigated an argument over whether his friend would receive carfare home. When George started shouting and threatening Henry, Harold, who was already angry at George for the paper clip, heard the screaming downstairs in the gym and raced out of class to Henry's rescue, only to find that Henry wasn't in any real danger. Without an excuse to support an attack against George, Harold returned to class, George settled down, and Don, who had been sleeping peacefully on the mats until the noise started, went with Henry to his office.

Don told Henry that he had been upset all weekend. He had argued with his girl friend and hit her. Then he had roamed the Village with some friends. He had taken some drugs, but he still hadn't been able to get his girl off his mind.

[Monday was always a busy day for Henry. A Tuesday after a long weekend could be especially busy. Three days at home for kids like Harold, Don, and George could give them a lot to talk about.]

At eleven forty the boys changed classes. Larry and Harold had math with Bill, George had math with Ed, and Don had his first math class with Jack. Jack began by reviewing the achievement test Don had taken previously. Don was still on a very basic level, and had trouble with subtraction and multiplication, even with addition. Jack chose an elementary-level programmed math text for Don and got him started.

HAROLD'S UNHAPPINESS
There was still some time before afternoon classes resumed. The boys drifted upstairs. Harold and Jack walked into the music room. Harold borrowed Jack's pipe, smoked it, then emptied the ashes on the floor. Jack asked him why he had done it. Harold glared at him—he wasn't in a mood to be criticized—then stormed up to Phyllis's office, pulled open the confidential files, and took out some papers. First Jack told him to put them back. When that didn't work, Jack grabbed some of the papers. Harold pulled them out of his hand. Jack wanted to take them away from Harold, but he

didn't want to use force. Harold read for a minute, put the papers down, and walked out, mumbling in a depressed rather than angry voice, "I'm a hopeleth cath. Life ithin't worth livin."

Jack tried to comfort him by saying, "Well, how about giving me a chance to try to prove different."

But Harold answered, "Fuck you, Jack."

Harold was suffering. He needed a lot of attention from Henry. He would have settled for Herb, his substitute therapist, but Tuesday was the day they both left early. So he didn't get it. He acted up.

After lunch Harold went to social studies. Jack had prepared a two-class unit for him and Larry. During the first class they were to read an article which claimed that the Kensington Stone, an archaeological discovery, proved that the Vikings had been the first Europeans to discover America. During the second class they were supposed to read an article which attempted to prove that the Kensington Stone was a forgery. Then they would try to come to some conclusions about the conflicting claims. It had seemed like a good idea to Jack but he hadn't counted on Larry's moods and Harold's academic difficulties. Jack wanted them to dissect the article and list the various kinds of evidence it presented, but Harold couldn't do it. If an authentic Kensington Stone proved the Vikings discovered America, he argued, then the Vikings didn't discover America if the stone was a fake.

Jack tried to help Harold see that even if the Stone were fake, the Vikings still might have discovered America. But Harold was unable to understand what Jack was getting at. He became more and more frustrated. He complained that Jack's lesson was shit and demanded a textbook that would tell him the facts instead of mixing him up. Then he began singing, louder and louder, carrying along Larry.

Jack was surprised and disappointed that Harold was able to divert Larry so easily. Harold's disruptive behavior he could understand, but Larry was going along with Harold even though he could do the work.

Wednesday, February 15

PROBLEM-SOLVING

When we got together for our Wednesday morning meeting, Jack was waiting to discuss Harold who had given him the old "one two," first in Phyllis's office, then in the social studies class. As we discussed Harold we again divided into two groups, newcomers and old-timers. The old-timers were impressed with Harold's improvement. Harold thought more of himself. He got along better with people. And he was moving closer to the women on our staff.

Stressing these improvements, the old-timers viewed Harold's provocative behavior as a temporary lapse. They weren't sure what was causing it, but they were certain that it wasn't anything to worry about.

After we "solved" Harold's problem, we moved on to Carlos who was becoming almost as disruptive as Nat. We had to admit that we didn't have a full program for him. Carlos almost always attended his class with Natalie and his two gym, rec room periods, but he seldom attended classes with Norm or Bill. Even when he went to their classes, he usually wandered out after a few minutes to disrupt whatever he got into.

Henry felt that Carlos's restlessness in school was caused by his problems at home. He thought that we needed to know a lot more about Carlos's family in order to help him. So we decided to hire a Spanish-speaking interpreter to help Henry interview Carlos's father regularly so we could find out what was going on at home.

Then we had another discussion about Nat. First, almost ritualistically, we recounted his most recent disruptive behavior, including the mess he had made by spreading a huge box of detergent all over the second-floor hall and rec room and allowing the sink to overflow, covering the whole floor with soapsuds. Then we debated whether we could possibly contain him for even a little while longer. We spoke with more exasperation and more certainty in our voices about excluding Nat. Yet we hadn't quite closed the door on him.

Natalie was very upset by the discussion. It had seemed to her that we had definitely decided to exclude Nat . . . as if the only thing left was setting the date. She had misunderstood us because she had taken the conversation too literally. She thought we were making a decision when we were simply engaging in a process. As Nat became more and more disruptive and demanding, it became increasingly difficult for us to work with the other boys. Our immediate impulse was to say, "Let's get rid of him." Then we thought, Well, perhaps we can help him control himself. We really have to try. If we still can't make it we will have to discharge him. We were gradually coming to a decision about whether we could contain him. But we hadn't made one yet.

LITTLE DEVILS

As we walked out of the morning meeting, Nat, Carlos, and George (speak of the devils) burst into Henry's and Herb's offices which were next to each other and "sat in," as if they were occupying them. They discovered they could telephone from one office to another and the "sit-in" became a "talk-in," Nat concentrating on Herb's phone, George on Henry's, and Carlos alternating between them. Then they all crowded into Herb's office. Carlos took out his knife to show Herb. George grabbed it, opened it, and poked

Henry's arm with it. Nat and Carlos looked at George like he was crazy. George turned to Herb, looked him in the eye, and jabbed the knife toward his heart, making sure to stop a good foot away. Abruptly Nat said, "Let's go eat," and the three of them cut out.

[That Nat! He was all right. Always saying the right thing at the right time. No sense kicking him out.]

After warm-up the three boys spent an uneventful first period in the gym with Natalie and Ed while the rest of the boys, except Manuel, had biology. At eleven o'clock when it was time for class, Natalie called Nat. He groaned, but came right away. Carlos followed him and sat outside Natalie's office as if he didn't want to let Nat have her to himself. Natalie reminded Carlos that he had shop, but he wanted to stay nearby. His jealousy was coming through loud and clear.

It wasn't Nat's academic day. He said he wanted to read, but before Natalie could hand him his book, he was playing with his "toy telephone."

"You said you wanted to read, Nat," she called to him, trying to remind him that he was the one who wanted to read. Nat didn't hear her or acted like he didn't.

"Nat!" a frustrated pause. "You know you're not supposed to play with the phones."

"You betta be down here Herbie or ah kick your ass" was Nat's answer, but not to Natalie. He still wasn't hearing her.

"Nat, you're not supposed to play with the phone," she demanded, losing her cool. Still no answer—like she wasn't there. That was enough to get anyone angry, even Natalie.

"Okay!" she huffed, "if you're not going to read we might as well go upstairs."

That got him. Looking surprised, and, a little anxious, he said, "Okay, okay, let's read, let's don't go upstairs."

He began to read the story, but he couldn't manage many of the words he had been able to read previously. By masturbating and rubbing his legs against hers he was able to relax enough to read for a few minutes. Finally he gave up. As he closed the book, he asked, "How long ah been readin this here book?" Before Natalie replied, he quickly answered, "Three days . . . ah finish tomorrow." This was impossible because he was still at the beginning of the book. "It too easy. Ah wants a hard one."

Natalie had blown her cool and Nat felt pressured. She was beginning to push him—like a regular teacher might. And Nat was pushing back.

As Natalie was working on Nat, Carlos was working on Herb to let him "have Natalie for two periods." Herb could see that Carlos was jealous. Carlos had had Natalie for himself until Nat had arrived. At first he and Nat had shared her as their "person." Then Nat moved in on Natalie, stroking her hair, holding her hand, and kissing her cheek. Carlos couldn't manage that kind of scene. During his most uninhibited moments Carlos might stroke her hair, but only very tentatively, very quickly, and very occasionally. Nat was flaunting his physical relationship with Natalie, and Carlos was jealous.

Herb thought it was still too early to confront Carlos with his jealous feelings. Instead he answered Carlos's request for two periods with Natalie by telling him that he didn't need another academic period with her. Carlos asked if he would have the other period if he needed the extra work. Herb said he would see when the time came.

Then Herb filled Natalie in on the conversation he had just had with Carlos and advised her not to be taken in by any sudden burst of energy and effort Carlos might show. When it was Carlos's turn with Natalie he wasn't in the mood to read, but he was determined to prove he was. He started to read, said the story was stupid, asked for another book, started again, then stopped to fool around with the telephone. Natalie asked him not to. Carlos asked what she would do if he didn't stop. Not particularly concerned about stopping him, she didn't answer, Carlos started to read again, stopped, wrote his name on the desk, drew a face on a piece of paper, took out a dri-mark pen and drew on the walls. Regaining control of himself, he tried to read, stopped, and asked for spelling and arithmetic on Monday. When Natalie agreed, Carlos told her not to give him hard spelling words, only easy ones. Then he continued reading until the end of the period.

[All that work—reading, spelling, arithmetic. He would certainly need two academic periods even though one was really too much for him.]

While Nat and Carlos were trying to please Natalie, George was doing just the opposite with Connie. During his English class he seemed like a caged tiger. Since it wasn't the first time he had been unable to sit in class, Connie wasn't surprised when George got up for drinks of water three or four times during the first ten minutes. When he grabbed her purse, taking out her keys, she still wasn't upset. But when he returned to class after his fourth drink with a bullwhip and started snapping it near her, George was in control of himself, but Connie was frightened. She quickly called Herb, who came in, ushered George out, and separated George from the bullwhip. Then, just as Herb was unlocking the door to his office for a talk, George grabbed the keys from him and started running away with them. By that time Herb decided Henry ought to handle the situation. So he called him and turned over George and the keys he was still holding.

George and Henry disappeared into Henry's office. Soon George was shouting at Henry and throwing playful punches at him. Henry grabbed him, controlled him for a minute, then let him go. George started yelling and searching through Henry's personal things and confidential papers. Henry asked him to stop. They talked. More jabbing, more controlling. Peace, more conversation. Then peace.

Their talk was over. Henry started walking George back down to the gym. George started pushing, so Henry grabbed him. George bumped his head and started screaming, "You hurt me, nigger, you hurt me." Herb, Harold, and Ed ran into the hall to see what was happening. By the time they got to the stairs Henry had let George go and was explaining to him that George had finally gotten Henry to reject him.

Henry placed the responsibility for George's actions right where it belonged, on his own shoulders. George preferred to blame others. Since he couldn't, he took off for the rest of the morning.

When he returned just in time for lunch, he looked sulky and angry and ready to slaughter someone.

NOT A KID

The afternoon was quiet but talky. Herb filled in for Henry with Carlos and Willie, Ed talked to Don, and Jack argued with Harold.

Willie was upset by the way George was acting. He asked Herb why we allowed the kids to act the way they did. Because, Herb answered, the school was for boys with problems that we didn't expect to disappear overnight.

Willie looked puzzled.

"I'm not like that. I'm not a kid."

"Well, you're here for some reason, Willie," Herb answered, letting the subject drop. Herb wondered if Willie was also asking why we had allowed him to get away with the five dollars he had stolen. He was busy making up for it in his own way. He had started a new project in shop, a large table. He had told Norm it was for the school and had hinted it was because he owed us something, probably the five dollars he had stolen when he had bought the coat he usually wore in class.

SCARS

H:rb also spoke to Carlos about having his eyes examined because he had been complaining about them to Natalie. Carlos wanted to have them checked but he didn't want to go to "some cheap clinic where they make ya wait and give ya a bad doctor." Like most of our boys, Carlos thought clinic service was cheap and second class. Because we had decided long before Carlos started in our school not to send the boys to clinics—for psychological reasons—Herb promised to send him to a private doctor. Since Herb was so concerned and sympathetic, Carlos took the opportunity to tell him about his other physical problems.

"See this scar here," he said, pointing to his scalp, "thas where my father crack my head open."

"He cracked your head open?" Herb asked.

"Yeah! Me and my sista was fightin—I din hit her but my father, he push me real hard and crack my head open on the steam . . . I took sick stitches. See this one?" Herb nodded his head yes although the second scar wasn't visible. "He crack my head here too."

After receiving more sympathy from Herb, Carlos continued displaying the scars he had received when he had been run over by a car, cut in a knife fight, and stabbed in the back. Herb asked Carlos if he could remember any time someone had been nice to him or he had been very happy. "Sure," Carlos replied.

"When?" Herb asked. Carlos thought for a couple of minutes, but he couldn't describe one happy incident in his life, or one nice thing a person had done for him. Herb put his hand on Carlos's shoulder and shared his feeling that things had been pretty rough. Then he told Carlos we would take care of his glasses on Thursday if we could find a doctor, but certainly by Friday.

NEVER BELIEVE THE ESTABLISHMENT

Unfortunately Jack didn't fare as well with Harold. Jack had asked Harold to read the second article about the discovery of America, one prepared by the government, which claimed that the Kensington Stone was a fraud. What Harold really wanted was a textbook telling him the facts. But he finally submitted, read all but the last two pages of the article, then threw it across the room, saying, "I don't believe it a fake."

"Why?" Jack asked.

"Becauth the Vikin did dithcover America."

Jack tried to point out Harold's faulty logic but Harold wasn't receptive. Harold claimed that the article was like the air force's reports about UFO's. He believed that the government denied their existence for its own purposes even though many people had seen them. "If the ethtablithment thay it not true," he told Jack, "then you know it true." At that point Jack gave up. He thought he had no other choice because Harold had his own way of thinking about things.

ANOTHER FULL-TIME STUDENT

Stanley came to school to talk about the Institute. He seemed eager to begin training but also concerned that his attendance at the Institute would prevent him from earning a high school diploma. Herb knew that Stanley needed some program to occupy him until there was an opening in the Institute print shop. So he told Stanley that he could work toward a high school equivalency diploma in school until the opening at the Institute developed. Connie and Jack would work out a tutorial program for him in English and math and he could hang around in the shops, music room, and rec room for as long as he wanted.

Thursday, February 16

THEM HIGH-CLASS PEOPLE

After the morning meeting, true to our word, Natalie drove Carlos to an ophthalmologist. At first Carlos didn't believe they were going to a private doctor. When they passed a hospital, he was sure he knew where they were going and declared, "Oh, no. I know where ya takin me."

"Where?"

"Ta a hospital! I tol ya I won go ta no hospital fa my eyes."

They turned into a nice neighborhood off Park Avenue. That convinced him.

"Yeah, this's more like it. Man . . . how'dya like ta be high class like them people?"

The doctor's office was plush, real "high class." Carlos looked like he felt he had made it.

And the doctor gave us a break on the bill.

And after lunch he went to an optician to be fitted for new glasses.

And after school Natalie drove him home.

And in his neighborhood he called to all his friends from the car window to see him with Natalie.

Carlos was really making it.

OUR SECOND PREGNANCY

And so was Manuel—his first therapy session with Herb. It started at the end of his class with Connie when Manuel said he was leaving school. Connie alerted Herb, who met them on the stairway. Herb asked Manuel what was bothering him, but got no answer. Herb said he understood Manuel didn't like to talk to headshrinkers. Manuel smiled. Herb suggested that Manuel think of him as a teacher like Connie, Bill, or Ed. He signaled Connie to leave and asked Manuel what was on his mind.

Manuel sat down next to Herb on the staircase landing where he remained silent for a few minutes. Then, he blurted out that he had gotten his girl friend pregnant. Herb had heard that story from Stanley a few weeks before. "Another false alarm," he hoped to himself. Manuel continued. The story was garbled. Herb could only get the general idea.

During the weekend one of Manuel's friends had noticed Manuel's ex-girl friend walking in the street with a bigger belly than usual. He had asked her if she was pregnant. She was. He had told Manuel about it. Manuel had been nervous since then, thinking about what he was going to do. He didn't want to get "hooked ta the girl." He was thinking of "takin it ona lam, cuttin out, runnin away." Herb asked him what he thought would happen, meaning if he ran away. Manuel replied that they would kill the baby. Herb thought Manuel was referring to an abortion but he wanted to make sure. So he asked, "What do you mean, kill the baby?"

"When i's out they kill it."

"When it comes out?"

"Yeah."

"How?"

"They throw it up in a air and catch it on a knife or sword."

Manuel seemed certain. Herb asked, "How do you know?"

Manuel didn't respond to Herb. He was too preoccupied with his own questions. What would happen to him if the police found out what he had done. What if they tried to make him marry the girl. No, he wasn't going to marry no girl. What if they caught him after he ran away? They'd never catch him. Maybe he'd kick her brother's ass so her brother wouldn't rat on him.

After Manuel had rambled on for a while Herb worked the conversation around to why he thought his girl friend was pregnant and why he thought he would be blamed. Manuel didn't have any rational reasons. He hadn't seen the girl. None of his friends had. The girl's brother had never been in touch with him. She really wasn't his girl friend anyway. She had made it with all sorts of guys in the neighborhood in gang bangs in the park and on roofs. He couldn't remember which friend had told him about her and he didn't even know why his friend had told him rather than some other guy.

The cause of Manuel's concerns was far from clear to Herb. It might have been a delusion—like the ants on the train, the ghosts under his bed, or the old people hanging from the trees in Puerto Rico. Or it might have been real. Not knowing, Herb decided not to question the reality of Manuel's concern but to deal with the anxiety it was evoking.

Herb explained why Manuel couldn't be forced to marry the girl and why it wouldn't be a good idea for a fourteen-year-old boy to get married, even if he wanted to. He told Manuel about abortions and birth control. Finally he said that the courts wouldn't punish Manuel for breaking probation because the girl had to have become pregnant before he was placed on probation.

Manuel seemed relieved to find out the actual facts because he evidently thought they would be much worse. Then, knowing that Manuel was very suspicious about people, Herb told him that he didn't have to worry that we might tell the court what he had done. He explained the difference between being caught doing something by the police, and talking to us about what he had been doing so we could help him stop doing it. Still anxious as he ended the discussion, Manuel couldn't decide if he should try to find out if the girl was really pregnant. He wanted to know, but he was afraid that people, especially her brother, would blame him if he seemed too curious.

TWENTY CENTS

It was an easy day. Even George was calm except for a couple of small incidents. During the morning he took twenty cents from Phyllis as she was preparing the envelopes for the boys' carfare. Phyllis gave him twenty cents less for carfare, so the score was evened up. During lunch George stuck his hand in Herb's pocket and took another twenty cents which he refused to return. He and Herb played cops and robbers over the money for a while. Herb told him he could keep the money if the school could deduct it from his allowance on Friday as they had done for the twenty cents he had taken from Phyllis. George didn't like the idea. Finally, with a smile on his face, Herb told George he could keep the money and Herb wouldn't take it out of his allowance. George smiled . . . then Herb added: "But I'll take it out of your carfare."

Everyone had a good laugh, including George, who answered, "Okay, take it out a my allowance." George seemed to take it good-naturedly, but Herb was worried about how he would react Friday when his allowance and carfare would be given to him twenty cents short.

Friday, February 17

EASY RIDING

Friday started off as peacefully as Thursday had been. Carlos brought his cousin Jimmy to school with him to talk about a job. George seemed calm. He even went to English, which he had skipped on Thursday. Although Connie was a little nervous after what had happened with the bullwhip on Wednesday, she tried not to show it. George acted as if nothing had ever happened. He worked consistently and quietly until Connie asked him if the word "sister" was a noun.

"No, I don't like my sister," George answered, responding to his own thoughts rather than her question. Then he told Connie that his teen-age sister had moved out of the state to avoid being sent "upstate." She had become friendly with some girls who were shoplifters. He called his sister a "cow" because she drank three quarts of milk a day and ate all of his food. As if that wasn't enough, his father ate George's food too. So when George liked the same thing his father liked, he had to eat first to make sure he got some. And that wasn't all. His father had stopped giving him an allowance because someone had stolen thirty-five cents from him and George had been blamed for it. But he didn't want his father's dirty money anyway, George added.

CLOSE SHAVE
It had been a good morning. Lunch and the trip were all that was left until the weekend. Herb gave out the allowances during lunch because he wanted to be the one to handle George in case he acted up about the twenty cents. George counted his money, found twenty cents missing, and good-naturedly asked Herb for the money. Herb, thinking George was joking, responded accordingly. George smiled and Herb thought the problem was over.

After lunch people gradually drifted into the rec room to wait for the trips to start. Nat started wrestling playfully with Herb. George joined in and grabbed for Herb's wallet. Harold, making it three against one, got the wallet and took Herb's money out. George became serious and suggested they split it. Nat, who was only playing, got worried and shouted to Harold to give back the money. Harold looked at both of them, smiled at Herb, put the money into the wallet, put his arm around Herb, and stuck the wallet back in Herb's pocket.

The boys were still drifting in. Herb was talking to Jack about the trips. Suddenly, George, acting tough but obviously just acting, demanded: "Where's my twenty cent, where's my twenty cent?" Herb reminded George that he had taken twenty cents the previous day from his pocket. Suddenly George had a fishing knife with a sharp long blade at Herb's back.

"You betta gimme that twenty cent, nigger," he threatened verbally but not physically.

"Come on, George, come on, cut it out," Herb answered, acting as if George were not really threatening him at all.

But, as George kept insisting someone had stolen his "twenty cent," he became more serious about it. The rest of us in the gym were getting anxious.

Connie started yelling, "George, leave him alone." Connie looked like she was beginning to panic.

Herb shouted back, "I can handle it."

Suddenly Harold moved toward them as if he was going to protect Herb from George. George's grip tightened— Herb could feel the point of the knife a little sharper in his back. Afraid Harold would panic George, he called out, "Keep away, Harold, I can handle it."

Harold stopped and turned away. That seemed to calm George momentarily. He lowered the knife and took a step back. Thinking the incident was over, Herb took a step forward. As he did, George grabbed him from behind and placed the blade of the knife against Herb's jugular vein. Scared now, Herb tried reminding himself that George had done the same thing to a little girl before he had been referred to the school and nothing had happened. That didn't help. He was still scared. Questions ran through Herb's mind. "Is the kid psychotic? Does he know what's going on? Should I try to get away?" Everyone was staring. Again George demanded his money. As Herb started to answer, Harold stepped forward to grab George. Herb yelled at Harold to get away. Harold stepped back about three feet, watching like a hawk. Herb made him back up some more. George gradually relaxed, let go, and put the knife away.

It was trip time. George left quietly . . . without the twenty cents.

Monday, February 20, through Tuesday, February 28

JEALOUS LITTLE DEVIL

George seemed quieter than usual when he returned to school Monday morning. Something was different about him. We nervously wondered what it was. During warm-up he eyed Natalie for a while without saying anything. Then he moved closer to her, haltingly put his arms around her shoulder, and asked her to take him to have his eyes examined. After what George had done to Connie and Herb the previous week, we were relieved to learn what he had in mind. So was Natalie. But Carlos didn't like it. George had his arms around Carlos's Natalie and he wanted her to take him to Carlos's eye doctor. Carlos definitely didn't like that. Natalie was his.

Carlos had to do something. He demanded to have her third period, Nat's period. Natalie, realizing Carlos was jealous, still couldn't give him Nat's period. It's Nat's period, she explained. But that made no difference. Carlos insisted he wanted her third period. And he kept insisting he was going to have her until Nat finally shouted, "NO! Ah be with Natalie. She's mine."

That ended the issue for Carlos, but not for George. Carlos might be willing to let Nat have Natalie third period, but George wasn't willing to let him have her first period. Instead of going to gym, George refused to let Nat and Natalie go into her room without him. Then, when Natalie let him come into her office with them, George refused to leave. Natalie sensed that George was preparing himself for battle. Rather than risk the big scene she expected, Natalie told him he could stay . . . if he was quiet. George agreed. Natalie realized her mistake when Nat was unable to concentrate with George in the room. George had to go. Natalie prepared herself for battle, but George left on his own, perhaps sensing he was about to be kicked out.

BAD NIGGER?

George still wanted attention. He knew Henry would play with him. Henry would argue with him if he took things from the office. Henry would argue with him if he used the phones. Yeah! Henry would give him lots of attention. So George went looking for him.

Henry could see that George was upset. He gave George the attention he wanted, then got him to talk about the threatening gestures he had made toward Herb with his knife. George was upset about his loss of control, but he was more worried about what we might do to him. Henry told him that we couldn't allow him to do things like that. "You know I wouldn't of hurt Herb," George claimed, trying to excuse himself. Nevertheless, Henry insisted, George had gone beyond the limits of what we could accept. He had been losing more and more control over himself, Henry explained. We didn't want that to continue. We had some rules everyone had to follow. If he couldn't keep his knife in his pocket, we would have to hold it for him.

That last idea sounded good to George. He knew he

needed our help to control himself. He offered to sell the knife to Henry for a dollar. Henry told him that we couldn't give him a dollar for the knife because he could buy himself another one for a dollar and change and reminded him that the going price was fifty cents and all the food he could eat. George agreed, broke his knife, and collected his money, two cheeseburgers, milk, and an ice cream sundae right away.

[Actually the established trade-in value for knives was all the food the boys could eat plus fifty cents for the first knife, twenty-five cents for the second knife, and ten cents for any other knives. That was enough of a pay-off to enable the boys to save face and feel compensated when they surrendered their knives, yet it wasn't enough of a pay-off to encourage them to turn the trading into a con for money.]

George was a happy kid when he returned to school from his snack. He really liked us. He wore Henry's gloves and Herb's jacket, he even smoked Jack's pipe. He was having too good a time to leave school without a lot of coaxing. Just as he was about to walk out of the hallway door into the street, he told Henry that he had a zip gun at home he wanted to sell. They haggled a while about the price of the gun and finally agreed on a dollar plus food. George started punching Henry aggressively but playfully. Larry butted in, pretending to rescue Henry. Henry told him to leave but Larry grabbed for George. George moved away, knocked into a garbage can, and started screaming, "Mothafuckin Henry's gonna push me inta the can," as if he actually believed it.

Herb, Bill, and Jack heard the noise, ran into the hall, and mistakenly decided that George was having a fit. As Bill and Herb grabbed George, helpful Larry shouted, "Don't let em push you out, George." George struggled . . . Bill and Herb held tight . . . George struggled harder . . . they held on even tighter. Henry shouted to them to let George go while Larry shouted, "George, don't let em push you out."

Finally Henry got through to Bill and Herb. They let go, but by then George was out of control and he rushed at them. They grabbed him and pulled him out of the door. As they let him go again, George kicked an empty can at them, just missing them. They grabbed him again. He kicked, punched, cursed, and spit, but they held tight.

By then we were all watching.

After a few minutes Henry calmed him down. As he did, Bill and Herb let go. Henry asked George to leave. George said he would if he could have a drink of water. Herb got him the water. He threw it at Henry and Herb, as expected, seemed satisfied, and left.

After George left, Henry and Herb confronted Larry about the way he had incited George. Larry smiled. The action was over, so Larry left.

We could finally start our meeting. Henry was angry at Bill and Herb for interfering when everything had been under control.

"There was no need for you to grab him," Henry told them. "He wasn't going to hurt me. There was no reason to use a tank to swat a fly."

Henry was certain that he was right. But Herb wasn't convinced that George was a fly. He remembered the knife at his throat. Bill felt that if they had made a mistake it had been a natural one. Henry and Jack disagreed. Henry felt George wasn't dangerous. He insisted that they had misinterpreted George's behavior and helped cause an otherwise avoidable scene. Jack agreed that George didn't look dangerous.

"George might hurt someone by accident," Jack admitted, "but he wouldn't harm anyone intentionally."

"Accidentally or purposefully doesn't count," Herb answered emotionally. "When he was cracking that whip near Connie and rubbing my jugular vein with his knife, I didn't give a shit about accident or purpose. I was just scared. No one should have to go through that much anxiety regardless of whether or not George would hurt them. That's too much to expect from us. And, Jack, you better face the reality that kids are dangerous and need to be controlled physically at times. We'll be counting on you when your time comes."

Henry agreed with Herb in part. He acknowledged the anxiety George had evoked in us, but he tried to reassure us that George wasn't dangerous. Again Jack agreed with Henry; Herb, Norm, and Connie weren't reassured. They argued that Henry's experience was different because his relationship with George was special.

"You're the one who buys George food and clothes and gives him his allowance. He treats you differently. You oughta be here when I'm in charge and you're gone. It's a different scene," Norm told Henry.

"But I don't buy him anything. I'm not special, and I don't think he's dangerous," Jack answered, trying to counter Norm.

Bill took a middle position. Earlier in the day, George had grabbed Bill around the neck and had put his thumbs on the pressure points which would have made Bill drop faint and limp if George had applied much more pressure. However, George quickly let go as soon as Bill tried to make him do so.

"I felt uncomfortable, very uncomfortable," Bill told us, "but George hadn't seemed that dangerous or out of control to me."

Our discussion narrowed down to one basic question. Could George lose control of himself and hurt someone even if he hadn't intended to do so at the start? Could George start by teasing and playing and end up angry, angry enough to hurt somebody seriously? None of us could say for sure and none of us wanted to find out the hard way. So we arrived at two compromise decisions. First, George would have to surrender his zip gun to Henry for his food and money *before, not after,* he entered the building. Second, Henry would explain to George that he wasn't allowed to hit anyone except for Henry, even in a playful or teasing manner. If he did, he would have to leave the building immediately for the rest of the day.

Since we couldn't agree among ourselves whether George was dangerous, we decided to ask the psychologist who tested the boys to test George during the week. We didn't expect her to be able to tell us very much that we didn't already know, but we were looking for something concrete that we could call evidence. If the results indicated that George had serious difficulties controlling his aggression, we would have to consider carefully whether we could continue to handle him in the school. None of us was completely satisfied with the decisions, but we were all able to accept them.

The next morning Henry met George as he was coming into school and told him about our decisions. George said he didn't have his zip gun. He had wanted to bring it to school for the food and money but he hadn't been able to find it. George was surprised that we thought he was dangerous. If we didn't want him to mess around, he told Henry, he wouldn't. He wanted to come to school. He didn't want to be kicked out. He seemed like he was ready to do anything we asked, or at least to promise to do anything.

After talking to Henry, George went to gym and English without causing any incidents. He was in control of himself, but very tense because he was controlling himself. After lunch he demanded that Henry buy him a pair of sneakers. Henry could see that George was setting him up for an argument and tried to avoid it. He reminded George that he had just bought him a pair the previous week. But George worked himself up anyway and got rid of some of his tension by throwing a mild temper tantrum.

[George had become our number one problem student. We had an interpretation of his behavior and were dealing with it. However, we weren't at all convinced that we could. We assumed that the way George experienced even the minor demands and rejections he met in our school was colored by the extreme degree of neglect, rejection, and physical abuse he had received at home. Each little thing at the school became a big thing because of what he had experienced before. At home he could never act out his hostility or rage, because he was afraid of the consequences. The permissive atmosphere of the school had encouraged him gradually, or not so gradually if you were on the receiving end, to let down his guard and act out his feelings. What we were seeing was the unleashing of years of pent-up rage, triggered by rather small events. We couldn't be sure that the dam wouldn't suddenly burst altogether and lead to some even more destructive behavior. We planned to make sure that it would not. We were employing a number of techniques to help George work through his pent-up emotions.

We were encouraging him to act out the feelings he had previously held in check, but within *clearly defined* limits, in ways not usually accepted in the ordinary, non-therapeutic real world. When he felt like hurting someone we encouraged him to hit a punching bag, a closet, or a wall. Or if necessary to stamp the person first class mail, curse him out, or do something direct and hostile but not physically abusive. We would then point out to George that he had maintained better self-control and congratulate him for it. Then since this usually left him with some unexpressed anger, we would pay him to tolerate it and calm him at the same moment with food, extra attention, some words of praise, a Ping-Pong game, or whatever was appropriate. We expected that George would gradually be able to be satisfied with less and less antisocial and more and more acceptable forms of acting out his anger and frustration.

We had achieved considerable success in helping George to express his hostility in symbolic or less abusive ways. However, again as we all had seen, this form of behavior had not completely replaced direct, severe, and dangerous aggressive outbursts. We hoped that within three or four months the severity of his outbursts would diminish to within tolerable limits, but we couldn't be sure.

Another part of this approach consisted of directing George's aggression toward Henry and Herb. They were the two people who were best able to help George in the working through of his hostility without reacting aggressively themselves, because of their training and their roles in the school. Here we had succeeded to a limited extent. When Henry was available, George directed his attentions toward him. However, when Henry was occupied, or absent, as he was on Tuesday afternoons and Thursdays, George's rage was diffused throughout the school.

We also expected that as George felt more positively about us, he would begin to be less defensive and more able to admit when he was wrong or when he was overreacting.

We had made some progress in making him less defensive. In the heat of the moment, George was still defending his aggressive outbursts by denying them and blaming others for provoking him. However, he was becoming somewhat able to see the situation more clearly and to admit his part in the interaction after he had calmed down.

George had been making progress in a number of ways. But we were gambling on two things—that George's loss of control would never be so complete that he would cause serious harm to anyone and that his aggression would decrease to tolerable limits before we and the other students reached the limits of our tolerance. At the time, most of us didn't feel very secure about our bet.]

A LITTLE SELF-CONFIDENCE

Nat had a good week. Monday morning we received two calls about him before school started. His parole officer wanted to know whether we planned to keep Nat in our program because he had to decide if Nat would be kept at home or sent to a state training school. Henry told him that we hoped Nat would remain in our school, but we weren't completely sure he would be able to do so. (By the end of the month we had made up our mind.) The second call was from someone who claimed to be Nat's mother. She told Natalie that Nat had been sick Thursday, felt better on Friday after she had given him some medicine, and was sick again that morning. However, Ed remembered hearing Nat tell Carlos the previous Wednesday that he wasn't going to be in school Thursday. So it was clear to us that someone was covering up for Nat. We decided to play it cool. If Nat didn't want us to know about something, we wouldn't confront him with what little we did know. Then Nat showed up for the warm-up despite the call.

After he had eaten, Nat went up to Henry's office to call his father at work. He dialed a number, got no answer, looked puzzled, even a little worried, and asked Henry why there was no answer when the store in which his father worked was always open during the week. Perhaps he had dialed the wrong number, Henry suggested. Nat tried again. Still no answer. Henry wondered what Nat was thinking, but Nat didn't want to talk.

Thursday morning, after the Washington's Birthday holiday, Nat seemed different to Natalie as he walked into her room—a little distant, stand-offish. He still had his father on his mind. First he called his father and told him he would see him later. Then he told Natalie that his mother was going to buy him a new jacket . . . not the hundred-dollar one he really wanted, but a nice twenty-two-dollar one because that was all she could afford. Then he started reading. Natalie felt he was short-tempered and hostile toward her. She hadn't done anything that she could think of and yet Nat's tone of voice and the way he looked at her were both angry.

After about twenty minutes of reading, Nat had had it. Natalie asked him if he wanted to go out for a soda. He asked for cigarettes instead. She explained that she had been told that the boys were supposed to use their own money for cigarettes, but she would buy him something to eat or drink. Nat laughed an embarrassed well-I-tried-to-jive-you-about-those-cigarettes-I-used-to-get-away-with-it laugh and said, "It's bout time for lunch, forget it. Let's go upstairs."

[Nat was having some second thoughts about his increasing dependency on Natalie. He seemed to be saying, "See, I really don't like you that much and I don't need you that much either."]

Nat continued his independent tack with Natalie till the end of the month. The following Monday morning he showed her a book he had brought from home which he said he had read with a friend the night before because there had been nothing else to do. Natalie tried to help him with one of the words he missed, but Nat told her to let him do it by himself. He tried again. She noticed that he was having difficulty keeping on the same line so she gave him a piece of paper to help him keep his place. That was better. "But why does he have difficulty focusing on the line?"

Natalie wondered. "Is it the small print? Maybe he needs glasses?"

Nat's reading was improving. He was able to recognize more words and sound out the others much better than previously. Perhaps he had actually read the story the night before. Natalie beamed with pride, and later told Herb, who decided to sit in on their next session.

The next morning, Tuesday, Nat became nervous when he heard Herb wanted to watch him read. He said he wanted to stay in gym instead and ran around the rec room like a frightened animal. Finally Herb and Natalie calmed him down and they all went into her office. Natalie took out his book and asked him to show Herb how he read. Nat started to run around the room. Herb tried to coax him to read a little, making light of Nat's resistance, but Nat was becoming more and more anxious. Finally he said he was hungry and wanted to eat breakfast. Nat obviously wasn't ready for Herb. Natalie took him to the luncheonette and Herb went upstairs to the rec room, feeling stupid.

[Nat was acting more independent, but he still wasn't feeling very secure—certainly not secure enough to read in front of "Mr. Big," the director of the school. For although Herb was "head horsey" and wrestler, he was still the authority in the school. Much as Herb liked to deny it, he couldn't avoid that role with the boys. He might be able to fool himself, but not them.]

CARLOS'S CONFESSIONS

Carlos brought his cousin Jimmy back to school Monday as we had suggested. After the warm-up he told Jimmy to wait for him in the gym while he spoke to Herb. Right up front he began by asking Herb if he thought he was crazy. No, Herb didn't think Carlos was crazy. He just had problems like all the boys in the school.

"Yeah," Carlos answered, "I got problems cause my father he always beat me in the head. Look a this scar here." Forgetting that he had told Herb the same story the week before, Carlos repeated the history of the battle scars he had received at home, then said, "Man, he beat me over the head so much he make me crazy."

"Did he really do all those things to you?" Herb asked Carlos.

"Din ya see the scars?" he answered.

"Well you're still not crazy," Herb told him. "You just have problems. Stanley used to have big problems. Now look at him. We can help you like we did with him."

Something about what Herb said pleased Carlos. From out of the blue he confessed that he had lied when he had come to the school . . . he really had a telephone at home. Herb asked Carlos to give the number to Phyllis. Carlos hesitated. Herb pointed to the bulletin board where all of us had listed our phone numbers for any of the boys to use, and asked him if he could trust us the way we trusted him. Carlos smiled and wrote his number down. Then they went back down to the gym where Herb spoke to Jimmy. He promised to contact some agencies which could help Jimmy and asked Carlos to bring him back after Washington's Birthday.

It was time for Carlos's class with Natalie. But first, Carlos made one more confession. Jimmy wasn't his cousin, only his friend.

[Carlos was beginning to trust us. That was the breakthrough we had been waiting for. He might make an about-face occasionally, but he was going down the right road.]

Carlos brought Jimmy back to school on Thursday and gave him the grand tour. First Carlos took him to reading where he proudly told Natalie that he had found a place for him to stay at a friend's house and he had been giving him food and clothing. Then he whispered: "Don't look at im. He don even know how ta write his name."

"Do you want me to teach him?" Natalie asked.

"She wanna teach ya how ta write your name. Okay?" Carlos said in Spanish.

"No, no, no."

"I's all right, she's a teacher—she don yell."

"Okay."

After Natalie had shown Jimmy how to print his name, Carlos said, "Les read."

Natalie took out an easy *Reader's Digest* book especially prepared for remedial reading. Thinking it was a regular book, Carlos said, "No, i's too hard—I can' do it."

Natalie showed him that it was a different kind of *Reader's Digest*—an easier kind. Carlos started reading, then smiled when he realized he could read it, especially in front of Jimmy. After he had shown Jimmy how well he read, Carlos took him up to see Henry. Carlos had a knife he wanted to sell for fifty cents and food . . . for two.

"Ya kin hold it," he told Henry, "but ya gotta give it back every day when I leave the school." Henry agreed, gave him fifty cents, and took Carlos, Jimmy, and George, who wanted to see if Carlos would get the same thing he had gotten from Henry, to the luncheonette.

Carlos asked George how much he had eaten, then asked Henry for more. He wanted three cheeseburgers and three milkshakes. Henry agreed. Carlos changed his order to two cheeseburgers and two sodas. Jimmy had one of each and George just wanted a soda. Carlos sat there not knowing what to do. He liked what was happening but he wasn't the kind to say so. Finally he grinned and said, "Henry—I like ya, man."

JEALOUS LITTLE DEVIL

As Carlos drew closer to us, especially to Henry and Natalie, Nat became jealous. Nat had his two periods with Natalie to flaunt, and he did so. Carlos couldn't brush off Nat's teasing as he did Don's ranking because Natalie meant too much to him. So he asked Herb for a second period with Natalie like Nat. Herb recalled the many jealous comments Carlos had made when one of the boys had been treated to food, clothing, or something special. He also remembered Carlos's recent openness. "Perhaps," he thought, "Carlos is ready for some confrontation." So instead of answering Carlos's immediate complaint with a simple statement that it would be impossible to give him a second period with Natalie because she was only in school for three periods a day, he responded in terms of Carlos's jealousy.

"You know, Carlos," he said, "you're kind a jealous of some of the other guys."

Carlos wasn't ready to admit that.

"No I ain," he answered. "It ain fair. Why should Nat have er twice an me once?"

Carlos was jealous yet unaware of it. In his mind he was being cheated. So Herb told him the realistic reasons why he couldn't have Natalie for two periods. But Carlos wasn't ready to be influenced by a realistic explanation. He was too jealous.

When Carlos found out he couldn't have two periods with Natalie he fought back by ranking Nat out. During his next English classes when he reached the phrase "the bright-eyed little dog," Carlos read, "the black-eyed nigger" and laughed. Natalie tried to draw him out by asking why he had changed the words but Carlos, not wanting to bite, answered, "I jus felt like it."

The next day Herb sat in during Carlos's reading session

as he had tried to do the previous period with Nat. Carlos was nervous. He read, but he made more mistakes than usual. After a few minutes Herb left. Carlos was still nervous. He was making mistakes still, even though Herb had left.

"How did you feel when Herb was sitting and watching us?" Natalie asked.

"Nervous, didn ya tell? I made a lotta mistake then."

"Why does it bother you when Herb watches us?"

"It don bother me. Yeah, it does, cause he wan me ta make mistake."

"Really?"

"No, he likes me."

Carlos changed the subject. He remembered it was his birthday.

"I neva get presen fa my birthday. They always give em ta my sista."

"Who always gives them to your sister?"

"My mother and father, they do."

"Is that really true, Carlos?"

"No! They gimme presens when i's my birthday—but thas the only time."

"Well, Carlos, I have a present for your birthday and I'm sure the school bought one too."

Those were the magical words.

"Wha?" he asked as his face lit up.

"You'll see at lunch," Natalie told him.

NO DUMB SCHMUCK—JUST JEALOUS

When Harold saw the attention Henry and Herb were giving Nat, Carlos, and George, he became jealous as well. He hovered around Henry, acting silly and infantile like Nat and Carlos, hoping to get a piece of their action. But Henry explained to Harold that he wasn't like them. He had more mature needs which we would satisfy in other ways. That didn't satisfy Harold. He was unhappy, he told Henry. His life was lousy and not worth living. Henry tried to find out what his specific complaints were but Harold couldn't be specific. He was just generally depressed and tired, too depressed and tired to stay in class.

The day after the Washington's Birthday holiday Harold was coming out of his depression. He even went to Connie's English class for the first time since he had been switched back from Jack to her. However he spent most of the time telling Connie that she bugged him, that all teachers were stupid, and that he was stupid too. When Connie looked at him doubtfully he added, "You think I juth kiddin. I really am dumb."

Connie wasn't buying that. She knew better and told him so.

"Oh, Harold, you know that's not true."

They continued talking and working on vocabulary until he threw down his pencil in frustration and told her, "I a product a my a'vi'ament. Gemme outta my houth. I hate my ol lady. I can't tell why. Ev'y time Henry ath me I don't know why. Maybe you know why. . . . You remine me a my mother. You keep makin me do the work over and over till I get it right."

"You know," Connie responded, "perhaps your mother and I do it for different reasons. I want to help you with your English, not to nag you."

That helped. Harold went back to work for a while, then stopped.

"What's the matter, Harold?" Connie asked.

"I'm a schmuck."

"You know you're not a schmuck," Connie answered. "If you want to act like one, okay, but I'm not going to believe you."

Harold smiled, then punched at her hand. Connie felt less uncomfortable about Harold's physicalness. She playfully punched back at him. They both laughed, then continued working until the end of the period.

Connie thought they had found a working arrangement. If Harold wanted to act like a clod, Connie would recognize that it wasn't really Harold, but Harold acting like a clod. He could act like a jerk, but he really wasn't a jerk.

Harold's English work was improving. When he had started with Connie, he had been almost completely unable to admit his errors. Whatever he did looked and sounded correct to him. As he started to evaluate his work realistically, he was able to notice his mistakes and correct them. This helped his spelling dramatically. He was able to correct his own spelling. He might have to try a word three or four times, but he usually spelled it right eventually without help. His spelling papers began to look like this.

1. also althorgh although
2. amongh am ong among
3. anmale anemale animal
4. answer
5. ane anthing anyh anything
6. anyway
7. apple

BIRTH CONTROL

Manuel had a productive week. He went to court on Monday, the twentieth, to see his probation officer. Since we had already told Manuel's probation officer that he was attending regularly and adjusting well, we weren't surprised that Manuel came back to school in the afternoon obviously happy with the results of his hearing. After telling Herb what had happened in court, he opened up his wallet and showed Herb a prophylactic someone had bought for him because he wasn't "gonna take no chances." Herb agreed that it would help keep him out of trouble. He advised Manuel also to watch the age of the girls he fooled around with and told him that he better not "put his penis into four-teen-year-old girls anymore."

The following day Manuel showed Herb the prophylactic again.

"I din use it," he told Herb.

"What do you mean?" Herb asked, wondering if Manuel meant that he didn't have any sex or he had sex without a prophylactic.

"The girl . . . she was too small," Manuel answered.

"Her vagina was too small?" Herb asked, puzzled.

"No, she was too small—too li'l. I was a head ova her."

"What does that have to do with it?"

"I like then my size, not small. I's no good to mess aroun with kids."

That sounded familiar to Herb, like the advice he had given Manuel.

"Was she a kid?" Herb asked.

"No, she's ol. She just too small. I won get on my knees fa no girl. I got a lotta girls, always runnin afta me ina street. 'Oh, Manuel—hi, Manuel.' What a pain. Once a girl's mother almos caught me screwin er. I heard er comin through the front door an cut out the back way. I get tire a girls soon."

Herb asked him how long that took. A week or two, he answered. Herb asked if he tired of girls after having sex with them. Manuel didn't answer. He said he just didn't like the girls after a while. Herb asked if his friends were the same way. No, one of his friends was a "sucker" who had been going with the same girl since the summer.

Changing the topic, Manuel asked who the four women visiting the school were. Herb told him they were Connie's friends. Manuel looked at Herb and smiled: "Boy, could I get one a them alone."

RANDOM CONVERSATIONS
Despite his comment, Manuel kept away from the women during lunch. He sat in a corner with Ed. "Stranger don belong ina school," he told Ed. "I ain gonna eat food stranger eat."

Manuel still seemed uncomfortable after lunch. Instead of working, he spent most of his time with Connie talking about ghosts and spirits who come back from the dead to haunt people at night. That was why he hated to go to bed. When he had to turn off the lights, he ran and jumped in bed. If only he had a bat to take to bed with him, he could kill the spirits if they came. He didn't know what they looked like because he had never seen them, but he was afraid of them. "So that's why he always looked behind the door and in the closets before he went to bed," Connie thought to herself.

[At the time neither Connie nor Herb realized that spiritualism was a fairly common belief among people brought up in a Puerto Rican culture. If they had, they might have understood Manuel's "confession" better.]

Manuel also talked to Connie about moving in with her. He asked Connie to draw the layout of her apartment. After she had drawn a floor plan for him, he told her, "Oh boy. Maybe I cone visit you. I's so high up, but I wouldn't be . . . I be scare ta go in—too many haunted room. I guess I could go in. I's so high. I like ta be high, accept once I got dizzy, on the Entire State Buildin."

He pointed to the floor plan Connie had drawn and said, "I wanna sleep in that little estra room. Then I could get up in a middle a the night and sneak out inta the city."

He described his favorite dream to her. In his dream he rode a beautiful white horse wherever he wanted: through peaceful valleys, along streams, then up across a mountain to a valley of sunlight. Then Manuel half-whispered regretfully, "I'n always lookin for a river like that in Central Park but I neva fine it. Thas bad bout the drean."

"My God," Connie thought to herself, "that's sad." She wanted to say something aloud, but nothing came to mind.

HEADSHRINKER

Changing the topic, Manuel asked Connie about headshrinking. Manuel had overheard Herb kiddingly tell one of the boys that his head could use a little shrinking and he half-believed that headshrinking meant what it said. Connie explained. Manuel laughed, then said, "There's nothin a matta with me. I been happy my whole life." But from the sly way he looked at her and the many times he had told her how unhappy he had been, Connie got the idea that Manuel had subtly meant just the opposite. And she smiled back knowingly.

WHAT GOES DOWN MUST COME UP

Larry started the week off feeling down. He didn't want to go to class. He had too many things on his mind. He told Henry that the management of his housing development was threatening to evict him and his mother because of the trouble he had caused there. His mother blamed him. She was worried that she would lose her job in the management office and have to pay more rent besides. He would have to work part-time or maybe even full-time to help his mother out. He might even have to quit school if they kicked him out. It was unfair, Larry complained bitterly, for the management to evict them because of things which had happened in the past, especially since he had stopped causing problems.

Henry asked Herb to join the session. After the three of them had talked some more, Henry and Herb promised to tell the housing authorities that Larry was under our care, that we believed he would not repeat his previous behavior, and that he shouldn't be evicted because of what had happened in the past.

Larry was even more depressed Tuesday when he came to school. Something was bothering him, but he wouldn't share it with anyone. After lunch he went up to the gym to "fly." First he used the parallel bars to swing around and around while he shouted that he hated gravity. Then he climbed up on top of the lockers, jumped up and down like a monkey, and continued to denounce gravity.

Henry walked in. Larry told him about the flying equipment he wanted us to buy for the gym. George walked in, saw Larry up on top of the lockers, and joined him. George caught Larry's excitement but not Larry's control. He started pounding his feet on the tops of the lockers, then screaming and pounding, then screaming, pounding, and jumping. Then . . . before anything else happened, Henry convinced George and Larry to get down. They both left the gym, but Larry returned with some barrels and boards which he used to build a shaky "flying machine" on top of the lockers. It looked dangerous. Henry tried to persuade Larry to dismantle it before anyone was hurt. Larry took it down. As he did, he became more and more depressed until he finally lay down on the couch in the gym and slept until school ended for the day.

Friday everything was quiet until Larry came to school. He was coming down from an LSD high. He seemed to be peering through a fog as he walked into the rec room. His coordination was shot and he walked stiff-legged. He was half out of contact with reality and half out of control. Yet, he was almost in contact. He peered at Herb and told him, "Man, I'm flying—Oo! Lemme fly. I'm a groove. Watch me go. I'm gonna build a flying machine."

Larry's high was contagious. We could see the ripples of energy starting to move through the rec room. Larry grabbed Herb awkwardly.

"Let's wrestle, baby."

The other boys caught the scene. They started drifting over toward Larry. Herb wanted him out of there. He gently nudged and guided Larry into the music room and closed the door. He told Larry to stay in the music room or Herb's office only—no rec room. When Larry agreed, acting like his optimistic self, Herb went upstairs with Carlos.

Things remained quiet for a while. Nat and some of the other boys wrestled. Larry wandered into the rec room, saw what was going on, and couldn't resist joining in. He challenged Nat. Larry wasn't playing around. Since he was much stronger than Nat, he threw Nat from one end of the mats to the other, held him down, and ranked him out about his size. Nat freed himself in a burst of aggressive strength, but Jack broke it up before he had a chance to retaliate.

Nat walked out into the art studio and burst back into the rec room in a crying and screaming rage, with a knife in his hand. Bill, who had seen Nat take the knife, sent someone up to get Herb, and ran into the rec room to help Jack. Jack grabbed the knife, took it away, and Bill held Nat until he calmed down. Then Nat went into the bathroom to change out of his sweat clothes. Jack followed, just in case. Nat started to put his pants on. Jack asked him something. Nat didn't answer. He walked back into the gym, took off his garrison belt, and ran toward Larry, swinging his belt with the heavy metal buckle on the free end and screaming

"Motherfuckin nigger!" Bill grabbed him again. Jack helped out. Nat struggled for a while as Henry tried to calm him down by listening to his venomous feelings about Larry. After a few minutes, when Nat was settled, Henry asked him and George to go for a ride in his car, until it was time to leave for the trip. Carlos and Willie asked to go along. Soon Nat was safely out of the building and in Henry's car. Henry started to make a comment to him about controlling his anger, but George interrupted.

"How can a bunch a fuckin Jews help us? Jews always cheat niggers. They got all the stores in Harlem. They always chargin too much."

Henry wondered what had set George off. "Perhaps," Henry thought, "he's angry because I didn't act mad at Larry who, after all, started it. Larry's white. That could be it."

Carlos continued the attack.

"Then some a them cheap Jews give a little money they stole ta help kids."

"And tell them all that garbage they shouldn't listen to anyway," George added.

"The garbage he's talking about is my telling him to control his anger," Henry thought.

"Someday niggers a gonna give Jews what the Germans did," George continued.

That hit Henry. "Am I treating someone who someday will kill Jews in the streets the way the Nazis killed most of my relatives?" he couldn't help but ask himself.

"Ya know," Henry said, "Whitey may be all fucked up. He may have done bad things. But," Henry continued despite himself, "he's got the guns and bombs. So you still have to find some way to live with him."

Henry didn't like that last part. He knew why he had said it. It wasn't for George's benefit, but as a warning to all the anti-Semites. George had triggered off Henry's fears and

Henry had responded in terms of his own fears. He wished he had stayed cool instead of rising to the provocative bait George had set out for him.

LARRY'S SISTER

Meanwhile back in the school, Herb had taken Larry aside to talk to him about what he had done. Larry tried to act innocent, but Herb told him what he did to Nat was the same thing he had done to George on Monday when he had been trying to convince George to leave. Larry was caught. He knew we were on to him. But instead of looking sorry, he smiled contentedly.

Larry came down to earth after the weekend. He skipped most of his classes except math and spent his time hanging around the gym and shop. He became more open with Norm and began to reveal some of his more bizarre thoughts.

At first, as if he were testing Norm, he bragged about taking drugs and his LSD trips, stealing cars, fencing stolen goods, and burglarizing homes. That gradually gave way to conversations about his faith in black magic, demons, spells, and the terrible powers of Satan. Norm took these conversations in stride, listened attentively, and reported what he heard to the rest of us. Then Larry introduced a new topic—his sister, a good-looking young girl in her early twenties who loved him and treated him like a boy friend. Sometimes, as they walked down the street arm in arm, Larry told him, they stopped and embraced, pretending to be incestuous lovers, in order to shock people.

Norm had never heard anything about Larry's sister. He and Henry checked Larry's records. There was nothing about a young sister. Larry's only sister, who was in her forties and lived out of state, had been out of touch with the family since his father's death.

What was it all about—this sister of Larry's? Was she a

figment of Larry's imagination, a delusion, or a real person? Should we try to find out from him or play it cool? We couldn't decide what to do. We couldn't put the picture together. Don't pressure him to attend classes or school, give him lots of rope, and watch him closely was all we could decide for certain. It would be a waiting game.

JACK'S TROUBLES

Although we didn't pressure Larry to attend class, he attended social studies consistently. He and Don started off the last class on a high kick, sitting on the desks, drumming and singing. Jack confronted them right away by saying, "Well, that's it for today. I guess you guys don't want world history."

"Yeah, yeah, we do," they insisted, not really meaning it.

Then Don began talking about sexual relations with an ape and the hugeness of a cow's udder. That continued for about twenty minutes, until Jack suggested maybe they ought to have two biology classes rather than world history. No, they wanted world history they insisted.

"But this isn't world history," Jack reminded them.

"What you give us isn't world history either. It's not like they give us in regular school with a textbook and questions to answer."

"That's what you want—a textbook and questions to answer?"

"Yeah, your frame-of-reference crap sucks, man. Teach us like they do in regular schools. Your stuff bugs me."

"Okay, if that's the way you want it. Where do you want to begin . . . Egypt, Greece, Rome."

Don wanted Rome—the wars and slaves. Larry liked the idea too.

"Okay, I have a reading I want you to do tomorrow. Today we can do a time line."

"We gonna have readings again? Let's cut out that source
material shit and have a textbook."

"Okay, if you want it, but it will be dull."

"Can we take it home to read? I can't read in class,"
Larry asked, not actually intending to read it at all.

The boys knew more facts about Rome than Jack had expected, and they had appeared really interested in the subject . . . maybe because they liked the story of history. But
that was the problem as well. History was like a story to
them—a fascinating story. They didn't want to stop and
separate the facts—for example, the wars with Egypt and
Carthage—from the fiction such as the legend of Romulus
and Remus, who were supposedly brought up by a wolf
pack. They were much more interested in the fantastic.
Whether or not it was factual didn't concern them. They
obviously weren't interested in developing educational
skills, forming and testing hypotheses, or resolving conflicting opinions. That bored them. They wanted the sta-
bility of knowing rather than wondering, and they especially wanted to be told a story. They were both like elementary school students in many ways.

In other ways Don and Larry were quite different from
each other. Larry usually preferred to sit quietly, passively
listening to what was being said, especially when Jack
spoke. Don was just the opposite. He couldn't sit quietly.
He constantly attempted to actively engage Jack in a dialogue about his own historical interests in bathrooms, sew-
age facilities, homosexuality, and war. Periodically Larry
made remarks about Don's unusual interests, implying they
were crazy or perverted.

[The dynamics of the class were unfolding fairly clearly.
Don was using Jack and the class very much as he used
Norm and the biology class—to pursue his own preoccupa-
tions, to test out some of his ideas, and to clarify some of

his questions. Larry was threatened by Don's preoccupations which were too bizarre for him. Periodically, Larry put Don down as perverted.

Occasionally the two of them got together against Jack and communicated the message—"Look, Jack, you're a creepy social studies teacher and we're not interested in this crap." But that only occurred when Jack insisted that they both engage actively in a topic of his choice. Despite these problems the boys were starting to attend the class regularly.]

BACKGROUND FIGURES

The other boys—Stanley and Willie—spent the last days of the month on a calm note. They went to classes regularly, "behaved" themselves, and kind of faded into the background. That was easy for them to do while we were all so busy with the activists—Larry, George, Nat, Carlos, and Harold.

CHECKUP TIME

The month ended with the first visit of our school doctor. We told the boys during the warm-up period that he was going to give all of them checkups during the morning. Manuel seemed a little nervous when he heard it. The other boys took it in stride. Around eleven thirty the word got around that the doctor was making them "drop their pants" and examining their "dicks and asses." Carlos and George thought it was a big joke. They hung around the waiting room outside Herb's office where the examinations were taking place and made comments each time one of the other boys entered or left. Carlos, who was especially stimulated, made a couple of comments about homosexual goings-on in the office, but he was quickly put down by the other boys because the physical exams were very threatening to many of the boys who were already concerned about their masculinity. They didn't want to hear the kind of talk that would make them anxious.

The boys were generally in good health. Manuel had a rash that required calamine lotion and Harold had psoriasis. There was nothing else our doctor could help us with.

A GOOD START

December, January, and February—the first three months of the school—were history. Our program was off to a good start. We had achieved most of our initial goals. We had gotten our full staff together, acquired our initial group of students, and established procedures and expectations which we all understood.

Our educational program was moving along, especially the classes run by the old-timers. The biology class had taken a permanent turn for the better with Stanley's full-time attendance. He provided the steadying, regularizing influence the class needed. With him in the group, there were three dependables—Willie, Harold, and Stanley. They outnumbered the casual attenders—Don and Larry—who were pulled along by the "steadies."

The math program was functioning well because we had made a number of schedule changes which enabled us to give the boys more individual attention. When Don was transferred to Jack, Harold and Larry moved much faster with Bill. Larry was working on algebra—he had taken algebra twice before but had failed it both times. So he needed a lot of individual attention and support to help him. After Larry had successfully completed several sections of a review book, Bill switched him to a programmed text and found Larry was able to work consistently without as much of the individual attention as he had previously required. This enabled us to transfer him to Jack and allowed Bill to give Harold, who was working on geometry, the additional attention he needed.

Harold was doing much better with the individual attention. Bill had tried a number of frustrating approaches with Harold until he had hit on a successful one. He had noticed that Harold forgot the meaning of the terms he used and lost his place along the road to proving theorems or solving problems. So he made Harold write down all the steps he would need to finish the problem, and definitions of all the terms and concepts. Although this was time-consuming and frustrating for Bill, who had to wait for Harold, it seemed to relax Harold and enabled him to proceed more logically. Harold's frustration tolerance was still poor. He still quit in the middle of problems and worked in the art media instead, but the time he spent working had been increasing steadily.

Don and Manuel weren't doing as well in math. They were still too defensive. Jack had been helping Don with fractions and decimals, although he should have been working on addition, subtraction, and multiplication, all of which were basic to fractions and decimals. Since Don wasn't ready to admit his severe deficiencies to himself, Jack was rightly taking it easy with him. Connie had just begun to work with Manuel. It would be a while before he would be able to face his limitations.

Marilyn's music program was in full swing. All but two of the boys were involved. Harold, Larry, and Willie were getting a lot out of the lessons. Don used the time, but not too constructively. Manuel claimed he wanted to play the piano, but he didn't act as if he did. Marilyn bought a chord organ for him because it was much easier for him to learn and required less practice. The organ was more like a toy than an instrument to him, but he seemed to enjoy the classes. Nat was Marilyn's real problem. Marilyn didn't want to continue Nat's lessons because he was too impulsive to even press down on the chord buttons while she played the melody on the organ. It was clear that we had to give up the thought of having him take music lessons.

The art program was firmly established. The art studio was a regular hangout. Carlos was wandering in during his period to work on his head a little and talk a lot. Manuel was painting a lot—in black—little people and things all in black—and talking a little. Don and Larry put in appearances, but after they had completed their sculptured penises they spent their time "rapping." Willie was the studio's best customer. He was spending at least one period a day working on an elaborate African clay mask with beautifully colored glazes. As he worked he occasionally rapped about his blackness and his African heritage.

George was also becoming a regular customer in the studio. However, he attended only because he wanted to listen to soul music on the radio. That brought him into conflict with Harold who liked hard rock music and acted as if he had squatter's rights and could decide which station should be played. It never reached a conflict stage because although Harold acted like he had all the rights, he "generously" proposed various compromises, which George accepted.

George had no choice. He had to accept. He was outnumbered. He was the only soul brother in the studio during that period. Even when Willie was around, George didn't get any backing because Willie dug folk rock music despite his black awareness. Bill realized what was going on and tried his best to make sure George got equal time.

Norm's shop was also busy. Willie was building a table for us, Larry was working on his secret sixteen-drawer box, Carlos and Manuel were both working on chairs, and Harold was playing around. Don popped his head in from time to time but just to rap.

The "newcomers" classes weren't working out as well.

Connie was doing an excellent job with Manuel and she had made the necessary breakthrough with Harold. However, she wasn't making it with George, while Don and Larry seldom even attended.

Jack was having little success with Harold, but doing slightly better with Don and Larry in social studies. Don and Larry usually went to social studies, but they weren't fulfilling Jack's expectations. They were getting things from the class but not what Jack planned for them. Jack was still a new teacher and would catch on. He was beginning to see the problems. That was the first step toward finding the solutions. Jack had to get with the boys, before he could get the boys with him.

8 March Roars In

QUIET WILLIE

The new month started off deceptively quiet. With no emergencies to press for our attention, we were able to spend our Wednesday morning meeting talking about the quiet ones, Willie and Manuel. Willie was trying to hide from us and we were trying to get a line on him. Herb believed Willie's detachment served to protect him from admitting that he still wanted the approval, attention, and affection he had never gotten at home and never expected to find anywhere else. He believed that Willie had experienced so much abuse and neglect at home that he had to maintain an "I don't care" shell to avoid feeling depressed and isolated.

The rest of us weren't convinced. Henry believed Willie's uncaring facade held back rage rather than disappointment. Most of us agreed with Henry, who thought Willie was afraid to show the anger he felt toward a rejecting and exploiting world for fear of retaliation by people and forces much more powerful than he.

Whatever his cool was covering up, Willie was different from the other boys. He wasn't disturbed. He wasn't even

247

disturbing. Whatever his problems were, he was handling or covering them up pretty well. Since he was dealing pretty well with his world we were tempted to let him be. What sense was there in releasing his dependency or unleashing his rage if we couldn't be sure it would help him?

WILD GUY

Manuel, our other quiet one, was coming out of his shell. We noticed that he had been teasing, pushing, and even ranking Carlos, Nat, and George. When he wanted something at the lunch table, he was much more likely to ask for it even if he knew others also wanted it. He was letting out just a little of the "wild guy" inside him and we were pleased.

Manuel was also revealing some more of his "secrets." He started one of his reading sessions by happily reporting that he had been able to read "a hard word ona subway," but he wasn't satisfied. He still wanted to read much faster.

"Learning to read is like learning to run," Connie told him. "A little baby first has to learn how to crawl, then to walk, and then to run. When you read, you can't just read fast at the beginning. You have to improve gradually."

Manuel didn't hear Connie's comments. She had lost Manuel with the word "baby." His mind was occupied with his own thoughts.

"I hate babies, they oughta die. Whadaya wan babies? People kill babies anyway," he said to Connie.

"What do you mean, people kill babies?" Connie asked.

"I's in a bible," he answered. "My mother read it, where they throw babies up in a air and when they cone down they get stab on a sword. Babies die lotsa way. Ya could take gas an you have a nice dream like sniffin glue. I hope she get a boy, even if i's not mine she should get a boy. My father, he like boys."

"Oh, does your father know about the girl?" Connie asked.

"Hell no. He break my neck. But I like hin anyway. He goes crazy sonetine. I like ta wrestle hin. He so weak I always win. My ol lady wansa get rid a me. She always ax me: Why don they get a school where you kin sleep? My father always go where I go. He follow me ta the pool roon. Maybe she wan me away so he won go ta the pool roon. He's ol, my father."

"How old?" Connie asked.

"Forty-one."

"Manuel, that's not so old," Connie explained.

"Well, he's real weak. He got asthma. He could die."

"Are you worried?"

"Yeah. If he dies, I kick er ass. She prob'ly make hin die . . . I know she wansa get rid a me. I call her ol lady to bother er. My brother fools aroun with me in a mornin. He throws a pillow an then he say I do it. He tell er Hit 'in! Hit 'in. Why you fraid? Hit 'in! Hit 'in! And she hit me. Las tine she hit me I push er. I din wanna hit er, but I hada get rid a er, so I push er."

Connie thought Herb ought to talk to Manuel right away. She brought him down to the rec room at the end of the period and signaled Herb that Manuel had something to talk about. Herb picked up the signal and tried to involve Manuel in a conversation about what was going on at home. However, Manuel wasn't ready, and he didn't become any more so by the end of the week.

UNWELCOME GUESTS

Carlos came to school with two friends. Herb and Ed saw them as they walked into the gym. They were nasty-looking guys in their twenties, sharply dressed . . . not like Carlos and his cousin Jimmy.

"Carlos isn't their speed," Herb thought. He asked Norm and Bill to take a look at the boys. They felt nervous too. Herb decided to hang around the gym for a while.

At the start of the second period, Carlos went down to Natalie's room with his two friends. He asked her to wait downstairs in her office while he went to put away his coat, left with his friends, and came back alone.

"Don worry," Carlos said to her. "They ain playin hookey. They're outta school. You scare?"

"No, I'm not scared, why should I be?" she answered truthfully.

"Maybe ya scare cause you think I'm like em, but I ain. I don hafta work, right?" he asked. "Then les go up ta the gym."

Natalie remembered that Carlos's friends were there and thought Carlos wanted to show off for his friends, but he didn't get the chance. Herb didn't like the looks of things. Carlos's friends seemed like they were looking for trouble. He wanted to keep things cool. So he told Carlos that he had to go downstairs or else his friends would have to leave.

Carlos went downstairs. He began to work, but he was extremely angry.

"Ya always say I don hafta do it, if I don wanna," he complained. "Now I hafta be down here."

"You don't have to work if you don't want to," Natalie agreed. "But Herb said you had to go down, so you have to stay here."

"Okay, then les read," he suggested.

Natalie took out the books. Carlos started to read but, as he did, he made mistakes to annoy her—at least it seemed so to Natalie. She became increasingly angry. Then finally she demanded, "If you're not going to work, suppose we just close the books and forget about it and not waste anybody's time."

"Okay, then les do that," he agreed, closing the books. Then anxious about what he had done, he added, "How daya espet me ta know it? I don know it. I'm stupid. I keep tellin ya I'm stupi."

Natalie disagreed.

"I know you're trying very hard to make me think you're stupid, Carlos, but I don't believe it and nobody else here believes it either."

Carlos wasn't buying that.

"I can', I tol ya I can' do it," he insisted.

Nevertheless Natalie took out his work again, calmed herself down because she was upset with him, and went over the words again. Following Natalie's lead, Carlos calmed down and worked until the end of the period.

Returning to the gym, Carlos found his friends had left, and he spent the rest of the day uneventfully.

PHILOSOPHIZING AND TERRORIZING

We had expected trouble from Carlos's friends. We were looking in the wrong place. The trouble came from George. He started the month off quietly enough. He spent the morning talking to Ed about religion. He told Ed that he often woke up in the middle of the night in a cold sweat, trembling, because he didn't know God. Even when he was awake he was afraid that someone was going to punish him . . . something was going to get him for not knowing God. He had been a Catholic, a Jew, and a Muslim. None of them appealed to him because, he claimed, all their religious books were a lot of nonsense. None of them told the truth about God. He asked Ed if he could use his math period to discuss religion. Ed agreed—George wasn't using it for math anyway.

George started the next day off quietly also. During the

first period, he hung around the gym playing basketball and Ping-Pong with Ed—laughing and joking happily. Toward the end of the period he left the gym, climbed over the Dutch door into Phyllis's office, playfully teased her by using the typewriter, and refused to leave until she got "help." Then he went to his English class with Larry and Connie.

The English class started off peacefully. The three of them, Larry, Connie, and George, were sitting around a table. Larry was leaning back against a bookcase. George was leaning against the wall. George worked quietly for about a minute until Connie corrected him. Then he went into his act—throwing chalk, banging on the blackboard, and shouting, "You're wrong, you're wrong."

Connie wanted to have an English class. Larry was finally getting down to work. She was tired of George's disruptions and she didn't want to put up with them. She looked sternly at George and gave it to him.

"If you want to bang on the board and throw chalk, you can go down to the gym and I'll work with Larry alone."

That did the trick. The chalk throwing and board banging stopped and the "you're wrongs" died down to a trickle for about ten minutes.

Suddenly without any apparent provocation, George took aim, hurled a pen across the table at Larry, and hit him point-first on his nose. Larry was stunned by surprise. Then, still immobilized, he glared at George and allowed every foul word he had ever learned to seep through the slits in his tight, but trembling lips. George panicked. Connie rose to her feet shouting, "George! Get out. Get out, George. I won't have you throwing things around hurting people."

But George was crouching in fear between the wall and the filing cabinet.

"Come on, George," Connie urged.

But George wouldn't budge. He was afraid of Larry who looked like a rumbling, shaking volcano preparing to erupt.

"Come on, George, leave by yourself," she urged him again.

George still wouldn't move. Connie reached to grab him. George slapped her hand away—hard. Connie thought about using the telephone at the other end of the room but she was afraid the two boys would go at it if she didn't stand between them. She shouted for Herb. Phyllis heard her and called Herb in the gym.

As it became clear that Larry wasn't going to go after him, George came out from behind the filing cabinet with a triumphant smile on his face, agreed to leave, and walked out the door. Connie rose quickly to close the door behind him. Just as she did, George stuck his arm back in to prevent her from shutting the door completely, and scraped his finger just enough to draw blood. George saw the blood and flipped.

"She hit me, the bitch hit me," he screamed. "I'm bleedin, I'm bleedin. I'm gonna kill your ass, bitch."

Connie relaxed her pressure on the door when she heard George's screams and he burst into the room again.

Herb walked in. George was yelling, Connie was quivering, and Larry was rumbling white and stiff in his seat. Connie told George to leave the room again. George turned to Herb, pointed to his arm, and said, "Look *at* she did. She hurt me, I'm bleedin—*my arm's* broke."

"What happened?" Herb asked.

"She hates me," George answered. "She tried ta hit me. She——"

"I told him to leave the room," Connie interrupted, "and he won't leave."

George became even angrier.

"I git er after school," he threatened, balling his fist. "She betta look out. I kill er."

"Come on, George, let's go out into the hall," Herb suggested, trying to separate him from Connie.

"No, nigger!" George answered. "She did it. I'm gonna git er."

Connie tried to tell Herb what had happened. George kept interrupting.

"She hurt me—she hurt me—she took a'vantage that I wouldn hit er back, the bitch. She hurt me. She took a'vantage a me."

"Why did she lock you out?" Herb asked.

George had an answer.

"She hates me. She knew I wouldn hit er back, that's why."

The scene continued a little longer. Finally George calmed down enough to leave with Herb.

Connie turned to Larry, who was still sitting silently in his seat. His eyes were glassy, his lips were white and tight, and his hands shook as he lit a cigarette. After a few more moments of silence his mouth opened.

"Maan, that guy just fucked up my whole moral code."

Connie asked him what he meant.

"I never touch nobody, no matter what, unless they hit me. Then I really let em have it. I know how ta control my emotions outside even when I'm goin wild inside. I never jumped nobody when I'm angry. I wait and plan and then kill em."

Connie was about to answer Larry when he walked out.

Out in the hall Herb was telling George he couldn't believe the only reason Connie had locked him out was that she hated him. George didn't respond. Herb asked him if he really believed his accusations. George repeated them again. Herb still wasn't convinced. He wanted to know whether George was likely to go after Connie if he was left alone. Herb looked straight at George and asked seriously, "Hey, George, you a little crazy now or can you really see what was going on?"

George gave Herb a kind of pouting look, which Herb took to mean that George's real complaint wasn't that Connie had taken advantage of him, but that she had hurt his feelings. Herb smiled at his apparent admission and thought the incident was over.

George leaned lazily against the wall as they began talking about nothing important. Just then Connie walked out of her room after Larry. Herb signaled her to keep going but she didn't notice the signal. She started to tell Herb her side of the story. George moved away from the wall. His body tensed. Herb stepped between them, interrupted Connie, told her that he believed George understood what had happened, even though George didn't feel like saying so, and declared the incident over.

Connie returned to her room. George jumped over the Dutch door into Phyllis's office and came out with an ink pad and a "Paid" stamp which he stamped on Herb's forehead, shirt, and the nearby walls. Herb laughed, then told George it was better for him to stamp people than to hit people. He could stamp him or Henry all he wanted to— gently of course—but not the other staff members. George moved teasingly toward Connie's door with the stamp, inked and ready to be used, held over his head. Herb gave George the look of disapproval George wanted and George stopped. Just then Natalie walked by and got stamped on the side of her face. She laughed, George laughed, and Herb laughed . . . a little. He was amused by the stamping but angry that George hadn't listened to him . . . and the incident ended . . . again.

George went down to the gym. Herb followed to warn

Ed, who was playing Ping-Pong with Manuel, that George was upset. George crossed toward the punching bag. As he passed Ed's end of the Ping-Pong table, he stopped and hit the ball back to Manuel with his hand. Ed asked George if he wanted to play a game. George mumbled yes, and picked up a paddle. Ed turned to walk away. As he did, out of the corner of his eye he saw George's paddle fly past Manuel's head, hit the wall, and ricochet into Manuel's back. George picked up another paddle, but Ed grabbed his arms before he could throw it. Manuel's face reddened. With his fists clenched in rage, he took a step toward George. Ed signaled Manuel to stop and led George out into the hall.

Ed couldn't understand what had happened. There hadn't been any arguments, no words, no sign that anything was about to happen—just a sudden, unprovoked explosion from nowhere. It was Ed's turn to be anxious. That kind of stuff was dangerous. He tried to talk to George about what he had done and why he had done it. George wouldn't respond. Not a word, not a nod, just a blank stare. At a loss for what to do, Ed called Herb who took over.

Herb thought that it was time to take a stronger position with George, a much stronger position. Herb explained to George that we had an obligation to the other boys and the community. If we felt he might hurt someone the court would want to know. Even if they didn't we would have to tell them. That would probably mean a state training school —the same one he was scheduled for before he had come to our school.

George went into his "I'm-not-dangerous" act, but Herb wasn't buying it. He told George that whether he himself thought so or not, the kinds of things he had been doing or threatening to do, like beating up Connie after school, were making us too uncomfortable. When George saw he couldn't convince Herb that he wasn't going to hurt anyone, he turned on his "I'll-be-a-good-boy-from-now-on." It appeared sincere to Herb. George seemed to want to behave himself. Whether it was out of guilt about what he had done or fear of what the courts might do to him, Herb couldn't tell. But he could sense George's genuine concern. So he considered the incident ended . . . again.

It was time to pick up the lunch from the local store. George didn't want the barbecued chicken we had ordered. He wanted hot dogs and pizza. Herb took him off shopping and bought him three hot dogs and a slice of pizza.

As soon as George got back to school, he bounded up the stairs to the gym where he told the boys, "See what I got. See what Herbie bought me." George was happy. Once again food had done the trick. He gave Larry one of his hot dogs and a cigarette, lit it for him, and smiled as if to ask "Is everything forgiven?" Then he took out three cigarettes, put one in Ed's mouth, one in Manuel's mouth, and one in his own mouth, lit them all, and gave Manuel and Ed the same smile he had given Larry.

Everyone went down to lunch. Since George had already eaten, he remained in the rec room while we ate. Suddenly we heard loud crashing noises coming from the gym. George was hurling the weights at the walls and the screened-in windows. He was still upset after all. Herb told George that although it was better for him to throw things at the wall than to hit people, if he was still too upset to do any work or to relax in the gym during the afternoon, it would be even better if he went to the movies.

George asked if he could go with somebody. Herb suggested Ed.

"Could I ask Willie?" George asked as he ran downstairs to the dining hall.

"No, don't ask Willie," Herb shouted, too late to be heard.

By the time Herb caught up with him in the dining hall, George had already asked Willie, who, in his usual passive way, was having a hard time telling George that he really preferred to stay in school.

It was Ed or no one, Herb insisted. George agreed to Ed. The two of them went upstairs for movie money. As they were walking back downstairs, George said he didn't want to go to the movie.

"Look here," he suggested, "why can't we both keep the two dollars it cost and tell Herb we went to the movies."

Ed refused. George asked if they could talk about religions in Ed's room instead of going to the movie. Ed thought that it would be okay because it had been George's decision to leave in the first place.

Around two o'clock George changed his mind. He wanted to go to the movie after all. Ed told him it was too late because school was almost over. George stormed out of the room toward Herb's office, with Ed close behind. Herb met the two of them on the stairs. Surprised to see them "back" in school, he asked what had happened. Ed started to explain but George interrupted.

"He wouldn lemme go. He made me sit in his office till it was too late."

Ed broke in to correct him. George shouted him down angrily.

"No, maan. He made me stay in his fuckin room till it was too late. He didn wanna take me. He made me stay."

Shit, Herb thought to himself. It's the same kind of scene George pulled with Connie this morning. He's getting lost in his own lies. His street language is starting to come through. There's no point in getting involved in an argument. No sense in making things worse by trying to prove who's right. Better cut it short.

Herb asked George to go for a walk and left the building

with him. Outside George quickly admitted the truth. But he had done it, he claimed, because he needed the two extra dollars and he couldn't wait for Friday to talk to Henry about money. His girl friend wanted to go to a dance Friday night. He had to buy the tickets that night because the church group holding the dance wasn't selling tickets at the door.

No tickets at the door. That sounded like a con to Herb or at least a face-saving excuse for trying to con the two dollars. Yet Herb couldn't be sure. Maybe George really needed money. Henry had told Herb that George's parents had been refusing to buy him clothes or give him spending money on the pretext that George had stolen a few cents change from his father. How would Henry handle it? Herb asked himself. Unfortunately he wasn't Henry, so he couldn't be sure. Herb believed it was a con, but he didn't want to do anything about it without talking to Henry first. So he reached a compromise with George: he would advance two dollars toward his allowance. We always did that for the boys. Friday they would talk to Henry about whether George should receive the two dollars as an advance or as extra allowance. If Henry decided that George should receive two extra dollars because his mother and father weren't giving him any money, we would forget about the advance. If Henry didn't think so, the two dollars would be deducted from George's allowance over an extended period. George seemed satisfied. At least he said he was. All the incidents were *all* over.

BAD NIGGER?
Friday morning we were all eager to talk about George. Even after talking with Larry and Manuel, we were unaware of anything they had done to provoke George. What had happened, we wondered. Psychotic delusions, rage dis-

placements, psychomotor epileptic seizures, and other possibilities crossed our minds. They could all be checked out in time. We had already begun the process. Our immediate problem was what to do about what George had already done. We decided that George needed a couple of days away from the school to cool off. He could still meet Henry at school after three in the afternoons if he wanted to.

The meeting broke up. Henry found George in the dining room and suggested they take a walk around the block. As they walked, Henry explained our decision. First George claimed he hadn't done anything dangerous. Then he argued against our decision until, finally, the inevitability of our decision sunk in. George's face clouded over. His bouncy, kidding mood vanished. His cocky, aggressive manner drained away and was replaced by a total depression.

Henry found himself thinking that he had just witnessed an instantaneous confirmation of the notion that depression is aggression turned inward against the self. He tried to kid George out of his depression. George continued his zombielike, staring, forward walk without even acknowledging Henry's presence. Henry reminded George that everything would be back to normal after only two days. That didn't work either.

When they completed their circle of the block, George sat down on the curb in front of the building. Henry tried to soothe George out of his depression. George remained motionless, silently staring into space. Henry continued for a good half hour, but it was futile.

Henry wasn't getting anywhere with him. He called up to Phyllis's window for her to get Herb. Henry asked George if he wanted to say anything to Herb. George walked toward the building, but stopped at the steps, sat down, continued staring, and began rocking back and forth, back and forth, back and forth, back and forth. The three of them stood there for another few minutes. Nothing was happening. Henry went back into the school to talk to Carlos, Larry, and Willie, who were all waiting for him.

Herb remained talking *at* rather than to George. We didn't want him out of the school permanently, he told George—no response. We were just trying to find a way to help him control himself so he could stay in school—no response. He would be back in a couple of days—still no response. We would handle it with his parents if he was afraid of his father—response. George spoke.

"Do my parents hafta know?"

"No!" Herb answered. It wasn't necessary to tell his parents unless he wanted us to.

George seemed relieved.

"You want to come in for a few minutes?" Herb asked.

George took a couple of steps toward the door, then turned as if he had changed his mind, walked a few steps away, and stared silently at Herb for another five minutes. Herb asked him if he was angry. No response, except continued staring.

Nat and Carlos came out to see what was going on. Carlos cracked a joke. George smiled. Henry returned. George was coming out of it. He started to excuse his behavior. He couldn't stand the way Larry and Connie had been arguing. Ed wouldn't take him to the movie. Connie had hurt him with the door. That's why he did it.

That wasn't quite true, Herb replied. Even if it were true, Henry explained, that didn't justify George's threats and dangerous behavior. George disagreed. But Henry and Herb didn't argue with him. They had confronted George's rationalizations. George was depressed and needed support and acceptance more than confrontation.

George was talking again. It was almost trip time. Who was going where with whom? Harold and Willie went with Jack to see *One Million B.C.* Henry took Larry to see *Funeral in Berlin*. Nat and George went to *El Cid* with Bill. Carlos and Manuel split after lunch. Stanley stayed at the school with Herb and Connie.

HIS OWN SONG

Stanley wanted to talk—about those "crazy kids" in the school. His group had been different, he told Herb. No crazy kids. Why did we keep kids like George and Nat? he asked. Why did we take so much from them? Why didn't we kick them out?

Herb explained that the boys only seemed different. They were the same. Stanley was different.

Connie told Stanley he was doing very well in English. He had just completed the last unit in his reading comprehension book. So she was going to start him on a new skill-building series. Herb congratulated Stanley, then told him that Jack had said that he was also doing well in math. Stanley smiled. Connie left the table.

Stanley changed the topic. He had decided to give up the guitar for the organ. . . . Herb was puzzled. Why, he asked. Stanley was bored with it. Oh, oh, Herb thought, but he was wrong. Stanley was tired of playing chords to someone else's lead guitar. He wanted to play melody too. He wanted to play his own song. With an organ he could play melody and chords, and maybe even sing. Herb smiled, feeling fulfilled.

It was a quiet end to a noisy week. We were all glad for the weekend.

Monday, March 6

MY FUCKIN FATHER

Friday had ended happily. Monday began angrily. Bringing a friend Don arrived early and looked like he shouldn't have been able to make it to school. His lower lip was cut through to the teeth, his face was puffed up, and his half-closed bleary eyes were black and blue. Someone had done a job on him.

"What happened?" we asked him.

"This is Lenny," he answered.

Lenny looked weird for those days . . . long, curly hair down his back over his ears, underwear sticking out from an open Mexican vest, dungarees, a sash for a belt, and high boots.

"Hello, Lenny," we answered matter-of-factly.

"What happened?" we asked Don again, since we didn't care about Lenny at the moment.

"Lenny's comin to the school."

"He is?"

"He's in court so he can come. His case comes up soon. I told him he could come here if the court lets him."

"We can talk about Lenny later," we insisted. "What happened to you? You're in bad shape."

"My fuckin father beat me up and kicked me out a my own house. So I stayed over Lenny's last night."

[We were angry about Don. We believed his story. His father had beaten him up before—not nearly as badly, but still it made sense from what we knew about the family. Maybe our anger was a cover-up for something else—guilt. Guilt about keeping Don in a home where his mother threw kisses and his father threw punches.

The dynamics of the family had become pretty clear in

Henry's sessions with Don and his parents. Mrs. Russo and her husband weren't getting along—no sex, no love. She was turning to Don. Mr. Russo was in a resentful, jealous rage with both of them. And he was taking it out physically on Don.

We had asked ourselves if it wouldn't have been better for Don to be out of the house in some residential setting where he wouldn't have had to contend with the triangle at home. We had decided we could help him. We had expected things to get worse before they got better and we had been right. That worried us. Don had brought us food for thought. We felt guilt, but anger was a much more comfortable feeling. Our anger wouldn't last long. Our doubts and guilt would hit us soon enough.]

Henry took Don to his office while we continued our morning meeting. He tried to find out more about what had happened. Don had stayed out overnight in the Village, high on pills. He came home, still high, got into an argument with his father, was beaten up, and spent the night at Lenny's.

How had he been getting along with his father before the fight, Henry asked.

"Fine, while the bastard was in the hospital. Then the son of a bitch came home to bust balls. 'It's too noisy—no music! I'm sick. Bring me this, bring me that,' " Don mimicked. "Expecting my mother to wait on him like a maid. He's a bad news fuck."

Don acted like he believed it was all his stepfather's fault, but Henry thought it was a front. So he asked Don if he could see the part he and his mother played in the problem. Don could. Henry then asked why he had gone to the Village for the weekend. Don said he didn't know. They talked a while longer. Henry promised to intercede with Don's parents. Then he allowed Don to shift the conversation to

Lenny. After a while Don went into the rec room and Henry talked to Lenny.

A PUSHER

Classes started. Manuel couldn't concentrate. Something was on his mind. After he had missed quite a few easy words, Connie asked what was bothering him.

"I'n nervous. I'n nervous," he answered. "Les keep readin. If I read when I'n nervous, I kin read better when I'n not."

However Manuel kept missing no matter how much he tried. He stopped abruptly to say, "I wanna hit a guy ina nose. I's private. I can' tell ya."

But he could and did.

The story didn't seem quite true, but Connie listened attentively without letting on. Manuel claimed he had been given some dope—a red mixture of LSD and some other stuff—to give to his cousin. His cousin came over to the house, shot the dope up his arm, and went crazy. Manuel brought him down to the cellar and told him to stay there until he "came down" from his high. But his cousin was too crazy. He ran away and was picked up by some cops in Times Square.

Connie controlled herself. No lecture, no advice, she reminded herself. Just tell him he ought to talk to Herb.

Manuel repeated the story to Herb with a change. His cousin hadn't been picked up by the police. He had just left the house high so he might have been busted. Manuel was afraid—afraid his cousin might tell the police who had passed him the dope.

Herb had heard about Manuel's "cousin" before. He was the "crazy kid" who sometimes destroyed things in the cellar, screamed, and saw things. Manuel spoke about him as if he were real, but Herb wasn't convinced. He sounded like that "friend" people talked about when they said, "I have a friend who . . ." He sounded like Manuel.

Manuel's story had the same unreal quality as his story about his pregnant girl friend. Is it a delusion? Should I challenge it? Herb wondered. No, better let it be. Deal with it as if it were true and reassure him that nothing would happen to him. Did he think his cousin would be caught? Manuel didn't think so. Did he think his cousin would rat on him? Not his cousin.

"See," Herb told him, "you don't have too much to worry about."

How about him, Manuel? Did he take anything, Herb asked. Sometimes he fooled around with marijuana but never LSD or heroin, and he'd never shoot up, because that was crazy. Manuel had said he didn't, but Herb wasn't sure.

PLAYTIME

Nat came to school with a friend about halfway through the first period. He went straight to class, but not to work.

"Man," he ordered Natalie for his friend's benefit, "gimme a mess a cake and some fa this nigger too."

After they had finished six Danishes between them, Natalie asked him if he wanted to read. No, Nat wanted to show his friend around the school. First, the rec room—see how the intercom phone works, ha ha! Then Norm's shop and Bill's studio. The music room—a piano to bang, a chord organ to bang, and a set of drums to bang loudly. He didn't bother too much with the third floor except Phyllis's office—more toys. Back down to the gym and the basketball court.

AM I CRAZY?

Eleven o'clock—change of periods. Carlos still hadn't come to school. Natalie stayed in the gym. And Carlos finally arrived.

"Hey, ya suppose ta be in ya office downstair, I's my time," he insisted.

"I didn't know you were in school," she answered. "Let's go."

Carlos led the way.

"I's my time you know," he reminded her again.

"Yes it is, Carlos."

With that Carlos started to read until he completed a story. Then he said, "I'm tire, les talk . . . les sell Henry a knife for all we kin eat."

No, Natalie couldn't do that, but she would take him out to eat if he was hungry. That wasn't it. Carlos wanted Henry to pay. He wanted to see if Henry would buy another knife from him. Why would Henry do a funny thing like that, he asked. Would Henry buy a knife from her for all she could eat? Natalie laughed. Who was Henry anyway—a psychiatrist? Carlos knew who he was.

"He thinks I'm crazy," Carlos told her. "He's always askin me question. A' you a psychiatris too?" Natalie laughed. "He thinks I'm crazy. When I was in Youth House he as' me if I saw elephanz on a wall."

Carlos laughed, then became serious as he told Natalie, "People thinks I'm crazy. They do."

"I don't think they do," she answered. "They think you have problems that bother you, but they don't think you're crazy."

"How'd ya get a job here? How come ya leave early? How come Nat has ya two periods and me one? I'm goin upstair . . . I'm gonna punch Herbie in a nose."

"Really?" Natalie asked in a way which said "I know you're kidding."

"Nah, I'm jus teasin. I'm sick." Carlos answered.

"What's the matter. Does something hurt you?"

"See these scar? My father gay me this. This one's from a brick. I got this from a car when I was run over . . . I'm crazy in a head. Man, I got headache and problem in my head."

"Do you think you're crazy?"

"No, but my head bother me with my problem."

"You ought to talk to Henry about your problems."

"Come on, les go up to Herbie. I wan my pascription glasses."

It was time for the next period. No Nat. Natalie waited in the rec room. Nat showed up about fifteen minutes later with his friend. He still didn't want to read. He was going home with his friend. Natalie thought something was bothering him. He wasn't friendly. He wasn't like her Nat. Natalie went down to her office to dictate, feeling a little rejected. Nat opened the door. She felt better . . . but only momentarily. He just wanted to tell her that he was taking his friend to the subway. He would be back in a while.

ANYONE FOR CLASS

Wasn't anyone interested in academic work? Not Manuel, not Nat, not Willie. Harold was absent. Don could hardly see through his swollen eyes. Stanley was interested and so was Larry. Stanley was really plugging away at fractions, decimals, and percentages. He was trying hard. He still didn't know which fractions equaled which percentages or decimals, but he was getting there. Larry didn't plug away. He just went to class.

MEETING TIME

After the boys left for the day, we spent our meeting talking about Don and Larry. Henry filled us in about his conversation with Don and told us he had made an appointment to meet with Don's parents. He suggested that Don should spend as much time as possible on schoolwork in order to keep his mind occupied, but he also believed that Don wasn't ready to work in a group. Connie and Jack offered to set up courses for Don which combined programmed instruction and guided independent study. That sounded great in theory. However, most of us thought Don didn't have enough interest or stick-to-it-iveness to work on his own. Since Connie and Jack were still taking the boys' promises literally, they wanted a chance—they thought it would be worth a try.

Then our psychologist gave us her report about Larry. She told us that Larry was able to function at the very superior level on his intelligence test and without difficulties. She suggested that he employed his acrobatics and daredevil behavior to counteract feeling damaged and depressed. She felt he used LSD and marijuana to withdraw from reality into a sea of tranquility just as an infant desires peace and gratification from its mother.

"That's wild," Norm commented when she mentioned the infant. "One a the first questions Larry asked in bio was if he could suckle at his wife's breast after she gave birth to a kid."

Since Larry's problems were emotional rather than academic, we concluded that therapy would be more helpful to him than education, even the ego-enhancing, self-concept building kind of education. We decided to avoid placing demands on him because we believed that his inability to fulfill our demands would make him feel weak and impotent, and more likely to want to "fly high" or withdraw. However, we felt that with his high IQ and good basic skills, Larry could quickly make up whatever academic work he missed when he was ready to work. In the meantime, he would have regularly scheduled psychotherapy sessions with Henry.

Tuesday, March 7

Tuesday started off slowly. Only five boys showed up for the warm-up, George, Carlos, Larry, Willie, and Manuel. It was pouring out. Maybe the other boys would be coming late, we hoped. We waited. It was time for the first period. Willie and Larry had shop instead of biology because Don, Stanley, and Harold were out. George went to gym. Carlos went with Natalie and Manuel went with Connie.

A BUM OFFA THE STREET

Manuel read a story about Africa. He was doing well. His basic vowel sounds were fine. Connie started to work with him on combinations such as "ie" in cities, chief, and field, and "ion" in champion. He was learning rapidly, but he had a lot on his mind. Connie kept quiet as Manuel interrupted his reading with comments.

"I don belong here. I'n too good fa it."

"Too good?" Connie didn't understand.

"No, I'n too bad. Why daya take a bum offa the street? You can' help me, I get in too much trouble. Wha's a use a helpin me if I get in trouble? If they throw me outta school . . . I'n gonna quit when I'n sickteen anyway. I can' stay out a trouble. I got too many frien's, junkies and things, in court I neva be a good guy . . . I don like bein a good guy. I like poolroons. When the cops come I stick my nose in an get in trouble. Anyway, when my frien's ax me, I gotta help em. They help me when I was small. Everyone useta pick on me when I was small, till they protect me . . .

"I think I wanna go ta Africa ta live. I's better then P.R. Ya could still have radio and TV and ya could trade teeth fa cigares. My frien, he tol me all bout Africa."

They browsed through *Life* magazine searching for

words Manuel could read. Manuel stared at two pictures—
a man walking in underwear, and a girl modeling a bra and
girdle on the beach. The pictures bothered him.

"Look!" he shouted excitedly. "People can walk round
like that anytime they wanna. Ain' they embarrass?"

Connie explained that they were models just posing for
pictures.

"No kiddin," he answered, surprised and not completely
convinced.

REMEDIAL TRIANGLE

Carlos and Nat continued playing out their games with Natalie. Carlos still wanted her for two periods while Nat still
wanted her for no periods. Carlos started the day in a good
mood because Natalie had agreed to spend the first period
time which Nat didn't want with him instead. First they
went for a walk. Then when they returned to the school
Carlos left Natalie for a basketball game with George and
Ed and she went upstairs to dictate.

Carlos and Natalie continued in their separate ways until
eleven o'clock when it was time for his regular class. Carlos
wanted to finish the game. He told her to wait, but she
walked toward the door to get some materials. As she did,
her bracelet caught on the knob and scratched her hand
against the door. Carlos laughed for a second or two, then
quickly went after her calling out, "What happen, what
happen? Did ya hurt ya hand?"

"My bracelet got caught. That's all," Natalie replied
matter-of-factly.

"Are ya hurt?" Carlos asked.

"No, I'm not hurt. I'm fine," she assured him.

"Good, then les go down fa readin," he suggested.

Natalie took out his book. As usual Carlos said it was
too difficult. As usual she said it wasn't, but if he really

thought so she would get him another book. He claimed he read too slowly, and, besides, if he made mistakes she would get mad, so he didn't want to read the book.

Natalie didn't want Carlos to think she would be angry at him.

"Carlos," she asked, "do you really believe I get mad when you make mistakes?"

"Not outside, inside."

"Carlos, when I become angry with you, you know it. I wouldn't let it remain inside, and I would never get angry at you for making honest mistakes."

Carlos liked her answer. It reassured him. He read fairly well, but he had difficulty with words beginning with "sw" and "gu," "st," "bl," "ch," "sl," and "sp." However, he seemed to pick the sounds up rapidly. He was also improving on his "s" and "ed" endings, to the point that he was more likely to read them than drop them. The session was interrupted by José, the Puerto Rican maintenance man, who came into the room to check the intercom system. After he left, Carlos asked Natalie if she would marry José.

"No, I wouldn't," she answered.

"Why? Don ya like Spanish people?" he asked.

"I like you," Natalie told him. "You're Spanish people. So I must like Spanish people."

"Yeah, ya do," he answered smilingly.

A few more minutes of reading, then it was time for the third period. Nat was supposed to have Natalie. However as she and Carlos walked into the gym, Nat announced that he wasn't going with her. "What's the matter?" she wondered, as she began to take Nat's indifference a little too personally. Carlos asked for Nat's time. Natalie explained that as long as Nat was in school it was still his time. Carlos didn't like her answer. If Nat had two periods with her, he threatened, he wouldn't let Nat study unless he had two periods with her too. Natalie looked hard at Carlos who backed down, offering a face-saving rationalization, "Nat miss the first period, so he kin have one with ya now."

Carlos was being generous, but Nat didn't accept his generosity. Nat still didn't want to be with Natalie. Carlos continued talking to her.

Natalie listened, but she was still concerned about Nat. She was feeling rejected and she wanted to know why. After Carlos finished talking, Natalie went into the studio after Nat.

"May I talk to you, Nat?"

"Ah aint goin with her," he said in an aside to Harold.

"You don't have to come with me. I just want to talk to you."

They stepped outside. He looked at her kind of bored, defensively bored.

"Are you angry?"

"Yeah."

"About me or something else?"

"Ah don know," he answered, obviously avoiding her question.

"Do you want to talk about it?"

"No."

"That's all right. I just wanted to know if you had anything you wanted to say to me."

"Ah'm goin home."

But he didn't. He walked back into the studio. Natalie returned to the gym.

SEX TIME

There they were in the gym: Natalie, Carlos, and Ed. Natalie asked Carlos if he wanted to play Ping-Pong.

"No," he seethed.

Natalie and Ed started to play. Carlos began to sing in

Spanish, at first to make them lose their concentration, then after a while because he enjoyed it.

"You know Spanish?" he asked Natalie.

"No, but I would like to learn the song if you'll teach me." Ed got a guitar from the music room. Herb came down and brought out his drum. A jam session was starting. Happy times. Larry and Harold, who had finally arrived in no mood for class, heard the music from the studio and came out to see what was up. Larry got another guitar and joined in. Harold ate peanuts and listened.

The jam session ended. Natalie played Ping-Pong with Larry. Harold sat on the side, watching quietly until he said, "Ya know, you don look tho good today."

Larry defended her.

"She looks great. Man, she even looks better than yesterday."

They continued playing. Natalie won. Larry said he was going to play another game with her. He was really going to beat her because he wasn't going to let any girl beat him.

"You shouldn't think of me as a girl," Natalie answered.

"Yeah," Harold added, "think of her ath one of the boy . . . but that hard phi-ikly ath well ath ment'lly."

Harold hit the punching bag for a while, then approached Natalie, saying he was going to mummify her. He grabbed her hands tightly at first, then gently. He put his hand on the back of her head and removed her barrette. As Natalie's hair fell loose he said she should let her hair stay down because she looked much younger.

"At least two years younger," Larry agreed.

"No, at least ten years younger," Natalie teased.

Becoming bolder and franker, Larry said she looked sexy with her hair down. Harold didn't like that.

"Don talk that way," he insisted. "She ol enough ta be your mother."

Natalie denied she was that old. They all laughed. Harold went back to the punching bag, and Larry and Natalie played the second game.

Larry won! It pleased him. It was twelve thirty—time for lunch. Natalie turned to walk out. Larry approached her from behind, gently put his arms around her, held her close, and whispered, "Now this is the way I mummify you."

MOTHAFUCKIN PSYCHOLOGIST

While all was peaceful downstairs George was going wild upstairs. After a great deal of waiting, we were finally having George tested. Henry had tried to prepare him for the tests, but George couldn't be prepared. He went into his act as soon as he saw the psychologist walk out of the morning meeting.

"I ain seein no mothafuckin psychologist, nigger. I ain crazy. You can make me."

Henry took George aside, explained the purpose of the testing in a way which he hoped would make them less threatening, calmed him down, walked him into the office, and left. As the psychologist took out her material, George started babbling "crazy talk."

"Look at the pink elephants, watch me fly, snakes on the floor—watch out—alligators. See, I'm crazy. You don hafta show me that things."

She told George he wasn't fooling her and kept preparing her material. George's first try hadn't worked. Time for a second offensive.

"I ain startin. You can make me. I punch your ass if you try. Gimme those test. I rip em. I mean it."

That didn't work either. George started an IQ test. He tried, but his panic was too much for him. By the time the psychologist asked him how tall the average American man was, he had gone to pieces.

"Thirteen feet."

"How tall are you?"

"Four feet six."

He wasn't putting her on, he really believed it. He regained control for a while, answering fairly accurately, until she asked him why brick houses were more desirable than wooden houses.

"Cause the big bad wolf might come and blow your house down," he answered.

Was he flipping, putting her on, or just keeping her away? She thought she knew. Again George regained control. The testing continued for a while. More threats, insults, refusals. Finally that was it. . . . He shouted.

"Sex maniac. She's a sex maniac," and out he bolted.

The psychologist gave George a few minutes to calm down, then went out to coax him back in. He agreed to try another kind of test. Again she felt his tremendous tension.

"Look at the picture and make up a story about it."

"This girl got raped. She went home and cried. They'll have a shotgun wedding."

"This one?"

"No more."

"This one?"

"Picture of a stupid girl."

"This one?"

"She's a spy. She comin inta the room ta try ta get a microfilm of the world's greatest five-piece band. She picked the lock with Henry's tiny knife. There's a lady's body in the closet."

"This one?"

"This boy got leprosy . . . and it's Henry's son, and he's gonna die. There's a priest leaning over him, givin him last wishes. It's Henry."

"This one?"

"Nope."

"This one?"

"A little boy. They're cuttin him open. It's a operation. They're takin out his appendix and after the operation the boy's body is in good shape and he lives happy ever after."

"This one?"

"No more."

George meant no more. He lost control, ripped the picture, then screamed, "I didn do it—I didn do it."

She tried to reassure him, but he kept screaming—"I didn do it." The more George screamed, the more he seemed to believe he hadn't done it. Then he was gone.

She went to find Henry. They spoke for a while. Maybe if Henry stayed in the room, his presence would calm George down. It was worth a try. Henry found George and convinced him to return to the office. The testing continued. After each card George asked for and received Henry's approval. It was moving along. The cards were finished. Time for the inkblots. George was especially tense about "those crazy cards." Once again Henry calmed him down. Suddenly George was up. He ran for the window, climbed out, leaned over, holding on with one hand, and threatened, "I'll jump. I'll kill myself. I'll kill myself."

The testing was over. Henry coaxed George back in, calmed him down, and took him out while we all went to lunch.

Henry knew how to relax George. First he took George for a ride in his sports car. They drove down the East River Drive across the loop to the West Side Highway and then crosstown at Twenty-third Street to the Village. Like all the kids, George dug Henry's car and liked to ride with Henry . . . especially when the speedometer registered a few miles above the speed limit. Then Henry had to gun it for a couple of seconds. Yeah, that felt good.

After the car ride Henry took George to lunch near the school. With a car ride and a big meal behind him, George seemed content. He was, until Henry made a comment about the psychological testing. George didn't like that. He headed for the door to escape from Henry's piercing words. Henry followed him out into the street at a medium-fast pace.

"What did he steal from you? What did that kid take?" a woman shouted.

How could I ever explain to this woman who George is? Henry thought.

[How could Henry explain George to the woman? Don't all niggers steal . . . and smell . . . and drink . . . and have a natural sense of rhythm?]

EASY AFTERNOON

The boys settled down to academic work after lunch. Larry went to world history. Stanley and Harold went to their English class together.

From social studies Larry went to English. They started working on grammar. He said he disliked grammar; he wanted to write something. Fine, write something, Connie told him. He did. He wrote

Peter flung the disc at Jim in which clipped him on the shoulder. Jim let out a scream of anger and pain as he fell to the ground. Peter had alread started running down the street to hide from Jim.

The cream of the small skulls found by John was very crisp from decay and it also needed to be mended.

The day was promising to end peacefully, but George wouldn't let it. The last period of the day found the boys in the gym. Ed was teaching judo, Bill was teaching tumbling, and Jack was trying to keep George out of the way by playing Ping-Pong with him. George lost interest. He began to knock the ball any which way, not even at the table. He wasn't even going through the motions. Oh, oh, was something wrong? Jack wondered. George interrupted the judo class. First he tried to throw Ed, then Manuel, then Willie . . . Willie? He had been in the music room all afternoon. The judo had brought him out of the music room. He was studying karate and he liked judo.

Ed was getting angry about George's interference.

"Okay, George, if you want to get involved why don't you let me demonstrate on you?" he suggested.

George accepted the offer. Ed threw him—gently—kind of, then told him he should get up quickly before the other guy had a chance to pounce on him. But George wouldn't move. He just wouldn't move. They couldn't use the mats with him on them. Should I drag him off, or not? Ed wondered. Screw it, he decided and walked away in disgust. That damn George, Ed thought to himself, what a pain in the ass.

Time to go home. George still wouldn't give up. He was no longer lying on the mats. He had another game—an old one for him. He wouldn't leave until he had bugged Henry a little. Smoke in the face, feigned punches at the midsection, and so on. The game was over. He had had his attention or whatever he had wanted, so he left.

STREET SCENE
Willie and Manuel had already left. The rest of us divided into groups as we left the school. Connie and George were up front, Norm and Bill were a long distance behind around the corner, and Larry and Harold were in between the two groups. George, looking back, turned on Harold.

"You mothafucker. You chicken bastard. I'm gonna kick your ass." Harold tried to ignore George. Larry egged

George on. Harold dropped back. So did Larry. George turned to go back after them. Connie reached out to grab him. George went into his sex maniac bit. People stopped to stare. It was quite a scene. A grown woman (white) holding a teen-age boy (black) who was screaming, "Lemme alone, you sex maniac, you sex maniac, lemme alone." Finally Norm and Bill turned the corner. George stopped as he saw them. Connie sighed. The people in the streets walked on. Norm, Bill, Larry, and Harold turned east. Connie and George continued west, Connie hoping George was finished.

Unfortunately, they had caught up with Manuel and Willie . . . two more kids for George to attack. First Willie—George grabbed his cap, ran away, got chased, threw the cap on the ground, stepped on it, then gave it back. Next Manuel—George ranked him out, challenged him to a fight, called him chicken, until Manuel got angry enough to swing. As George ducked Manuel's punch, he bumped into Connie and felt compelled to start his sex maniac act, which ended the thing between him and Manuel.

Things seemed cool until Jack got into the picture. Jack had left the building late, as he had been talking very briefly with Carlos's father, who had arrived unexpectedly, looking for Henry. When Jack reached them, Connie and George were up front talking. Manuel and Willie were about two paces behind. Jack joined the boys.

George dropped back to "devil" him. He grabbed Jack's scarf, pulled it, choked him a little, then took it and refused to give it back. Jack let him keep it because he wanted to avoid a physical confrontation. After a block George returned the scarf. It was Connie's turn to leave. After she had left, George started on Manuel again.

"You talk big when people's around. What you gonna do now she's gone."

I'm someone? Doesn't George see me? Jack wondered, feeling slighted. Manuel didn't respond, but he looked frightened. Jack stepped between them. George eased off.

They reached the subway. It had been a long day. Jack didn't want to have to continue watching over George. Could he leave him alone with Manuel, he wondered. George had to take the uptown subway, Manuel the downtown train. The day was over. It's a good thing George doesn't have to be tested every day, Jack thought to himself.

Wednesday, March 8

UNEXPECTED VISIT

Jack started our morning meeting with a summary of his conversation with Carlos's father. Mr. Rivera had come to school unexpectedly to see Henry. That surprised us because Henry had been trying unsuccessfully to make an appointment to see him. Carlos had told Natalie the truth about his father. Carlos was getting drunk with his friends. Mr. Rivera was worried that the police might think Carlos was getting the liquor from his bar in the living room. Mr. Rivera also thought we were too nice to Carlos. He wanted us to be harder on him.

What was going on? we asked ourselves. Something was up. Carlos had seemed especially suspicious that we wouldn't keep our promises to him, that we wouldn't pay back Natalie the money she spent on him, that we might even fire her. There was the new "don't tell the others" bit with Natalie and now Mr. Rivera's visit. Why had *he* come to the school?

Connie had the key. Carlos had told her he had overheard Henry and our psychologist talking about his mother. He had heard that his mother had cancer. He had told Henry it was a lie. He found out it was a lie, but he wouldn't tell Connie how he had found out.

So that was what was going on. Carlos had probably asked at home about his mother. That probably was what had brought Mr. Rivera to the school. Henry said he would talk to Carlos, then make an appointment to see the Riveras.

DON'T TOUCH

Connie wanted to talk about her difficulties with George. She was upset about the slapping, pushing, grabbing, the sexual accusations, and the scenes in the street. She wanted help. She wanted to know what could she do to avoid that kind of involvement.

We weren't sure why George was acting up with Connie. However we felt certain that she made things worse when she tried to use physical force to control him. We couldn't be sure, but we guessed he experienced some sexual stimulation from the contact, became anxious, and acted aggressively in order to keep her away.

One thing was certain. We didn't want Connie to touch George. He couldn't handle it. Should we remove him from her class? Connie didn't want George transferred. She wasn't afraid of him, she insisted, just concerned about his behavior. Herb thought Connie might have been denying her fear. She felt sure she wasn't. So she got her wish. George would continue to go to her class. We would observe whether his behavior would improve as Connie limited their physical contact.

[Connie was definitely doing wrong. By pretending to herself that she wasn't afraid of George, she was keeping herself and George in a situation which would probably worsen.]

DISRUPTIVE BUT NOT DANGEROUS

It was time for warm-up. We wondered what the day would bring from Carlos and George. After warm-up George told Jack he was ready to go to the social studies class he had requested. It would be his first class with Jack, even though the March schedule had been in effect for more than a week.

Jack talked to him about general social studies things. George knew quite a few historical facts, but they were pretty confused. He was very weak in basic geography. He didn't realize that New York City was part of New York State. He didn't know what a state was and he didn't know the difference between countries and continents. Although George could read fairly well, he had a lot to learn. The period went well, ending a few minutes early. George went down to the music room.

When Connie went looking for him for their second period English class, she heard George's favorite drumbeat coming from the music room . . . bam-bam-bam, bam-bam. George was pretty good on the drums, especially on loud marching rhythms—bam-bam da-bam bam bam-boom. Connie went in to call him. The time between periods was just about over. However, George wasn't ready to leave. He was working himself into a full hour session. The same beat over and over. It mesmerized and "trancified" him. Connie sat waiting, powerless, impatient, frustrated, and angry.

George was getting real loud. Herb came in, saw the two of them, and told Connie not to wait for George in the drum room. If George wanted English, Herb told her, he would go upstairs by choice. Connie waited anyway. So Herb stayed. How can she sit here? Herb asked himself. The noise is almost dangerous. Yet Connie sat there silently for five, maybe ten minutes, until George stopped.

"Can I go to English now?" he asked.

"It's your time. If you're ready, let's go," Connie answered.

George rose carefully—carefully placed the drum sticks on the base drum and left—just as if he were in perfect control of himself. But was he? Herb didn't think so. Connie did.

Connie and George went upstairs to English. Connie asked him if he wanted to follow the schedule they had made up, or what. Yeah, he wanted to follow it. What was it? Vocabulary and reading. She gave him a list of fifteen words.

"Write down the definitions. If you don't know them, look them up."

"No, you write them down, my arms a tired from the drums."

Connie refused.

"You do it," she told him.

"No, you."

"No, you," she insisted.

"Okay, I'll do the damn shit," he agreed.

In two minutes George had written down the definitions of twelve words he knew.

"Finished. That's all I know."

"Then look up the others."

No answer. Tick-tack-toe on the paper. More silence. Then up he went on top of the bookcase.

"I'm gonna jump. You betta believe me, I'm gonna jump."

"George, come down."

No, yes, no, yes, no, yes, then down he came right on top of the table. The telephone was next. George called Norm, Phyllis, Herb, Henry, almost everyone. Connie remembered not to grab him, but he was wild anyway. Finally she tried to grab the phone from him. He struggled, broke her bracelet, felt anxious, ran to the window, threatened to jump out, and started to open it.

Henry and Herb ran in, moments apart.

"George, get the hell away from that window now!" Herb shouted. Down off the window, up onto the bookcase, down onto the table, back to the floor. Three of us, one of him. Those were good odds even against George. Phyllis came in. Herb was wanted on the phone. He left—two against one, the odds were still in our favor. George was quiet. Henry had calmed him down. George was ready for more work, or so he claimed. Connie agreed. Henry had his doubts, but George and Connie wanted to continue the lesson.

Bam! Off George went again . . . the phones, the bookcase, the table, the floor. Then one good nudge and he had pushed Connie out of the room. He tried to close the door against her, and picked up an iron bar that one of the boys had left in class. Connie called Herb, who took over for the remaining few minutes.

George wouldn't talk. They sat in Herb's office for a minute or two until Henry joined them. After Herb filled Henry in about what had happened Henry told George that he would have to leave early because he had threatened Connie with an iron bar. He offered to drive George to the bus terminal to make it easier for George to accept his medicine.

"Do I hafta miss lunch? Can we go after lunch?" George wanted to know.

"We wouldn't want you to miss lunch. We'll eat first, then leave," Henry told him.

George felt a little better, but he still tried to argue that he hadn't really threatened Connie. It was a futile attempt. He knew it. He quickly gave up and sat silently for a couple of minutes. George looked sad, but not depressed and certainly not angry. Still he needed to make at least one defiant gesture before he could accept their decision. He got up, went out into the hall to the water fountain, and filled his mouth with water. Then he walked up to Herb as if to squirt him in the face, then into Connie's room as if to squirt her. He returned to the hall, glared at Henry and Herb, blew air at them to show them that he really didn't have any water, then laughed ecstatically as he ran down to the gym.

[George was able to laugh. He still needed the last laugh, but he was able to laugh and kind of admit he deserved the consequences of his own behavior. It was a positive sign.]

WHAT CARLOS BELIEVES

Natalie spent the first period with Carlos because Nat was late again. Carlos seemed hostile. Natalie wondered if she was just being especially sensitive because of our meeting about Carlos. Then when the first thing he said was, "I ain gonna read," she knew he was in a mood.

Carlos told Natalie that he was worried about his mother because two years before she had almost died after an operation. He was going to quit school so he could work to give her money.

"How would your mother feel if you quit school?" Natalie asked in order to encourage Carlos to stay in school.

"She wan me ta stay in school," he answered, "but I'm quittin in a few months, when I'm sixteen."

Having gotten that off his chest, Carlos read for the rest of the period, then they went out for hamburgers.

On the way back to school Carlos said that he and his two friends, the boys who had been to the school, had bought a gun—for protection. They wouldn't go out and shoot anybody with it, but if anybody messed with them, they had a gun and could protect themselves. Herb could offer him twenty dollars and all the food he could eat for a week, but Herb would never get that gun from him. She asked who carried the gun.

"Who da ya think?" he answered. "I'm gonna carry it cause I'm the boss. But don worry I ain gettin inta any trouble. I jus need it fa patection."

When they returned, Henry asked Carlos about his mother. As we suspected, Carlos had asked his father about what he had overheard. His father had called us liars who were trying to poison Carlos's mind against his own family. Henry asked Carlos for his permission to talk to his family about it. Carlos agreed.

SEX TIME AGAIN

Things got sexy during lunch. Harold asked Natalie to sit next to him. Carlos and Ed joined them, then Connie, Larry, and Stanley. Carlos started the conversation by teasing Ed that he was Natalie's boy friend. Harold answered adamantly that Ed was already married.

"Don't worry, love, there are other fish in the sea," Larry added.

"Da ya like ta scheme with ya boy frien?" Carlos asked.

"Scheme? What does that mean?" Natalie answered.

"Kissin and things. Don ya know that?"

"Pass the ketchup, love," Larry interrupted.

"You know, Carlos, those aren't the kinds of questions someone discusses at the lunch table."

"I'm jus teasin, ya know tha."

"I know, Carlos—I'm not angry."

Harold took over for Carlos.

"You don't look like a teacher," he told her. "Connie look like a teacher. You dreth casual."

"I do?"

"Yeah, like your blouth. It outthide your thkirt."

"Are you sure you don't mean sloppy?"

"Well, yeah—but it nithe. Maybe I come vi-hit you nekth week."

"Okay, Harold, but please call me first. In my neighborhood I don't answer the downstairs bell unless I know who it is."

"Well, when I bang on the door, you'll know it me."

Natalie felt it would be fruitless to insist he should call first. Knowing Harold, she realized he would do what he wanted anyway.

After they had finished eating, the boys wandered up to the gym to spend the rest of the lunch period. It was Natalie's turn to supervise them. Nat walked in and avoided her until he asked her to play a game of Ping-Pong.

George and Harold were both in the gym. Harold was showing George how to punch the bag. George walked away, started wrestling, then came up to Natalie after she had finished the Ping-Pong game with Nat and asked her to tell him a story. He sat down a while, listened, got up and walked away again. It was Harold's turn to sit with Natalie. Other boys and staff drifted into the gym. Don, who was wearing sweat pants, asked her to sew the pants he had ripped earlier. Natalie took them. As she was walking out of the gym, Larry came up to her from behind, crossed his arms around her, and roughly pulled her close to him, not gently as the previous day.

"Let go. What do you want?" Natalie demanded uncomfortably.

Larry smiled and answered in a quiet voice.

"If I told you, love, you wouldn't want me ta tell you."

As Larry let Natalie go, George put his arm around her. But he released her almost immediately.

Then Nat came over, wrapped his arm around her, and kissed her on the cheek.

Carlos, who was standing watching, shouted to Nat:

"Let go, let er alone."

"See Natalie," Harold said, "I told you to wear a weddin band."

It was just about time for the first period of the afternoon. Henry walked into the gym, called George, and left with him. Jack's social studies class started off well. Don seemed especially interested. Larry was being carried along. Natalie walked in with Don's pants. Larry got up, stretched his arms out, and tried to embrace her.

"Please stop," she demanded.

Don broke in. "Leave her alone, can't you see she's my wife. See, she sews my pants, leave her alone."

Larry moved between Natalie and the door.

"Please let me out," she demanded . . . in an almost pleading voice.

"No, love."

Natalie turned to Jack.

"I guess I'll have to stay here, since Larry won't let me out."

But when she turned around again, Larry had moved out of her way.

TWO JOINTS

At the end of the period Larry left for English while Don remained for math. However Don wasn't ready for math and Jack didn't press the issue. They started talking about the wars between Rome and Carthage. Don interrupted.

"Man, I got a great idea. You get a whole country on heroin, then withdraw the supply. They hafta go cold turkey. Then you walk in and take over."

Don remembered the two marijuana cigarettes he had brought to school. He showed them to Jack who lectured him about the trouble he could get into. Don listened without hearing.

After class Jack told Don it would be better if he left the marijuana in school. Don refused. Jack insisted. Don still refused. Jack asked Norm to help out since Norm was in charge Tuesday afternoons in the absence of both Henry and Herb.

"You know why you showed the marijuana to Jack?" Norm asked Don.

"No, why?"

"Because you wanted to give it to him."

"Come on! That's bull shit."

Norm knew he was right. He felt certain he could get it. He tried another approach, then another and another. Finally Don handed the marijuana over and left.

Jack followed him out. Don turned around.

"You know, those reefers cost me a buck . . . I should at least get back the money I paid for em. Just like you buy knives."

Jack didn't think so. Reefers and knives seemed different to him. Don kept pushing him. Jack grew weaker and weaker until he finally gave Don the dollar. Poor Jack, even after he gave him the dollar, Don was at him complaining.

"Man, I needed those reefers. I never should of given em to you guys. You burned my brain with that psychology shit."

"Well, why did you show it to me if you didn't want to give it to me?" Jack asked.

"Because I wanted you to smoke one with me . . . no, I didn't."

[Jack was right about the dollar. We didn't buy reefers from kids like we did knives. Jack was a new teacher. He would learn how to handle the kids' pressure. He would learn to follow his own judgment and common sense.]

BAD NIGGER?

Meanwhile George, Henry, and Herb had set out for the bus terminal in Henry's car. George was pleased about the special treatment he was getting, but not pleased enough to behave himself. As soon as the car moved he began shouting "Fuck you" and "Pull over" at passing drivers, and "You want to get laid" to the girls on the sidewalks. Henry told him to stop. George stopped yelling at people but toyed with the gearshift and beeped the horn instead. Henry pulled over, stopped the car, and said, "George, either you behave or you will have to leave the car." George answered, "No no, I'll be good," and kept his word until they approached the bus terminal. When he saw they were almost there he gave Henry the wrong directions to prolong the trip. Henry confronted him. George started to beep the horn. Henry said he wouldn't pull over again because it would only prolong the trip, which was what George wanted. George wasn't quite ready to leave. It took another three or four minutes of "why-can't-we-drive-around-the block-again" and "you-can't-make-me-get-out" before he finally left on a happy note.

Throughout the ride Herb marveled at the really dependent, childlike way George related to Henry. It was very different from the aggressive hostile stance George took with other staff members. No wonder Henry doesn't understand the way we feel about George, Herb thought. With him, George is like a little kid.

Thursday, March 9

BEAUTIFUL MORNING
The weather was beautiful, the boys were beautiful. The classes were beautiful. The beautiful Vocational Institute called to inform us that Stanley would begin his training the following Thursday. The whole morning was beautiful.

WRESTLING THROUGH HISTORY
While most of the boys spent the afternoon in the gym, Don and Larry went to social studies with Jack. As the three of them walked upstairs to Jack's room, they passed Natalie

on the stairway. Larry decided to hug her, but Jack grabbed him and pulled him along. Suddenly Larry twisted Jack's arm behind him and held it there the rest of the way up the stairs. When they reached the top, he asked Jack to arm-wrestle.

"Okay, after class," Jack answered. "But right now we have world history."

"No, I wanna arm-wrestle now."

"Wait till after class."

Larry decided to arm-wrestle Don. Jack got out the history books and notebooks and waited impatiently until the wrestling ended. Then Don announced: "Okay, let's have world history."

Jack was relieved.

"Good," he said. "Today we're goin to start a unit on 'Why the Roman Republic became a dictatorship.' "

Jack put the question on the board. The class went well for a few minutes until Don asked, "Tell us the answer."

"No!" Jack insisted. "I want you to piece the evidence together and get your own conclusions."

"No, you tell us."

"Well then, I guess that ends the class for today. You guys asked for this course and I'm ready to give it to you. When you're ready, we'll start. We'll try again Monday. Right now I have a couple of calls to make. See you Monday."

Jack walked out, made his phone calls, and came back. The boys were still there, but Jack sat down without trying to teach anything. Don tried to get Jack's attention by changing "dictatorship" on the board to "dick-taker-ship," but Jack ignored him. Don tried again by asking him what he thought of "dick takers," but Jack didn't answer. After a few more minutes he told them that the class was over. And it was.

The three of them went down to the gym where George and his friend Lonnie were boxing. When Jack walked in, Jack thought they looked serious and told them to stop. Ed, who was sitting on the Ping-Pong table, told Jack that they were hitting with open hands. Jack hadn't seen Ed sitting there when he came in. But even after he did, he told the boys a second time to stop because it seemed to him that some of the blows landing weren't open-handed. Ed insisted that he was in charge of the boys so it was his decision to make. He reminded Jack about our procedure—if you don't like the way another staff member is handling things *don't interfere,* talk to him privately or walk away.

After the boxers finished, Don and Larry had a go at it. They looked like a trapeze artist and a gorilla wrestling. Fortunately they spent so much time grunting, shrieking, jumping, and flying across the mats that they never got to wrestle. After they finished running around, Nat and George took their turn next, while Larry and Jack played Ping-Pong.

Don was sitting with Connie. Something was on his mind. Perhaps it was his earlier wrestling match with Larry.

"Faggot—playin with Jack's balls," he called out.

"You're the real queer—and you know it," Larry answered.

That made Larry feel better, but not better enough. He still had to knock over some chairs and hurl a weight halfway down the gym away from everyone. Jack was concerned about what Larry might do next. Determined to stop him, he threatened, "Larry, if you keep it up, we're going to have to treat you like George and send you home for the rest of the day—I mean it."

Connie looked at Jack with, "What's that all about? There's no danger" in her eyes. But Jack disagreed.

BAD NIGGER
Meanwhile, Herb was in his office talking with some visitors about the program. George walked in, sat on Herb's lap, and put his arm affectionately around Herb's shoulders. The visitors looked at Herb, wondering what George was doing on his lap. Herb asked George what he wanted. George asked for allowance and carfare. There was more to it than that. He also wanted carfare for his friend Lonnie. Before Herb could answer, George got up, ran into Phyllis's office, and started to type on the electric typewriter. Herb coaxed him out without much trouble and George left, but not before he had taken Phyllis's cigarettes without anyone noticing.

ENCOUNTER FOR NEWCOMERS
It was time for the afternoon seminar for interns and new teachers. Jack became the center of attention as soon as he said he had been unable to teach world history because Larry and Don refused to take notes. He was quickly criticized by Natalie for placing demands on Larry and for not meeting the boys at their level.

Jack agreed. "My whole approach to them was wrong," he admitted. "They tried to communicate with me several times. When Don asked me to answer the question, when Larry said let's take world history, and when Don deliberately pointed out what he had done to the word 'dictatorship.' Each time I closed the door in their faces."

Connie continued the onslaught. She felt Jack had been too punitive when he told Larry he would have to send him out for the afternoon if he didn't stop throwing weights. She thought Larry wasn't dangerous and didn't need to be told to stop. Jack agreed. He wasn't sure what he had felt at the time, he answered, but he thought it had probably been discomfort with Larry's behavior rather than concern that Larry might become dangerous.

Ed joined in. George and Lonnie had been boxing each other with open hands. Natalie and Connie, who had been in the gym, agreed. Ed had been handling the situation. Jack shouldn't have interfered. Utterly defeated, but obviously growing from his experiences in the meeting, Jack agreed again. Ed kept going. He began to explain to Jack that it was important for George to learn to express his aggression in sociably acceptable ways. Herb thought Jack had had enough and interrupted Ed. We had been very critical of Jack. Now it was time for us to support him.

Natalie demanded the floor. She had a problem to bring up.

"I'm not getting the kind of guidance that could really help me. I want real guidelines where I know exactly what I'm supposed to do when these things happen. It's one thing if a boy embraces me in an infantile way. I can accept this, as I do with Nat. But with Larry, it's a very real thing. I think I'm stimulating him and I'm very uncomfortable with it. And the more I feel uncomfortable, the more he seems to do it. And Carlos is being extremely protective. I think he really gets upset when he sees the boys handling me, especially Larry. The adults around me, except Connie, just place themselves in a vacuum when it happens. I need far more than a catch-as-catch-can session to discuss this."

Herb said he thought he had explained to Natalie why the boys were getting physical with her. He felt he and Henry had given her a lot of supervision. Natalie disagreed. She still felt uncomfortable. Herb explained again. He believed that it was as natural for some of the boys to kiss her and touch her as it was for them to sit on Henry's or his lap. They were doing it because we were encouraging them to regress. Herb wasn't sure about Larry, but he thought it was good for boys like Nat, Harold, and George. He told Natalie that whether it was helpful or not, she was the one to control it. "If you feel uncomfortable with some of the boys," he announced in his supervisory voice, "you'll let them know it clearly enough for them to stop it. Connie does. It's up to you and only you to control their behavior. Your reactions should set their limits." Natalie didn't say anything. Although it was becoming easy for her to complain to her professor, she was still unable to tell him that she disagreed.

Friday, March 10

FISHIN

The week ended with an all-day trip. Norm had volunteered to take the kids fishing on his day off while we had an administrative day. They met him at six thirty and caught an eight o'clock boat around New York Harbor. That is, Manuel, Nat, Willie, Harold, Carlos, and Norm. George and Stanley didn't like fishing. Larry and Don said they wanted to go, but six thirty turned out to be too early for them.

There was something settling about the fishing trips. There were seldom any fights or even arguments among the kids who had a great time fishing and eating, eating and fishing. They even got along well with the other people on the boat. They all got something out of fishing. Norm liked the fresh air. Willie and Harold liked fishing. Nat and Carlos liked playing on the boat and got excited when they caught something. Manuel liked to watch the last gasps of the dying fish, especially the ones he caught.

9 March Trips Out

Monday, March 13 through Friday, March 17

STEALING DRUNKEN WEEKEND

Monday Larry came to school high. He had two stories to tell about the weekend. Herb was free, so he heard them first. They were like Manuel's stories. The details were vague, the relationships disjointed, and the motives obscure, but the central themes were there to connect the pieces.

The first story was more intelligible than the second one. Friday evening Larry and his friends were sitting in front of his building drinking beer and wine. Policemen came out and saw them drinking, but Larry saw them first. So he wiped the fingerprints off his bottle of rum (Rum? weren't they drinking wine and beer, Herb thought) with a handkerchief and threw it into the bushes. One of them, a mean son of a bitch, told him, "Pick up your bottle."

"What bottle?" Larry asked.

"Pick up your bottle," the cop said again.

"I don't have a bottle," Larry answered, because he knew the cop just wanted to get his fingerprints on the bottle to frame him.

The cop drew his gun, pointed it at him, and said, "Pick up the goddamn bottle a liquor."

297

Larry thought he had to do it.

"Okay," Larry replied, "but remember, you told me to pick it up. It's not mine."

The cop was going to let him go after he picked it up, but another one came over and said, "What's going on here? Take him down to the station."

(What about his friends? Where were they? Herb wondered.)

The sergeant in the precinct, who recognized Larry, said, "Uh! You picked this kid up again. What'd he do this time?"

"Drinking, that's all," the cop answered.

"That's all? Fill out a white JD card for him and let him go."

Larry's head was full of questions for Herb. What could happen to him? Would the cops tell his probation officer? Would he get into trouble with the court? Herb started to respond, but Larry interrupted him with a story, a much less coherent story, about Saturday night.

Larry and a friend had taken a battery out of a telephone company car in the company parking lot near his housing development. They just borrowed it to start his friend's car —something about it was parked illegally some place. After they had taken it out, Larry changed his mind, so they left without it. Just as Larry was climbing over the fence— something about swinging from a fifteen-foot bar on a rope —a cop saw him and started shooting. Larry could see the bullets just missing him. (He saw the bullets?) He dropped down and ran, but the cop caught him from behind. Larry thought for a moment, then continued his story. Yeah, he had twisted his ankle when he dropped from the rope. That's how the cop had caught him. The cop was trigger-happy. He was waving a gun in Larry's face. Larry was afraid the gun would go off so he hit the cop—something about he swung and missed—he didn't hit him—something about he jumped back from the man when he realized he had a gun. (But wasn't that why he had swung and hit or missed him in the first place?) Then the man pistol-whipped him on the side of the head. (Man, wasn't he a cop?) Suddenly, Larry was surrounded and brought to the office. Since they confessed that they were going to borrow the battery (his friend must have been caught too), they were set free without charges because they had confessed and had left the battery there.

The story seemed like a dream that somebody might lose as he tried to tell it to someone else. Was it drugs again, Herb wondered. Were the stories true or was Larry in some kind of delusional state? Herb kept his questions to himself. His intuition told him not to confront Larry. Instead he reacted as if the story made complete sense and he believed it. He told Larry that if he continued messing around, he would get into trouble. Then the court would insist that he be removed from the community and sent elsewhere.

After finishing with Herb, Larry told his story to Bill, then to Henry. While he was talking to Henry he suddenly began making faces. He told Henry that the organ sounded like it was going to devour him. What did he mean, Henry asked. All day long he had heard the same tune on the organ, Larry answered. "Silent Night, Silent Night, Silent Night." He hated it. And the music was like a monster eating at his back and neck . . . like it was eating him. All day he kept hearing it . . . all day it kept eating him. It just wouldn't stop.

Henry didn't hear music. Larry was hallucinating. Was he high on drugs? Was it a psychotic episode? Again the same questions, this time on Henry's mind. Henry couldn't be certain. Larry wouldn't say. They talked for a while. Then they stopped.

It was time for the Monday afternoon meeting. We were waiting for Norm. Where the hell was he? we wondered. He was outside in the rain, getting wet. Larry was standing outside on the back fire escape in the rain—staring straight ahead, depressed, unwilling to leave. Norm tried to talk to him, but he wouldn't respond. Herb went down, but he did no better than Norm. Henry came down. Jackpot. He was the one Larry was waiting for. They talked some more. Henry reassured him. He left.

Henry came back up. We all filled each other in about Larry's other hallucinations during the day. Even after hearing about the whole day's events, we still didn't feel certain that we understood what had happened. We thought Larry had been tripping on LSD, but we couldn't be sure. Was he in danger of hurting someone? We didn't think so. He had no history of hurting others. But what about himself? That was a different story. He had hurt himself plenty already. We decided to follow up on him immediately. Henry was busy. He had an appointment with Carlos's parents. Herb would make a visit to Larry's home as soon as the meeting ended.

SOME VISIT

Larry's mother was still out working when Herb got to the house. Larry and Johnny, his nineteen-year-old friend whom he had once brought to the school, were sitting in the living room. Herb knocked. Larry opened the door, saw Herb, and dropped his mended lower jaw in astonishment. Herb walked in without waiting for an invitation. Johnny looked at Larry, said hello, and excused himself. The whole thing took a few seconds, and Johnny was gone.

Herb told Larry that we were concerned about him because of what had happened during the day. So we thought someone should stop by his house to talk to him. Larry sat stony-faced, acknowledging nothing. Herb asked him if he knew what we were concerned about. Larry only glared back.

"You nervous or suspicious about something?" Herb asked.

"Not yet, but you're gettin there," Larry replied.

Herb repeated his question.

"What do you think we were concerned about?"

"The organ."

"What about the organ?" Herb asked.

Larry laughed skeptically because he knew Herb knew about the organ. He was down from whatever he had been high on in school. He wanted to tone down what he had previously told Henry.

"I didn't mean the organ was gonna eat me. It was eatin at me. I wanted to say it was eatin at me."

"Whatever it was, it bothered you a lot."

"It was like a monster."

"Like a monster?"

"Just like a monster."

Larry continued. He had heard "Silent Night" when he came in and had continued to hear it most of the day. Herb asked him if he had been worried that the music was just in his mind. Larry didn't answer. Herb looked him dead in the eye and said, "You know, most guys in our program have funny thoughts, but we can't help them until they first tell us about them."

Larry reacted. Yes he had heard "Silent Night" over and over again.

"Sometimes people hear things mostly in their imagination," Herb told him. "Did you ever hear things before?"

"Yeah," Larry said, "but only after my father died. For about a month after my father died I kept hearing someone calling me. I'd turn around, but, man, no one'd be there."

Herb thought it would help if Larry understood why he had heard "Silent Night"—if at least he had the feeling that there was some reason behind why he had heard it the first time. He explained to Larry that when Larry had come to school at eleven o'clock, the portable organ had been moved upstairs to the top floor because the piano in the music room was being tuned. He had probably heard "Silent Night" coming from upstairs and thought he was hearing things. Larry smiled a sign of relief, but they both knew Larry had heard the music almost continuously later in the day when it wasn't being played.

Herb asked Larry if there was anything else he thought we might be concerned about.

"Yeah," he replied, "the weekend, but don't tell my mother bout Saturday night. I'll talk to you if you don't tell her bout the telephone company."

Herb wondered why Larry was only concerned about Saturday and not about Friday, but he didn't ask. He promised Larry not to tell his mother anything at all unless he asked Larry first, then asked if he could wait for her.

Herb thought that Larry seemed fairly open. He hoped that Larry would talk about a couple of things that had been puzzling us. We had tried unsuccessfully to get Larry to talk about his "sister," the nurse, the one who had cared for him while he was in the hospital. Herb asked him specifically whether the nurse in the hospital was really his sister. Larry made a "thud" face like he had just been hit by a blow over the heart.

"No," he whispered. "She's not my sister, but I think of her like a sister."

Larry was very intense, very emotional, almost in tears as if he were about to lose everything. For the first time Herb felt real contact between them. It was Larry—no pretense, no act, real Larry.

"Please," Larry continued, "say she's my sister—tell everyone to say she's my sister."

"If you need to think of her as your sister, I'll try to talk like she is," Herb promised. "But maybe someday, before you leave the school, we'll help you so you won't need to think that."

Larry had made another puzzling statement to Norm. He had told Norm that the guy who broke his jaw was killed. We thought his jaw had been broken in a fall. What exactly had he meant by that? Herb asked. Larry explained. On the way home from New Jersey after the fight—he didn't remember what the fight was about—he and his friends got on a bus. Larry couldn't see too well. He was dazed from the pain. Everything looked fuzzy. Some guys got on the bus with them. As he walked to his seat, a big bulky guy winked at him. It was a sign. He dozed off and woke up, nodding in and out. He saw his friend Johnny talking to one of them. They had seen Larry get it. They knew the guys— bad motherfuckers—they would get the guy that did it. He made a date to meet Johnny in the Port Authority bus terminal in Manhattan three weeks later. Larry didn't have to worry anymore. The guy would be taken care of. The next thing Larry knew he was in New York.

Herb began asking questions. Who was the guy? Had he gotten on the bus with them? Was he the big bulky guy or someone else? Larry didn't know. He had been too dazed— nodding in and out. But he knew the guy had been taken care of. How did he find out? Had Johnny met the guy at the bus depot?

"No," Larry answered, "the guy didn't show up. That's how."

"What?" Herb asked, completely surprised.

"If the guy was taken care of he wouldn't show up—if not, he would."

A couple of more questions and Herb stopped.

They had been talking for quite a while. Herb's last question challenged Larry's story too much. It used up Larry's tolerance. Herb changed the topic. How about showing me the apartment, he asked. He had noticed only one bedroom and was curious. He was right—only one bedroom—a tiny one with two single beds against opposite walls with only about two feet between them, a dresser covered with knickknacks and religious figures and a cardboard clothes closet. Where did his mother sleep? In the bedroom. Where did he sleep? In the bedroom. Both of them in the same room? No, one in the living room. Herb made a mental note of that. He would ask them about it when Mrs. Keating returned. First he had to check with Larry about what he was going to bring up with her. They agreed on the topics and made small talk until Mrs. Keating arrived.

"What happened now? What did the boy do this time?" she whined in her singsong voice when she saw Herb. Larry was doing well in school, Herb assured her. He only wanted to visit with her to find out how things were at home. He complimented Mrs. Keating on the apartment. Then he asked her why she and Larry shared the same room when one of them could easily sleep in the living room.

Mrs. Keating smiled, embarrassed but not ashamed, and answered, "He won't sleep in the living room."

"I don't like the couch," Larry explained. "It's not comfortable."

"Did you always sleep in the same room as your mother?" Herb asked Larry.

"No! Not until we moved here." Mrs. Keating answered for him. "He had his own nice room when we lived with Grandma, didn't you? And a nice cot too, but he won't bring it here. I don't know what to do with the boy. He never listens."

"There doesn't seem to be much privacy," Herb probed.

"I know, but I can't get the boy to listen to me. You know how he is."

Larry defended himself again.

"She gets up before I do to go to work and goes to bed at nine so we never see each other in the room. Anyway, either she's asleep or I am."

"That's true. I guess it's all right. Don't you think so?" Mrs. Keating asked, smiling.

Herb remained silent.

Mrs. Keating continued, smiling—still smiling. "He's much worse lately. I don't know why, after all I have done for him. Look at these black-and-blue marks. Do you think it's right for a boy to do such things to his mother?"

Herb looked at Larry, who said nothing. Herb asked her how she had gotten them. The two of them had been involved in a lot of wrestling and biting, she told him. It would usually start for fun, then Larry would grab her in a bear hug, knock her down, get on top of her, and bite her or press her against the floor so she couldn't move. Sometimes she knocked him down. Her favorite hold was the bear hug too.

"I was only playin with er," Larry interrupted. "I didn't hurt er."

"If he didn't want to hurt me, why did he give me these?" Mrs. Keating whined, pointing to her black-and-blue arms and legs.

"You know why," Larry answered, apparently referring to something he and his mother understood.

"You know you weren't playing," she retorted, still smiling. "How can you say that in front of him?"

Herb asked when the fighting had started. Mrs. Keating answered that it had begun shortly after she and her husband had been separated. She had been very physical with

Larry as a child. She cuddled him and gave him a lot of affection, even though her husband had always objected to that. Herb asked when she had stopped cuddling him.

"When Larry was about nine years old," she answered.

Larry looked at her angrily.

"I made it stop. I didn't do it anymore," he insisted.

Larry was angry about something. Herb didn't know what it was, but he could see the veins in Larry's throat tightening. Mrs. Keating giggled and continued.

"I was always very athletic, not like my husband. He didn't like wrestling or anything like that, so I taught Larry how to do push-ups and how to play ball. Now I'm old and I can't take it anymore, and he's not playful either. He's trying to hurt me."

Larry jumped up out of his seat, screaming hatefully, "Well, look what you do to me, look at what you did to me!" as he showed Herb scars from when his mother had stuck his hands in a fire, banged his head against the floor, and beat him. Herb looked at Mrs. Keating. She smiled again. Then she admitted that when Larry was about nine, she took his hands and put them in the fire to teach him not to play with matches because it was the only way that she could think of to teach him a lesson.

Larry continued on the offensive. Hadn't his mother tried to stab him a few weeks before with an arrow just because he was shooting some arrows at a box in the living room.

Mrs. Keating corrected him. "They were hunting arrows and the box was leaning against my chair. I could have been hurt," she whimpered. "I tried to get the arrows away from him to break them. He pushed me and I became full of temper and tried to stab him with the arrow."

"Yeah," Larry added. "It went right through my underwear and cut me here. She could of killed me."

"And you could have killed me," Mrs. Keating whined. "You know that too, don't you?"

"She's always tryin to stab me," Larry answered immediately.

Herb's head was starting to spin. Larry was growling at his mother, but she was smiling back lovingly at him . . . as they talked about killing each other. Herb commented that he didn't think either would kill the other. Mrs. Keating disagreed. She wasn't sure. Maybe she would kill Larry, she answered, smiling angelically.

"But he's your own flesh and blood, your son," Herb reminded Mrs. Keating, who answered, "Well, sometimes I get very angry. I know it's terrible but I could get full of temper."

Larry looked at her unresponsively.

"Do you think Larry might kill you?" Herb asked.

"Yes, I do. I really and truly do," she answered.

Larry laughed scornfully.

"What are you laughing at?" Herb asked him.

"That I could kill er," he answered.

The conversation was interrupted when Johnny walked in without knocking, with a bag full of groceries. Johnny put the groceries away in the kitchen where they belonged and retired to the bedroom and TV set. Just like he lives here, a part of the family, Herb thought to himself. That's funny.

The conversation continued as they talked about Larry's father and their family. Larry insisted that his father had been a good man. Mrs. Keating disagreed. She claimed that Larry idolized him only after his death. When he had been alive, he was a bad husband and a bad father. That's why they had separated. Herb asked about the family, especially Larry's sister and Larry's father's children by his other marriage. Mrs. Keating told him that she hadn't seen them since the funeral because they were mean, selfish people. They only cared about themselves. They had no interest in her or Larry, not like her mother.

Larry tried to disagree, but Mrs. Keating raised her voice in order to drown him out. Larry spoke anyway. His father *had* brought him to see his other children. If that was true, Mrs. Keating answered, it must have been in the middle of the night because she didn't remember it. She repeated her claim that Larry had not seen his stepsisters or stepbrothers since the funeral, while Larry insisted that in the hospital his sister had visited him. Did anyone visit Larry, Herb asked Mrs. Keating. Larry's aunt had visited him, but she was sixty years old. He did have a sister, Julia, who was in her thirties, but she hadn't visited him in the hospital. Perhaps, Mrs. Keating added, Larry had confused his aunt with his sister. After all, he had not seen very much of either of them.

Herb said that it was difficult for him to believe that a sixty-year-old aunt could have looked like Larry's thirty-year-old sister. Mrs. Keating disagreed. She explained that people on her husband's side didn't show their age very much. She was serious. It seemed strange to Herb but he didn't say anything.

Mrs. Keating changed the subject. She really wanted to know what had happened Friday. Herb asked how she knew about Friday? Larry had told her. What had he told her? Well, on Friday Larry came into her office and asked for four days allowance all at one time. She refused and told him that she was going to New Jersey for the evening to visit a friend about business. After work she and Larry argued and wrestled about the money. After he beat her black-and-blue all over her arms, she gave him the money, then left. When she came back late at night, she found out that he and his friends had been picked up by the police.

"He stays with boys who aren't allowed in the development. He knows Johnny is one of them. Johnny is *not* supposed to be in the building. You know that."

"If Johnny's not allowed in the building," Herb asked, "and you don't want Larry to hang around with him and the other boys, why do you allow him in the house?"

"The boy won't listen to me," she replied. "I tell him. They're always in the house. Sometimes I come home late at night and find them, boys *and* girls, having a party, drinking, and God knows what else. I try to kick them out, but they won't leave. Sometimes they hide under the beds or behind the furniture where I can't find them. The boy had a party a while ago when I went to New Jersey. The house was full of children when I came back. I was going to kick them out, but it was raining."

"What did that have to do with it," Herb interrupted.

"I felt sorry for them. I couldn't chase them out in the rain, so I made them promise to leave as soon as the rain stopped. Do you think they kept their promise? When I woke up in the morning there they were sleeping all over, even under my bed."

Mrs. Keating was complaining, but she seemed to enjoy her complaints. Her face was beaming, smiling, animated. Herb said he thought that she wasn't very effective in getting rid of Larry's friends, including the ones that were supposedly barred from the development. Mrs. Keating smiled. Johnny was obviously a welcome guest.

Herb asked Mrs. Keating if she went to New Jersey often, since she had mentioned it a few times. She smiled as she said not as often as she wanted to because Larry always got into trouble when she went away on business.

Herb wondered what kind of business Mrs. Keating had in New Jersey and why Larry acted up when she went out there. Was it sexual? Larry acted like it was. Herb didn't ask. Instead he asked about the trouble Mrs. Keating was having in the development because of Larry. How likely was it that they would be evicted? Mrs. Keating didn't answer. Why hadn't she accepted Henry's recent offer to send a letter to the Housing Authority on their behalf? Again she didn't answer. Herb challenged her.

"You don't seem too eager to have a letter from us."

"Yes, I am," she replied.

Herb looked at her questioningly. If she were really eager, he told her, she would have asked Henry for the letter. Larry interrupted. He didn't want a letter, he didn't want to stay in the development. He wanted to live some place where he could have a pet.

Mrs. Keating agreed. She wanted to move too. However, she wanted to move to a larger apartment in the same development, as the management had promised. But Larry had gotten into so much trouble that the management wanted her out even though she worked for them.

"And I'll lose my job. Then how will we live? I told him. I explained it (she cried without tears), but he wouldn't listen."

"Then let's move," Larry shouted.

"But where?" Herb asked. "To another apartment or another place?"

No one answered him. Each one was listening to himself. Larry and his mother screamed and shouted each other down. They didn't even realize that they disagreed.

It was just about time to leave. Larry and his mother were too confused to be reasoned with. Herb thought authority was necessary. So he laid down two laws to go into effect immediately. Larry and his mother were not to sleep in the same bedroom anymore. And they were not to wrestle with each other or become involved physically. Herb avoided a discussion about why they were not to do so or what would happen if they did. He just communicated the attitude that he was the authority and he was telling them what to do and what not to do. He gave Mrs. Keating his home phone number, told her that he wanted her to call him if either of the rules were broken, took down the lawyer's address, and left.

Herb was flooded by reactions. There's something sexual there—no doubt about it. Bear hugs, getting on top of each other, sleeping in the same room practically next to each other, and the way they went at each other—whore, prostitute, scrunt—that sounded like cunt with a little added, maybe runt. Visiting a man on business at night—could be that was why Larry acted out. Jealousy? Is that part of Larry's problem? Her damn inappropriate smile, like she never had a hostile thought—perfect innocence. How could anyone think ill of her without being bad himself? Is that part of Larry's problem? She wasn't fooling anyone, not even Larry, about those kids. She liked them in the house and probably encouraged them. And Johnny, there was something weird there. Definitely. The moving bit was really confusing, as if she and Larry had been talking about different things. How often does that happen? Was that part of Larry's problem? And the way she supported Larry that he wasn't drunk and his sixty-year-old aunt could look thirty because her husband's side of the family didn't age fast. Wow!

I'm glad, Herb thought, that I made a couple of rules. If they listened, it might cut down on some of the sexual stimulation. That's some mother. We'll have our hands full with her. God, there's a lot of sex in that apartment—and where does Johnny fit in? Is he part of Larry's problem?

DECISION TIME

Herb had a lot to report and we had a lot to discuss at our next meeting. Herb's home visit had given us the additional information we needed to understand why Larry was calling Natalie "love," putting his arms around her, and making sexual advances to her. Before the home visit we knew that Larry wasn't quite copying Nat. The home visit clarified just what he was doing. Larry was transferring some of the physical, sexual, assaultive wrestling type behavior that he engaged in with his mother to Natalie. The grabbing, overpowering, and obvious sexuality were probably what was upsetting Natalie.

[What was coming from Larry and Don was the real stuff —sex. That was one of the reasons why the two of them were so upset. We wanted to keep that down or channel it better. Nat and George were different. They were infantile and dependent—at least we thought so. That could, should be encouraged, at least for a while.]

When Larry arrived in school, Herb asked him what he thought about his visit to the apartment. Larry played it cool: "Nothin much," he answered. "It was all right." Herb asked about what had happened since his visit and learned that Larry was sleeping in the living room on his grandmother's cot.

Herb told him about our decision. Larry wanted to know why other boys could put their arms around Natalie but not him. Herb explained that what he was doing was different from what the other boys were doing, more like what he did with his mother. He had to stop it with his mother and with Natalie. Herb offered no explanation, just a it-was-good-for-some-boys-to-touch-and-kiss-staff-and-for-others-it-wasn't-good. Although he might not understand it, Herb told Larry, he should follow the rules anyway.

Larry also wanted to know what Herb had told the rest of us about his visit and whether Herb thought he was crazy. Clearly Herb still had some more reassuring to do during the week.

First he explained to Larry that he had told the staff everything he knew because there was no reason to hide it.

Then, in order to dispel Larry's fear that he was crazy, Herb attempted to describe his impression of what had happened in Larry's house in a way that would appear less threatening to him. He told Larry that we didn't think that he was crazy in Larry's sense of the word. We thought he was the kind of person who became confused and had strange thoughts when things were very important or very troubling to him. Larry nodded his understanding. Herb continued, he was confident that we could help him as we had helped Stanley and Harold.

ANGRY RIVERAS

While Herb was visiting with the Keatings, Henry and our interpreter were visited by Mr. Rivera and his daughter. Henry had told the interpreter before the Riveras arrived that he wanted Mr. Rivera to admit that his wife had cancer. He had explained that Mr. Rivera might deny it. If so she, the interpreter, would have to reassure him that it would be helpful to everyone if he shared the truth with us. When the Riveras arrived, the interpreter began.

"I've been told that you have a great many problems. Your son has difficulties and your wife is sick. I understand she is very ill."

"My wife? She's fine," Mr. Rivera answered. "My son drives her crazy. That's all."

The interpreter continued. "We know your son is difficult. But your wife is also ill. We understand she has cancer."

"Who told you that? My son?"

The interpreter didn't know how to answer that question. She asked Henry, who said, "Tell him that he himself told me the first time I visited his apartment while Carlos was still in Youth House."

She did. Mr. Rivera remembered the visit. He admitted that his wife had cancer. However he still insisted that Carlos was so bad that he was driving his mother to the grave, and about to get him, Mr. Rivera, in trouble.

Then Mr. Rivera told the interpreter that he wanted us to get tough with Carlos . . . to make him behave so there would be peace at home. Or else, Mr. Rivera threatened, he would have to get rid of Carlos.

That or-else-he-would-get-rid-of-Carlos sounded ominous to Henry. It reminded him of Stanley's home and Don's home, and Larry's home and others as well.

Henry could sense Mr. Rivera's tremendous resistance. He realized Mr. Rivera half-believed that Carlos was killing his wife. Henry knew he had to convince Mr. Rivera otherwise. So he told the interpreter to tell Mr. Rivera that people died of natural physical causes not aggravation. Carlos wasn't to blame. If he continued to blame Carlos, Carlos's life would be ruined.

In a complete turn-about Mr. Rivera agreed with Henry. The interpreter smiled at Henry in a way which communicated her admiration for Henry's accomplishment. Henry found it difficult not to bask in the warmth of her admiration. For the moment he allowed himself to believe that he had really won Mr. Rivera over. Of course, he hadn't.

Carlos had missed school Monday and Tuesday. So when he hadn't arrived by mid-morning Wednesday, we asked Natalie to call his home to find out why he was absent. However, before Natalie could call Carlos, she met him on the stairs.

"I was just going upstairs to call your house," she told Carlos.

"How kin ya call my house, I don have a phone?"

"I thought the office had a number for you?"

"No," he insisted. "Nobody's got a number cause I ain got no phone."

"No?"

"No!"

Natalie knew there was a telephone in his house, but she didn't pursue it because it was obviously upsetting him.

Carlos told Natalie that he wanted to quit school. Something about Henry's visit was bothering Carlos, but he wouldn't say what. He wanted to read, not talk. He couldn't do that either.

So they made small talk for the rest of the period. Natalie thought that Carlos seemed friendly, but there was that ominous note. He felt bad about Henry's visit. He wouldn't tell Natalie what had happened at home. He wouldn't tell anyone. He wouldn't tell us Wednesday and didn't come to school Thursday or Friday.

NAT MAKES IT

Nat made up for Carlos's anger at us by returning to the fold. He was almost over whatever had gotten between him and Natalie. He wanted her attention again. Taking the direct approach, he telephoned her room from Henry's office. Was she busy? No. Did she want to play Ping-Pong? Yes. Then she should come get him in Henry's office where he was hiding underneath a desk.

When it was time for Natalie to move her car, Nat put his arm around her, kissed her on her cheek, and explained: "Ah always kiss you good-bye when you leave."

Nat came in late the following morning. He looked depressed to Natalie. She asked him what he wanted to do.

"Nothin, ah'm goin home," he answered.

He wandered around a bit, then came back with George who had a plan to get us to let Nat go with him to the movies. If Herb said Nat couldn't go, George would disrupt Nat's reading session in the office and then Nat would have to leave school early like him.

"If I knock two times," he told Nat, "answer the door, cause that means that Herb won't let you go. Okay?"

"Okay."

Nat started to read. A few minutes later George knocked two times on the door.

"Should ah open it?" Nat asked Natalie.

"I am not going to tell you what to do," Natalie told him permissively. "You have to make up your own mind."

Nat was really back in the fold. He didn't want to leave.

"Forget it, George," he answered. "Ah cain't go."

[Nat was back physically, academically, and emotionally. We were well on our way with him. We knew what we wanted to do and we were sure we could do it. Nat still had a few surprises in store for us, but the road ahead was clearly in sight.]

PEACE AND TRANQUILITY
COME TO GEORGE, TEMPORARILY

We had a nice peaceful week with George. He started off on the right track by attending his social studies class. However, almost before Jack began the class, George told him what he wanted to do. He wanted to draw a map of the United States. After he had drawn a fairly good rough outline of the map, Jack asked him where different places were. George got a couple correct, then placed Texas in Florida. Jack corrected him. "No, that's Florida."

That killed it. George didn't like to be corrected. He lost interest and walked out of the room as Jack followed him into the gym. George told Jack he didn't want social studies. He wanted the sandwich Henry had gone out to get for him.

After George had eaten his sandwich, he still didn't want social studies. He wanted to talk to Henry. So Henry took him for what he thought would be a short walk around the block.

George started a conversation about the school but quickly turned to his family. How come they wanted him to be so good when they weren't? Why should they punish him when they did the same thing? How come Henry wanted him to be good? Look what his family was doing. His father was stealing from his boss. Every chance he got he stole things he was supposed to deliver in his truck. Their stereo, TV set, and all kinds of electric things his mother had were stolen. His sister wasn't any better. She had been convicted of shoplifting. And his aunt in New Jersey was hiding out from the police, so his mother was living there taking care of her kids. The black leather jacket his mother didn't want him to wear because he looked like a hood—his father had the same jacket and no one bothered him about it.

"Why do you have to be like your parents?" Henry asked.

"Because they want me to," George answered.

Henry understood George's predicament. George's parents were constantly telling him to be good. But did they really mean it? Henry didn't think so. They themselves were delinquent. Did they really want a son who would be "better" than they were? Henry didn't think they did.

"Parents say many things," he told George, "and do other things. You don't always have to go by what they say or do. There are better ways."

George didn't like Henry's point.

"Nigger, you ain so fuckin good either," he insisted.

"No, I'm not," Henry admitted. "I have many problems."

"So maybe you should see a shrink too, Henry."

"I have."

"The nigger's seen a shrink."

Their conversation continued inconclusively . . . Henry trying to substitute his image for the confused models the Jacksons offered their son and George resisting and trying to provoke Henry.

Tuesday George came to school early, angry, loud, and hungry for attention. Since we were busy meeting, he had to wait . . . and George didn't like waiting. He pouted a while during warm-up and even refused to eat, but only for a while. After a few minutes and a few smiles from us, he put down three donuts in a hurry.

George was in a bad mood about something, a real bad mood. Henry talked to him for a while, but he remained sullen. He was in a drum-playing mood, an all-morning drum-playing mood—two hours or more of unbelievably steady pounding until lunchtime.

The drums were great for George. It was a blessing to have something to occupy George when he was uptight, but two hours of constant pounding full force was getting to everyone, even way up on the third floor. We knew we couldn't take much more of it as a steady diet. It was too much for us.

After lunch George wanted to work on an airplane model. Henry asked Connie to sit with George in the rec room while he worked, since Manuel was absent. Connie was surprised at the amount of patience George had with a model—a lot more than with people. He was friendly as he talked and worked, even when he discovered that a part was missing . . . until a part he had glued on popped off. Then he screamed, "You son of a bitch, whore. You broke it."

Connie hadn't even been near it. She took George's curses in stride and laughingly answered, "Well, George. You hit just about every curse word in that sentence."

George laughed too. Henry came down and encouraged him to continue screaming because yelling was better than hitting.

"You're a jerk. You're a fool," George insisted. "You want me to throw a temper tantrum."

"That's right," Henry agreed. "I do want you to throw a temper tantrum and you know why."

It worked, George settled down, and Henry was able to leave.

George remained calm for quite a while until he became frustrated with the model again. He grabbed Connie's hair and pulled it. Connie wasn't about to let him do that without putting up a defense.

"George, if you're going to pull my hair," she told him, "I'm going to pull yours."

That was the wrong strategy with short-haired George. There wasn't nearly enough hair to hold onto. When her active resistance failed, she tried passive resistance, going limp against his chest. That was the right strategy. George dropped her hair, put both of his arms around her, hugged her affectionately, and allowed a tender "Aw, Connie" to escape.

That was a little too much intimacy for George. Embarrassed by his show of feeling, he let her go and immediately began to curse her again in order to avoid the intimacy. His words were abusive, but their sting was gone. They were actually almost pleasant.

George came late Wednesday at eleven o'clock. He went straight to Connie's room and asked for donuts and coffee. After he had eaten five donuts, he asked for a book, not to read in class but to take home. He took out a grammar book which he had brought to school. They started. George obviously wasn't in the mood.

"What's a noun?" Connie asked.

"It's a verb."

"What's a verb?"

"Oh, just a word."

"George, just what do you want to do?" she asked, after only thirty seconds of grammar.

"Read my comic book," he answered as he unrolled it.

After he had finished his comic book he worked on his model airplane until the period ended. It wasn't English, but it was peaceful.

George was definitely coming along. We knew how to

help George. We could see we were getting to him. His rage was diminishing and his ability to love was growing. If only we had a soundproof drum room for him . . . if only we had a Henry just for him . . . if only we could keep the group to nine, we could handle him—unquestionably. But people were complaining about the drums, Henry had other boys to see. We would soon be expanding the program to at least twenty boys. Time and numbers were against us.

Thursday morning our psychologist gave us her report about George. It confirmed what we had been thinking. She reported that George was very suspicious of other people's motives and even more afraid that he was going to be hurt or overwhelmed by them. His fears were so intense that he had to defend himself against even mild criticisms which he experienced as major infringements of his integrity. She felt that he was capable of uncontrolled rage during which he could be extremely dangerous. And she believed that after he had acted it out he became so confused that he was often unable to remember his behavior.

We became silent. We had been talkative while she reported about George's intellectual and academic functioning. But when she spoke about uncontrolled rage and lapses of memory, that was scary. Although we had more than suspected it from his behavior, she was confirming our fears and it was hitting us hard—almost stunning us.

We asked her to suggest an approach for dealing with him. She continued: George was an extremely infantile youngster who could become very dependent on the adults who satisfied his basic infantile needs. Feeding would be one way of relating to him. Physical contact would be another. If we could somehow contain his rage for a while and develop a very dependent relationship between him and an adult, we could help him develop to a point where he could adjust to the world without all of his pent-up rage. However, until that happened, she thought there was a real possibility that George would hurt somebody.

We were exactly where we had been before hearing the test results. George couldn't function in class—we had an idea why. He was full of rage—we had an idea why. He was dangerous—we had all come to realize that. We had an approach which we thought might work—if we had the time and manpower. We had placed our bets. We would see if we had chosen well.

Speaking of the devil, George came to school late, looking like he was up to something. He walked into the rec room and asked for Nat, who hadn't arrived yet. Ed asked him if he wanted to play ball. No, he needed Nat. Nat was supposed to bring something to school for him. "What?" It was hush, hush, big-secret stuff. George left the gym and checked each room for Nat. No Nat. Then George said he was going home. Instead he started a Ping-Pong game with Ed, quit, went into the art studio, spun the potter's wheel, made inkblots for the "crazy psychologist upstairs" who was testing Manuel, burst into her office, and offered them to her.

George was getting bored. Henry wasn't in on Thursdays. Whatever George had planned with Nat wasn't coming off because there was no Nat. He went looking for Herb, told him he wanted his subway tokens to go home, then left the office without his tokens to play the drums.

Connie went looking for George at the start of the second period. He wasn't playing the drums. He was in Natalie's office dialing the phone. Connie's immediate impulse was to stop him. She grabbed the receiver and yanked it. As soon as George put up a struggle, she realized her mistake and disengaged herself. The fun was over. So George left the building.

He returned to the gym about fifteen minutes later. Herb

was talking to Larry. Ed was sitting nearby with Harold. George took out a pint of sherry—the cheap kind. He offered to sell it to Herb. Herb laughed, said he didn't want to buy it, and asked George where he had gotten it. George claimed he had bought it in one of the nearby bars with his brother's draft card.

George repeated his offer to sell the wine. Herb said he would *take* the wine for his party Saturday evening if George wanted to *give* it to him. George wasn't ready to give it away. He asked Larry and Harold if they wanted a drink. They refused but not without saving face. Harold broke the seal, acted like he might take a swig, but said "No." Larry also opened the bottle, stuck his finger in it, tasted it, and said he never drank wine either. After offering everyone in the school a drink and finding no takers, George needed his own face-saving device. He left, returned a few minutes later with a dollar in his hand which he said he had gotten from some bum who bought the pint of wine from him. At least he had made a sucker out of some bum. Having saved his face, he was ready to leave for the day.

NOT SO QUIET ONES

While George and Nat were beginning to find some inhibitions, the withdrawn ones, Manuel and Willie, were beginning to lose some of theirs. Manuel missed school Monday and Tuesday. When he came on Wednesday Herb took him aside to ask him where he had been. Manuel seemed annoyed—secretive, bothered. If he had to answer, he wasn't going to say more than he wanted to say. He smiled a funny smile and said, "I din feel good. I slep late."

Herb thought it was more than that, but he didn't see much sense in pushing it.

Manuel was equally definite about his desires with Connie. He didn't want to read. He wanted to go shopping for glasses. He didn't want just any frames. He wanted black frames with a silver line along the sides. He wanted something to eat. He was definite about that too. He wanted a hamburger and an orange drink for breakfast.

As he ate, Manuel told Connie that he had been sick Monday and Tuesday. Then he admitted that he hadn't really been sick on Tuesday. He left the house in the morning, goofed around, came home for lunch, told his mother that he had only a half day of school, and goofed around for the rest of the day.

"A guy needs a day off once in a while. Right?" he added.

Connie smiled to herself. That was progress, if it was true.

[We were trying to get Manuel to be less constricted, less "goody-goody." If he acted out a little, it would give us the opportunity to convince him that his fears and suspicions about us—and perhaps others as well—weren't justified.]

Manuel was also beginning to stand up to the boys, especially George. However, he was still using us to protect his rights for him. He complained to Herb that the boys were stealing his music time. That's why he wasn't practicing, because the boys were stealing his time. Actually, even when he was the first one in the music room he left when someone wanted to use it. Herb had been encouraging Manuel to tell the boys to wait until he finished using the room. However Manuel wasn't ready for that.

Manuel's thinking was still confused, but he was keeping fewer secrets from us. They were coming out in almost every reading session. During one class when he couldn't read the word "crib," Connie said, "You know what a crib is."

"Yeah," he answered. "I slep in one. Did Herbie sleep in one?"

"Yes, Herbie probably did."

"Herbie came out wearin glasses. Ya know, a guy was born in a army uniform."

"That's just a joke."

"No, no, i's really true. There's a guy born in a army uniform. He was born dress."

Connie led Manuel into a discussion about birth in order to correct him. Instead, she learned about another of his distortions.

Manuel believed that he and his older brother had been inside his mother together at the same time. They had lots of fights inside his mother. He even knocked his brother out once. His brother was older because the doctor pulled his brother out of his mother's stomach and left Manuel there. Then two years later he came and pulled him out too. That was why Manuel was younger.

Connie didn't want to admit to herself that Manuel actually believed what he said, but he did. Even though Manuel knew that it took nine months to be born, he clung to the idea that he and his brother were inside his mother together. He even remembered kicking his mother's stomach and hurting his brother. He was a little embarrassed about the idea, but he believed it.

Willie was also moving out, especially with Manuel. He began by teasing Manuel whenever he beat him in Ping-Pong. When that proved to be safe, Willie started a grab-your-hat-game. He would grab Manuel's hat and run outside, laughing. Then he would run back in the building, let Manuel grab his hat, and run after him. We had been congratulating both of them and telling them that there were some kids who had to control themselves more, and others, like them, who had to express themselves more.

Willie was also playing with George. He stood in front of us with George, put his arm around him, and whispered in his ear for a good two or three minutes, "Yeah, yeah, what about this, bzz, bzz." George was cool. "Uh, I don't know, we'll see." We didn't know what they were whispering about, but Willie looked as if he was trying to use George to get something he wanted. It seemed like he was cooking something up. Then we realized that wasn't it. Willie was too slick to do things out in the open, right in front of us, almost calling attention to himself. He was teasing us. He was telling us, "See, I'm cooking up something, but you don't know what." He was calling attention to himself. He was agreeing with us that it was all right to kid around.

Yet like Manuel, Willie was still far from spontaneous or assertive. Like Manuel, instead of standing up for himself, he still complained about the boys who interfered with his piano practicing. When we gave him the same answer as we had given Manuel—better to stand up for yourself than complain to us—he didn't like it.

"I'm not complaining about them," he answered.

"No, Willie, you're not complaining about them. But that may be your problem."

"My problem is that I don't get enough time to practice in the music room."

"Your problem is that you don't want to admit your feelings."

MAGNIFICENT MASOCHIST

Harold cut school Monday and Tuesday. We called his house Tuesday evening and learned that he hadn't been home for a few days. No one had heard from him since Friday. Something was going on. He was the main topic of our Wednesday morning meeting. We realized that we had been too successful in making Harold aware of some of his limitations, and not successful enough in providing him with the satisfaction and attention he needed to like himself. Immediately we resolved to give him as much approval as possible. That wouldn't be easy. We expected that the more we attempted to provide Harold with success and acceptance, the more he would try to push us to reject him.

A few minutes before our meeting broke up, Harold called to ask us, "What cookin?"

"We were wondering what happened to you," Herb answered.

"No big deal. I okay. Ya want me ta come ta thkool?"

"Of course you should come to school."

"You really want me ta come?"

"Yes, silly, we really want you to come."

"Okay I come."

"What time?"

"Lun'htime."

"Can't you make it earlier?"

"Eleven, maybe."

"Good."

We were pleased that Harold was coming, puzzled about what he had been doing, and determined to be nice to him no matter what. He came at eleven as he had promised and immediately began his game. First he pressed Herb to let him go to a stamp exhibition on Friday when the boys went on a trip. Herb got that I'm-being-manipulated feeling, which he didn't like. He explained to Harold, as he had done many times, that he could go to stamp exhibits or the UN, his two favorite trips, whenever he wanted to. We would not provide a special trip for him.

[Harold still had that knack for turning people off and getting turned down. Still Herb should have thought some more before acting. Harold had been told repeatedly that we would not set up a special stamp trip for him. Herb should have made an exception . . . probably.]

Then Harold started on Connie. Would she take him to the auction down the street, the one she had taken Manuel to? She would try her best, she answered. She would if it were at all possible.

[Connie wanted to take Harold. It would be a good move, the kind we had talked about in the meeting. Harold felt unwanted, unloved, unneeded. She would take him, if she could. But she didn't know what might really stop her. The only obstacles she anticipated were the demands of the school and the other boys. She didn't anticipate Harold's skills in getting rejected.]

It was time for social studies. Harold went on his own. Jack didn't have to get him for the first time in weeks. They had been working on a time line of colonial America the previous week. Instead of ordering the items chronologically, Harold had organized them into subject groups. Jack felt he had to correct Harold, but he wanted to do so without putting Harold down. He told Harold, as gently as he could, that subject headings were not the same as time lines. But Harold insisted.

"Well, I like ta do it thith way."

"Harold, it isn't what I asked you to do," Jack explained again. "It's not the same as a time line."

"Why?"

"Because you can't see the relationship between events under subject headings the way you can under a time line. The time line lays out the events according to when they happen. So you can see the dates and the importance that one event had in relation to another event."

Harold grabbed for his papers to tear them up.

"No! Don't tear them up, they're still good. They're important, but they're not the same thing as a time line. Now what I'd like to do with you today is . . ."

Jack did it. He corrected Harold without putting him down. The class was going along beautifully. Jack felt his plan was working. It was, but outside forces were about to interfere.

Jack was writing on the blackboard. George opened the door. Jack didn't like his back turned toward George when he wasn't sure what condition George was in. He looked over his shoulder. George had one of his self-satisfied smiles on his face. While Jack's back had been turned, he had done something to Harold. Jack didn't think it was much. He hoped it wasn't much. He was wrong. Harold jumped up, knocked over his chair, and started after George. Jack put his arms on Harold's shoulders, to calm him rather than stop him. Harold could have broken away, but he didn't. Jack told George to leave. George started to walk out the door with his back to Harold who picked up a wastebasket. Jack grabbed his arm as he threw it, and it fell short.

Meanwhile Connie had arranged her afternoon so she could take Harold to the auction. After lunch, when everyone had finished eating, Harold was still teasingly playing with his food while Connie was waiting impatiently. Harold fiddle-faddled around a while longer, then finally finished. Connie got up to go. Harold still wasn't ready. He wanted Connie to get his allowance and carfare for him so he could go right home after the auction. Connie went upstairs, got the money and her coat, and returned to the dining room. Harold wasn't there. She trudged upstairs to the rec room to look for him. There he was, playing Ping-Pong. Connie was becoming even more impatient. Her foot was tapping rapidly and firmly as she said, "Okay, Harold, let's go if we're going."

That's what Harold was looking for. He smiled slightly and said innocently, "In a few minute. I playin."

Connie got that I-have-to-wait-until-*he's*-ready feeling and raged at him.

"Well, there's no point in going since it's already started, unless we leave now. It gets boring at the end."

Harold was angrily satisfied as he replied, "Well then, juth forget it, damn it. Gi me my money anyway."

"No," Connie retaliated. "The money can stay here until it's time to leave."

She went back upstairs, deposited the money with Phyllis, took off her coat, then came back down to the gym. Harold came over to her, smiled, and said, "Come on. Les play a game."

"Play a game. He has a nerve," Connie thought as she responded as Harold probably wanted her to, by explaining to him that she was much too irritated to play a game with him. She had tried to be agreeable, she told him, but she had been slapped down.

Connie's statement was the rejection that Harold had been hopefully expecting.

"Go ta hell," he shouted. "I hate you."

A few short hours before we had all resolved to give Harold special attention, acceptance, "nice nice," and success. But Harold was a tough opponent. Harold intensified his attack the next day. He had been good to Jack the day before. He had to make up for it. Not to go to class on time was all right for openers. Jack went down to fetch him from the gym where he was playing Ping-Pong with Ed.

"Harold, it's time for social studies class," Jack called from the door.

"I juth want to play Ping-Pong a lil bit more. I been in math all day with Bill. My head hurt. I need a few minute reth," Harold answered.

Jack submitted with a, "Fine! You can play Ping-Pong for five minutes, then come up to class. I'm going up. I'll see you in five minutes."

Jack went into his room and continued to work. Ed followed him up about a minute later.

"Aren't you playing Ping-Pong with Harold?" Jack asked, surprised to see him. Ed explained that Harold had been playing Ping-Pong in the gym with Bill for at least fifteen minutes before Jack called for him. That conflicted with what Harold had told Jack. Jack didn't like that. Harold had also promised Ed that he would go up to social studies as soon as Jack called for him. Jack didn't like that either. He returned to the gym and confronted Harold, who innocently denied that he had been playing Ping-Pong very long.

"Ath Bill," he suggested to Jack.

Jack was getting nowhere, just frustrated.

"Well, Harold," he said in a controlled but angry voice, "if you don't want to take social studies that's okay. I'll just wait here for the five minutes anyway."

As he waited, Harold said to him, "Thee, I never play a game, we juth volley."

"No, you never play the game of Ping-Pong," Jack answered.

"What do you mean?"

Jack told him what he had meant.

"Well, you've been playing a game all morning. It's called con."

Five minutes later Harold was upstairs in social studies working—slowly—unbelievably slowly—unbearably slowly. By the end of the period he had added only three events to his time line. Harold was satisfied but Jack wasn't. Jack knew he was supposed to give Harold approval, but Harold's passive resistance had worn him down. Jack just couldn't take the frustration any longer. He had to say something or explode.

"Harold! I don't see how we're ever going to get through a year's work if you insist on fooling around like this."

"I can take two year ta take thith course. I only need three credit in hithtry and I have two now."

"No, you need three and a half credits."

"No!" Harold insisted. "Only three credit. Thath what my guidanth teatyer told me."

"Harold!" Jack argued back, "I talked to Herb and you need three and a half credits."

But Harold wouldn't admit anything.

"Herbie don't know what he talkin about," he insisted as the discussion ended because Jack was too angry to continue it.

Harold had really gotten to Jack. Damn it, Jack thought to himself, he knows he needs three and a half credits. Herb told him and me together. I'm going to insist that he conform at least structurally to an academic situation. If he insists on being late for class that'll be the end of class. He won't have class that day. God damn it! If he wants credit, he's going to have to attend class and do the work.

Harold tried for one more rejection. Natalie was going to the beauty parlor in the afternoon. During lunch Harold asked her if he could go along. When she said yes, he told her never mind, with a look of surprise which seemed to say, "You're really going to take me?" A few minutes later, Harold had changed his mind again. He wanted to go. Natalie told him to check with Herb first. Harold knocked on Herb's door. There was no answer. He called out.

"Herbie, I goin ta the beauty parlor with Natalie. Okay?"

Herb didn't answer "No." So Harold thought he had Herb's permission.

[Herb hadn't even been in the office, but he hadn't said no. It was a beautiful Harold bit.]

Anyway, the trip was a good trip, a therapeutic trip because Harold couldn't get Natalie to reject him no matter what he tried. He started by coughing up saliva and phlegm and spitting it on the floor of the school, then in the streets, and finally on parked cars. Natalie wouldn't respond. He asked her to buy a book for him. Natalie wouldn't refuse. He asked her to take him to a stamp store. Natalie wouldn't say no.

As they were about to walk into the stamp store Harold told her he was going to steal some stamps. That made Natalie nervous. She asked him not to. Harold agreed. Then after they had gone inside he suddenly turned pale and ran for the door because he was afraid that he really would steal some stamps. Natalie told him that she was sure he could control himself.

"You thtill new," he said. "You don know about me yet." Another supportive statement from Natalie and they were on their way back to the school.

[Harold got rejection from Jack and acceptance from Natalie. Was it because of their different personalities or their different situations? What would have happened if their positions were interchanged—if Natalie was his social studies teacher and Jack his tripper? Would Jack become a good guy? Would Natalie get involved in the same kinds of things that plagued Connie? Probably.]

It wasn't all bad with Harold. Harold had made a new group of friends—"the Diggers." He had lived with them in one of their free apartments and ate their free food during the five days that he hadn't slept at home. He liked the Diggers, he told us. They understood the good life. He liked them and they liked him.

The Diggers were pre-hippie commune types. They ran "free stores" and provided free services to lost and lonely people. At first we were skeptical about Harold's story. We would find out later that he hadn't been exaggerating.

FAMILY AFFAIR

Henry continued to work closely with Mr. and Mrs. Russo. They were arguing constantly at home. Henry believed that he had brought the hostility between them out into the open by uncovering the partnership Mrs. Russo and Don had formed against Mr. Russo. Henry felt that their sudden awareness of the hostility between them had frightened them. With that in mind, Henry tried to reassure the Russos that their conflict and anger would diminish rather than increase. Although the relationships among the Russos were changing, Don's behavior at home wasn't. Henry thought it would be a while before that happened.

Don wasn't getting along any better with Lisa either. Lisa was still annoyed about Don's possessiveness. She had been threatening to break off with him, but she wanted to talk to Henry before she made a final decision.

When Henry got together with Lisa and Don, he helped them resolve the immediate issue between them. But Lisa was clearly moving further away from the kind of serious involvement Don wanted.

STANLEY MAKES IT

Before the week ended Stanley departed for the Institute and a new student, Lenny, Don's friend, arrived. Stanley had told Herb that he wasn't going to come to school during the week. He wanted to treat himself to a last taste of freedom before he began training at the Institute. He called the school first thing Monday morning to find out how to get to the Institute by subway. Herb offered to call the Institute to find out what subway he should take and what stop he should get off at. He also offered to meet Stanley in the city for a drink after his first day of work. Stanley said he wasn't sure if he wanted to meet Herb Thursday. They left it open.

Herb would be in school all day Thursday. If Stanley wanted to meet him, he could call sometime before the end of the day.

We had done all we could to pave Stanley's way. We had arranged for Stanley to get release time to come to the school. We had talked to Stanley's social worker at the Institute about procedures that might help Stanley adjust to the new place. We had suggested that he ask Stanley's boss, who was known to be fair but tough, to tone himself down a little with Stanley. We had told the social worker about the tremendous progress Stanley had made, in the hope that he would view Stanley more optimistically than their staff had done in the initial intake meeting. Perhaps equally important, Henry had made arrangements to continue giving Stanley driving lessons.

Stanley called Thursday afternoon. Herb met him after work in a midtown cocktail lounge. As they walked in, Stanley looked around and said, "Ay, this is a sclusive place."

"Did that make him feel nervous?" Herb asked.

"No. He felt good," he answered with a big smile on his face. A waitress came by and offered him hors d'oeuvres. Stanley didn't know what to make of that.

"A' they free?" he asked.

"Yes," Herb answered.

Again he smiled.

Herb asked about his "job," as Stanley called his training. Stanley's day had been boring because his instructor was out. Stanley didn't get involved in printing. He just worked around. He delivered packages from receiving and took care of some papers. He didn't learn anything about the machines. The people seemed nice, but the girls were kind of ugly, and besides, they were Spanish. The guys told him that there were good salaries and a good union. Stanley said he still liked IBM, but maybe, he added, he would have gotten bored in the IBM department.

Herb encouraged Stanley to talk about the money he was going to earn. Stanley enjoyed that. He said he was going to save most of it. Herb suggested Stanley might find that he was spending more than he planned to. Stanley smiled and said, "Yeah, well, maybe I won't save so much."

He told Herb that he was going to buy clothes, because he only had one pair of pants and he didn't have the clothes he liked. Herb asked him if he wanted to come down to the school occasionally. Stanley didn't think so because it meant money out of his pocket.

"I don know why I did it," he said to Herb, "but I asked ta work from nine to five instead a nine ta four."

"Why?"

"Ta make money."

"Then what do you mean you don't know why you did it? Do you mean that you're not sure if you can work the extra hour or not?" Herb asked.

"Yeah," Stanley answered.

Stanley was also worried about this guy who had been talking to him. He didn't really want to get involved with him, but maybe he would. The guy was married, but he talked about screwing women all over the country, and he had promised Stanley that he would fix him up with some girls. Stanley didn't trust him because there was something wrong about him.

There were some other guys in the print shop that he liked. He didn't know how it happened, but he had lunch with four guys in the program. He was surprised that he had made friends so easily. It had been a good first day. Stanley thought he was going to like it. Herb thought so too.

Monday, March 20, through Wednesday, March 22

WINTER'S LAST DAYS

Winter's last days were pleasant ones. Perhaps it was the nearness of the vacation. Whatever the reason, all the boys kept busy in the class making an extra effort, all except for George.

Early in the week Herb was showing some visitors from Columbia University through the school. As one of them had just remarked about how well adjusted the boys were, they passed Connie's door and heard an argument starting. Herb opened the door to shouts of "Cheating bitch." The visitors looked in curiously. Connie looked back embarrassedly.

"Everything's under control—George is fine," she told Herb, who wasn't convinced.

"Do you think George can work?" Herb asked in a way that reminded Connie of the many times she had been unable to disengage herself from George.

"No, no, I don't think so," Connie agreed. "We'll go down to the rec room instead."

That didn't work. George was angry at Connie, not English.

Norm's turn was next. As soon as George went into the shop he started messing with the other boys' projects. Norm told him to stop. He did, but he started playing with a power saw instead. Norm didn't like playing around in his shop. He told him to stop. Again George listened. Then George quietly picked up a hand saw, walked up behind Norm, and ran it over the veins in Norm's wrist with just enough pressure to cut the skin without cutting the vein. Norm could take the kid's aggression. He kept his cool. So George wasn't satisfied. He picked up a handful of sawdust and threw it at Norm, then another and another. Now Norm had enough. He showered George with the stuff, told him to "Get out and stay out," and ran out after him into the hall as the visitors were passing by.

It was a sight to remember—two sawdust snowmen running out of the room into a group of university people who had been listening to the commotion through the door. Herb smiled as he thought to himself: "See, I told you we have problems."

George ran back into the shop. Norm followed him in and gently attempted to move him out explaining to the audience that everything was okay. Finally, just as he got George out of the door, he reached back with his foot and kicked Norm in the shins. Norm's face turned red with anger.

George became anxious when he saw just what he had done. He took the offensive.

"You threw sawdust at me, nigger. You threw sawdust at me," he shouted as if he had done nothing to provoke Norm. "I wanna work on my plane in the room." Norm refused. George asked if he could get his plane and some tools from the room so he could work on them in the gym. Norm and Herb looked at each other. Although they weren't sure whether George could control himself, they decided to take a chance and let him get the tools. But George sat down in the shop and began to work.

Norm gently nudged him out of the room and closed the door. George screamed, "Mothafucker. I'm gonna get you," and kicked the door down with one good blow. Herb shouted "Stop!" at the top of his lungs. George did a double-take, gained control of himself, and marched off toward the stairs.

Herb caught up with him, talked to him very briefly, walked him into the dining hall, and took the drums out for him. George played the drums for a while. Then about fifteen minutes later he returned, asked for his tokens, and left without saying anything.

APRIL FOOL IN MARCH

The boys gave us our April Fools' joke early because they were going to be on vacation April first. In the middle of our afternoon staff meeting we received a telephone call from Macy's department store. They had caught a young man, Harold Stern, stealing stamps. He had given them our name as a reference. Herb started to handle the situation over the phone until Harold took the phone on the other end and laughed. He was drunk at Larry's house. Larry's friend Johnny had called us up. Herb told them to take a cab back to the school because he wanted to talk to them.

Norm and Herb were waiting for the boys when they returned to the school. Larry and Johnny were high on pills. Harold was drunk half out of his mind.

"You're drunk as hell. What's up?" Herb asked Harold.

"We were jutht kiddin you, Herbie pal, and you fell for it."

"Kidding—that doesn't sound like why you called," Herb answered.

"Here come the headthrinkin thtuff. Okay, why did I call? Read my mine—go head," Harold challenged.

"You can knock it if you want to, but it's more than coincidence that you told us you were caught stealing stamps. That was why you were sent here in the first place."

"Tho!"

"So it sounds like you want us to treat you like we did when you first came here. More attention."

"That thit."

Herb explained why it wasn't shit. Then he asked Norm to take Larry and Harold to a movie so that they would keep off the streets and out of trouble while they were high. Larry refused to go with Harold, he wanted to go with his friend Johnny. So Norm took Harold to a movie by himself.

Herb wanted to keep Larry and Johnny out of trouble. Since he had to go to Hofstra University that evening to teach, he took them with him out to Long Island.

As the three of them rode along, Larry began boasting about his past escapades. Johnny joined him.

Herb asked, "How are you two making out now that you're not stealing? John, you don't even get seven dollars a week from us and you don't have a job."

"We got ways—it's not hard to get money," John answered.

"What do you mean?" Herb asked.

"Queers, man, homos—they'll always give you five bucks to let them blow you."

Larry hadn't expected Johnny's revelation. It was too much of a put-down.

"But, man, those queers're weird. They're disgustin. I gotta be high to take em," Larry added to protect his reputation with us. "I almost killed one the first time it happened. I was passed out in a party when this queer bastard zipped my pants down and blew me. I was so high I couldn't feel nothin but wet. I would of killed the prick if he didn't whip out ten bucks."

JOHNNY: Sometimes we roll em if they screw around with us. They have it coming, the queer bastards.

LARRY: Time Square is full of queers—you can't take a piss without some queer starin at your dick.

JOHNNY: And they got pimps who set them up. They give you the money for them and you meet them somewheres. Just like a whore.

LARRY: Sometimes you take the money and don't meet them.

HERB: Then what happens?

LARRY: Nothin. Them queers know we'd kick the shit out of em.

[Larry had made his point. He didn't have to feel ashamed or guilty because he wasn't a queer. How could he be one? He didn't like them. They were disgusting.]

The topic changed to crime. Johnny told Herb he had all kinds of connections. He had been into things for a long time, or so he claimed, ever since he was a kid. Then Johnny checked himself and changed his tune to his special story for social-working-bleeding-heart types. He was an orphan. He had kicked around from foster home to foster home, one worse than the other, until he was finally sent away to a treatment center. They had been good to him there, but when he returned to the city he got into trouble again, then reform school. He hadn't been caught since then.

Larry changed the topic to cars.

"Man, drivin's cool. Like flying if you go fast enough. Once——"

"Don't let him ever drive your car, Herbie," Johnny interrupted. "He'll crack it up like he did his mother's and them cars we borrowed."

"Really?" Herb asked.

"Yeah, man! I love crashes, you never know what's gonna happen. It's a groove," Larry answered.

"What do you mean, John, borrow a car?" Herb asked in a delayed reaction.

"We see a car that's open, so we jump the wires, ride it, then leave it."

"That's not borrowing. That's stealing."

"We don't keep it."

"But you don't ask permission either."

"If they're stupid enough to leave the car open, it's their fault."

Herb didn't answer. Larry had just stepped down on Herb's foot—the one on the gas pedal—lightly, but noticeably.

"Get your goddamn foot off! Now!"

"Man, don't you wanna fly?"

"Keep your fucking foot off the pedal and stop kidding around."

Larry smiled and cooled it. The conversation continued for a few more minutes until they arrived at Hofstra. Herb took them to the cafeteria and he gave them some spending money, so they could pass the time.

After class Herb was surprised to find Larry and Johnny sitting outside the door. They were excited about something. Johnny and Larry confessed to Natalie, who was also at the class, that Larry had messed up Herb's car. That's what they were excited about. They had disconnected some wires and some fuses so that it couldn't start. Herb wasn't sure if it was true or not. When he investigated, he found it was true. Larry roared with laughter while Johnny played innocent. Larry didn't like that.

"If you're innocent, how come you held the flashlight when I did it?"

Finally, Larry put all the parts back, and Herb was able to start the car. It was five minutes to eleven when Herb dropped the boys off at the subway . . . a long day but very revealing.

VACATION TRIPS

We had planned four trips for the boys. The first was on the last day of school—a good way to end school and begin a vacation. The boys were going to an expensive restaurant, then to a Broadway movie.

When it was time to go, Connie and Jack got the group together and started for the subway. There was plenty of fresh-fallen snow. So despite warnings by Connie and Jack the boys threw snowballs at everybody and everything. They hit a few buses and barely missed an old man along the way. Connie and Jack both finally decided that it was useless to try to stop them, especially when Jack got hit on the ear with a snowball. Once they got down into the subway, they quieted down a little. The trip to Grand Central was uneventful except for the fact that Larry, George, and Nat rode between the cars, Harold continued spitting, and the boys continued cursing.

The restaurant was swank, very plush. The boys were greeted by a maître d' who took them to a special table upstairs. When they sat down at the table they immediately became confused about whose silverware and water goblet was whose. A couple of them, George in particular, were intimidated by the rich atmosphere. Harold looked at the menu and picked the most expensive meal—T-bone steak for seven dollars. Some of the other boys said they wanted the same thing. Connie told them to look at the other side of the menu where there were other steaks listed at four dollars. Harold started in.

"What the matter. Don't be cheap, the thkool pay you back!"

"Yeah," George chimed in, "the school robs a bank every week anyway! If Henry was here he'd get us the steak! and Herbie too, and Bill, but not Norm. He's cheap too."

Meanwhile the waitress stood waiting.

Manuel and Nat couldn't read the menu—Connie took time out from her argument with Harold and George to read it to them. George looked at the waitress.

"I don't like none of this crap sept lobster. Gimme lobster."

The waitress looked at Connie.

"The lobster will take a while—can you wait?" she asked.

"Not really, we have to leave for the movies soon," Connie replied.

Connie's comment gave George something to gripe about. Or perhaps he really felt put out about the lobster. He argued with Connie about the lobster, then turned to the waitress and said, "Gimme a damn cheeseburger and make sure the cheese melts."

Nat wanted "a mess of fried fish," but the restaurant didn't serve fried fish.

"Then gimme swamps," he said.

Neither Connie nor Jack knew what swamps were. Nat couldn't explain because he had never eaten them. Willie figured out what they were. "Shrimps." Nat had ordered shrimps. More arguing about T-bone steaks.

Meanwhile the waitress waited.

Finally, everyone chose the four dollar steak or the roast beef.

Then the waitress made a mistake. She asked them what they wanted to drink.

"Scotch, bourbon, gin, rye—Sneaky Pete, Five-Star."

The waitress looked helplessly toward Jack this time—another argument. Finally they settled on Cokes, ginger ale, orange soda, and other less potent beverages. The waitress started to walk away, but before she could get herself out of hearing range, George declared to Connie: "An the bitch betta not take her sweet-ass time with the food."

Sodas and salads arrived and were consumed almost instantaneously. Feet and hand tapping began. None of the boys had ever eaten in a restaurant which cooked food to order and they weren't used to waiting.

"Where's the jukebox?"

"Where's the bathroom?"

"Where's the food?"

"I want another fuckin Coke."

"I want two," added Harold.

Another round of drinks—two for Harold.

The more uncomfortable the boys felt, the more they cursed. Fortunately they had a special table upstairs—by themselves. (Was it coincidence or had the maître d' known what he was doing?)

The waitress brought a loaf of warm bread. The boys got a kick out of that.

"Fresh bread—they got their own bakery."

The food arrived, very pretty-looking with little sticks designating whether the meat was rare, medium, or well, and parsley for decoration. Everyone seemed satisfied except George who pushed his plate away as the waitress placed it in front of him and told her, "I wouldn give this shit to my daughter."

The waitress took it admirably.

"What's this wood for?"

"Rare, medium, and well sticks," Connie explained.

"What's this green stuff? It tastes like shit!"

"Parsley," Connie explained.

"What's this loose bird turd for?"

"Sour cream for the baked potato," Jack explained.

Everyone dug in. It became relatively quiet.

After a few minutes Larry made a big point of saying that he wanted to bring his aunt and his cousin for dinner. He had a lot of questions for Connie and Jack. Exactly how much would it cost for the three of them to have drinks and the best steak that there was? How should he go about making reservations? Should he ask for an upstairs table or a downstairs table? And so on. He asked Connie if she would lend him thirty dollars. He asked Jack. Then, "Anybody got thirty dollars?" A grandstand gesture.

"Why doya want to spend money on them?" George asked.

"Well, it's the ladies' birthday," Larry answered and let it go at that.

They made their way through lunch. The bill arrived. Connie paid it and left a tip. Nat picked it up. It looked large to him. He showed it to George who said, "The next time Henry takes me to eat, tell him I don want any food, just gimme the tip."

Nat pretended to pocket the tip. Connie wondered if they would have another scene. But she didn't have to worry because he put it back, crumpled but whole.

One more little incident. Harold had done his thing. As they walked out the front door, he took out the loot from under his jacket. One ashtray, seven books of matches, and two champagne glasses.

It was an interesting and good experience, Connie thought to herself, although a little nightmarish.

[The restaurant had been a "happening." The boys had been uncomfortable. However, they had enjoyed it. Perhaps it would have been better if they had gone through a rehearsal! The maître d' will greet us and treat us like we're special. Don't let that bother you. You are. Your glass is to your right. You don't have to eat the green parsley. It's a decoration. One thing for sure, our boys had been to an "expensive" restaurant.]

The following Tuesday Henry took Nat and Carlos to the movies while Norm took most of the other boys on a fishing trip. On Friday Herb and Jack took the boys to the amusement park. Carlos showed up with a friend.

As soon as tickets for the rides and the spending money was divided up, Don and Manuel took off by themselves. They had both brought extra money. Perhaps they wanted to spend it without sharing it with the others. The roller coaster attracted the boys' attention first.

"Let go on the roller coather," Harold suggested.

"Yeah!"

"How many tickets do you need?"

"Six tickets."

"Six tickets! Ain't worth it," Nat declared, chickening out in a face-saving way.

Carlos joined him. They were both afraid. The others went on.

"Come on, there's custard," Nat said to Carlos as he walked down the path. Carlos followed. Three girls passed. Carlos looked at one of them.

"Hiya, baby."

"Fuck you, spic."

"Back ta you, *puta*."

"Ha!"

After the ride the others joined them. They reached the Loop-the-Loop. Nat didn't want to ride that one either. Jack didn't blame him. All it did was make you sick by turning you around and upside down at the same time. But the others shamed Nat into it. He looked sick when he got off and said he wasn't going on any more "sick rides."

The group split in two. Herb, Nat, Carlos, and his friend walked on. They reached the drive-your-own-hot-rod cars. The line was long but that didn't matter. They all wanted to go on. They waited. It was almost their turn when the ticket-taker yelled to a kid in front of Carlos to put out his cigarette. It had nothing to do with Carlos but he got involved.

"Why can he smoke? I don see no sign. He kin smoke."

"Who asked you—fresh kid," the man answered as he grabbed Carlos by the shoulders and turned him toward three different No Smoking signs.

"I din see it. I din see it," Carlos pleaded.

"Then shut up next time," the man answered angrily.

Herb watched, waiting to calm things down if need be. However, Carlos kept quiet.

Carlos and his friend had squeezed their way ahead of a few people so that when they got into their cars Nat and Herb were still half a dozen people behind. Finally Nat and Herb got into a car and started around the course. Shit! When they reached the halfway mark they could see the ticket-taker push Carlos as he got out of his car. Carlos pushed him back. It looked like they were about to start fighting. There was nothing Herb could do. Herb couldn't stop the car. He had to wait until they reached the end. By the time the car came to a stop, the man had his jacket off and was asking Carlos to fight. Carlos looked afraid, but he wasn't backing away. He looked scared, but he was getting ready to defend himself and his *machismo*. Herb rushed over, grabbed Carlos, and lifted him over the guard rail separating him from the man. The man kept cursing and screaming and daring Carlos to fight. He looked like a crazy man. "Why the hell did he start with Carlos?" Herb wondered. Herb held Carlos, who pretended that he didn't want to leave (more *machismo*), and screamed: "I kill im, I kill im. He push me cause I din know how ta drive. I don know how ta drive a car. I's not my fault I don know how ta drive a car—i's not my fault."

When they rejoined the others, Carlos told the boys he had a fight with a big man and beat him up. Later when they met Don and Manuel, Nat had become part of the story. It became: he and Nat had a swing-out with two men and they would have killed the men if Herb hadn't interfered.

The group stayed together for the rest of the afternoon. No arguments, difficulties, or incidents. Time for one more ride before returning home—the fun house. As they walked through they all noticed a big-breasted sloppy woman with tight-fitting knitted clothes, admiring herself in the funny mirrors. She just couldn't drag herself away from the mirror especially when she noticed the boys staring at her. When they reached the end, Nat and Carlos decided to go back to the woman. They returned about five minutes later with a story about the good time they'd had with her.

It was a fun trip. Lots of food and fun, only one incident, and a hint of sex. The surprising thing was how well the boys had managed their money. No one was broke. Everyone had saved his carfare. Some even had extra besides. And no one was late for the return trip home.

VACATION CONVERSATION

Although we didn't see Stanley during the vacation, we heard from him and his social worker at the Institute. Stanley's social worker called Herb at home to say that Stanley hadn't come in. The social worker had called Stanley's house, but there was no answer. He was concerned because it was the second day in a row that Stanley had missed. Herb assured him that Stanley was just about over his truancy and lateness problem. However Stanley seemed reluctant to work on the large presses and spent most of the time on smaller machines. The worker thought Stanley was probably afraid that he wouldn't be able to work them. Herb said that Stanley had reported just the opposite.

Four or five minutes after Herb hung up, Stanley called him and said that he had overslept. Herb advised him to get dressed as quickly as he could and go to work because his worker was waiting.

"That's why I called," Stanley answered. "I ain't sure I wanna work there."

"Well, do you want to?" Herb asked.

"Yeah."

"Well, then, you're late already. I won't hold you up any

more by talking. Hustle up and get there as soon as you can."

Stanley called again on Saturday. He wanted to make sure Henry was going to give him and Harold driving lessons on Sunday. Herb said he didn't know and gave him Henry's office number so he could call him direct. With that off his mind, Stanley began to talk about the Institute. He said he liked it better than he had thought he would, but he still didn't like it that much. That meant to Herb that Stanley wasn't sure if he would make it or not and wanted to leave himself an out.

Then Stanley's voice dropped as he said, "I left early Friday."

Oh shit, Herb thought to himself. Is he screwing up?

"What do you mean?" he asked.

"I left a couple a hours before quitting time."

It sounded as if Stanley had just walked off early. But he hadn't. It had been Good Friday and almost everyone, except a couple of people who had to clean their presses, had left early. Again, Stanley was worried about having anything less than a perfect attendance record. So Herb said, "Well, I guess if everybody was leaving, it was the thing to do. If there's nothing doin except a couple of people cleaning presses, there's no point in hangin around."

Stanley felt better. He told Herb that he could have left even earlier but he had waited for his paycheck which was seventy cents short. Stanley had caught the error and had gotten it corrected—that was real progress for Stanley. Before, he would have merely sat and wondered why they were "cheating him."

Stanley was finished talking.

"Well, I'll call you during the week or something," he told Herb.

"Good," Herb answered. "I'd like to hear how you're doin."

10 Post-Vacation Blues

Monday, April 3, through Friday, April 14

We added two more boys to the school after the vacation. One of them, Sam, was an old-timer who had been in the pilot program for almost a year, the other one was new. With Don's friend Lenny who had been added the week before the vacation, we were up to eleven, not including Stanley . . . five blacks, two Puerto Ricans, and four whites. We had real integration, with very few of the problems people expected.

PHASE TWO

Before the vacation we had decided to put Phase Two of our plan for Nat into effect on our return. Natalie had become very important to Nat. It was time to use the relationship to get Nat to control some of his behavior. Natalie had been spending two periods a day with him, doing more or less whatever he wanted. We changed that. She would continue to mother Nat, take care of his allowance, buy him things, and play with him. However, we designated the first of his two classes with Natalie as an academic period. If Nat wanted to spend the first period with her, he would have to do academic work, reading, or math. If he didn't

350

want to work, he was still free to do whatever else he wanted, but not with Natalie.

Herb met with Nat the first thing Monday morning after the vacation and explained our decision to him. Nat accepted it without any show of emotion at the time. But, within a few minutes, he developed an attitude. He cut up the protective window screens in the gym with a pair of wire cutters from the shop. He grabbed Herb half kiddingly but half seriously by the tie, just tight enough to choke him a little. Then, perhaps most important, he refused to go to his "academic" class with Natalie. By the third period Nat had calmed down and wanted academics. We began to feel cautiously optimistic about our decision. However, after lunch, Nat was like a tornado getting into everything, telephoning everyone, and stealing keys like they were gold.

NAT'S GIRLS

The following day Nat showed up with a girl, Brenda. He introduced her to some people as his sister and to others as his girl friend. We wondered how Nat would act with his girl around. He surprised us by spending two periods reading with Natalie while Brenda sat quietly outside Natalie's room looking at picture books while Nat was in class.

During lunchtime we got a better picture of their relationship. As soon as Brenda and Nat entered the dining room, she told Nat where to sit. Then she demanded, "Gimme soda, put mustard on my bread, pick up my fork," while Nat obeyed meekly. "We should have it so good with Nat," we thought. After lunch, and after his girl had left, Nat spent the afternoon hugging and kissing Natalie almost continuously.

The following day Nat worked on reading and math during his academic periods and ran wild during the afternoon. Toward the end of the day he "borrowed" Bill's keys, found

Natalie, brought her up to the storage room, turned on the lights, and whispered,

"Look at them mattress. We could go to sleep. No one could find us." Then he locked the door and quietly gave her the keys.

"Things are getting pretty sexy," Natalie thought as she found herself for the first time feeling uncomfortable about Nat's attention.

Our real surprise came the next day when Brenda returned to the school with a seven-month-old baby, Nat's baby. Our little Nat was a father. Nat who stroked Natalie's hair, held her hand, rubbed her leg, and kissed her cheek was a father. We were all amazed, especially Natalie.

NAT MAKES IT

The following week Nat added a third academic subject to his morning schedule—social studies with Jack. He did beautifully in social studies. All the difficulties and absences Jack experienced with Don, Larry, and Harold were made up for by his sessions with Nat. One good class after another. Scarcely a disruption. Scarcely a missed class.

Afternoons were a different story. That was the time when Nat paid us back or made us pay for what we were doing for, or rather to him, in Phase Two.

He switched from noisy disruptions to quiet little fires in ashtrays and flaming Ping-Pong balls. Bill tried to get him to stop. Coaxing and friendly persuasion didn't work. Nothing dangerous was happening. Things were still under control, but Bill felt he had to take out the big gun.

"Nat," he told him, "you have to leave early because you didn't stop setting fires."

Bill called Henry who was pleased to see Bill take a firm stand with Nat. However we weren't bad guys. Since Nat had to leave the building early, Henry used the time to buy him the clothes we had promised him.

By the end of the week the afternoon disruptions had all but disappeared. Nat was quieting down. He was making it.

MUCHO CORAJE Y ANGER

Carlos was angry and upset when he returned to school after the vacation. Something had happened between the trip to Palisades Amusement Park and his return to school —Henry had met with Mr. Rivera again. When Henry spoke to Carlos, he tried to relate Carlos's anger to his concern for his mother. Carlos took out a knife and threatened to cut Henry if he spoke about his mother.

"Ya all liars. Is all bull shit. My fatha tol me the truth."

He believed his father, not us, he insisted.

Carlos was trying to make himself believe. But it was obvious to Henry that Carlos was really aware of the truth and was holding back his anger at his father for lying to him.

When it was time for his class with Natalie, Carlos was still too angry to go with her or to even talk to her until he got rid of some tension by punishing the punching bag. Then he asked Natalie to play Ping-Pong. As they played, he told her about his trip to Palisades Amusement Park and his "fight with two men" but wouldn't talk about what was bothering him.

Tired of her company, Carlos conned Nat into a crap game downstairs. When Herb came down to break it up, Carlos took out his knife and teasingly pretended that he was going to cut Herb with it. Herb told him he had to stop or leave, even if he was only playing. He took Carlos upstairs to Henry's office where they talked for a while. Then Henry took Carlos for a drive.

QUEERS AND BEERS

As they drove, Carlos bragged about his relationship with homosexuals. He told Henry that he let them look at him, photograph him, and fondle him in the nude. He didn't mind, he explained, because they gave him rides in fast cars and bought him beer. Henry thought that Carlos was probably involved in other sexual activities which he wasn't able to talk about, but he didn't probe.

During the week Carlos continued to talk to Henry about homosexuals, hinting that he might have been involved in other ways with them. Carlos had convinced himself that he had been taking advantage of the homosexuals rather than vice versa. Although somewhat ashamed about his relationship with them, Carlos was able to hide his feelings from himself. Henry tried to challenge his view in order to make him feel uncomfortable about his homosexual behavior. Henry's confrontation didn't seem to work.

Carlos also began to act much more sexual in the school. He used words like "cocksucker" and "motherfucker" in front of Natalie for the first time. He joined in Don's sexual discussions and told homosexual jokes.

Then Carlos outdid himself. He sneaked up behind some male staff members and rubbed his penis against their rears. Most of them laughed it off. Herb didn't. He got angry, and the angrier he became, the more Carlos sneaked up behind him. Finally, in a fit of rage, Herb picked Carlos up, pinned him against the wall, and told him to stop or else.

After Herb had calmed down, Henry took him aside in the hall.

"Why the fuck are you so uptight about homosexuality?" he asked.

Herb stretched his hands out forward, palms up, symbolically pushing Henry away, and answered, "I don wanta talk about it."

"You have a school full of kids busting with sex, most of it homosexual—since all human beings have their homosexual tendencies—and you don't want to talk about it."

Herb grunted. The conversation ended. Henry felt he had

helped Herb to see something. Herb thought Henry had bugged him.

GIVE ME THE MARIJUANA

The next week was even worse for Carlos. Something had happened at home during the weekend. Carlos walked into school scowling. Something was bothering him. He hardly spoke or ate during the warm-up until he took Natalie aside to tell her that he had been smoking pot over the weekend. Not only that, he continued, he had some with him in school.

Natalie alerted Herb. Herb brought Carlos to his office where he confronted Carlos with what he had just told Natalie.

"I's not true, I was kiddin, I neva in my life smoke pot," Carlos protested.

Then without any urging from Herb, he took out an envelope and produced five marijuana cigarettes. Herb asked for them, Carlos refused, rummaged through the supply closets, and stuffed some boxes of ball-point pens down his shirt.

Before Herb could say anything the phone rang. Herb started talking. George came in—Carlos grabbed the phone.

"Fuck you, fuck you, *maricon, maricon,* fuck you, *maricon.*"

HERB: Get off the phone, Carlos, it's an important call.

CARLOS: No deal! . . . *maricon, maricon,* fuck you.

HERB: Carlos, you can't stay in school if you're going to curse into the phone.

GEORGE: Don't listen to him.

CARLOS: Fuck you, *maricon, maricon.*

Herb hung up, frustrated and angry. He had blown his cool.

CARLOS: I ain givin you nothin.

HERB: Then you'll have to go home.

CARLOS: Good! Who wan's this fuckin school. I's crummy anyway.

Carlos started to walk out. Herb recouped. Carlos was walking out with the pens and the pot. Herb followed Carlos. George, who didn't want to miss out on the entertainment, followed Herb.

Carlos changed the subject as he walked downstairs.

"You always buy everybody else things and me nothin; Willie and Nat got jackets. When do I get somethin? You promise me pascription sunglasses, I wan em now! And shrimp too, like Henry got Nat."

By then they were out of the building.

"Don follow me, I ain givin you nothin," he told Herb.

"You still have the pot," Herb insisted.

"They ain marijuana. I was jus foolin you, Herbie, I was kiddin. I's tea, roll-up tea."

"Come on, Carlos, give me the cigarettes."

"They jus tea."

"Fine, then give em to me anyway."

"Why should I give em?"

"Why not? They're just tea."

"They marijuana. You know it. Why should I give em ta you? I as' fa shrimp and ya din give me it."

"This is as far as I go. If you walk any further you're goin by yourself."

Carlos walked a few more yards, then stopped.

"Okay, I' tell a truth."

Herb thought he had Carlos: "Not here, let's go back in."

When they went back inside the building, Herb asked for the cigarettes. Carlos ran upstairs and disappeared for a couple of minutes. When he returned, Herb again asked for the cigarettes.

"I's jus a joke, jus a roll cigarette. See."

The five cigarettes were gone. There was one in their place, but it was different. Carlos had hidden the pot.

"Come on, Carlos, you showed me five marijuana cigarettes. Now where are they? Why did you show them to me if you didn't want us to know?"

"They gone now."

"Where?"

"I threw em in a back yard."

"Okay! Show me where and we'll look for em."

"You can fine em."

"Just show me where."

"They not there. They down a toilet."

The contest continued until Herb realized that he wasn't about to get the pot. He would have to settle for the pens.

NOBODY LOVES A STOOL PIGEON

When Natalie called Carlos for their second period class, Carlos said he was never going with her again because she had ratted about the pot. Natalie reminded him that he knew the policy about secrets. But Carlos wouldn't talk to her. He only wanted to talk to Henry. So Natalie went upstairs to get Henry who was already busy with someone else. Henry asked her to stay with Carlos. Maybe, he suggested, Carlos might change his mind about her.

When Natalie returned to the gym Carlos flew into a screaming cursing rage. Then he ran into Connie's room. Natalie's intuition told her she ought to keep away from Carlos. But Henry's suggestion and her own guilt dragged her up to Connie's empty room after him.

Carlos started to play with the phone. Natalie moved next to him and asked him to stop.

"Shut up," he told her.

Natalie put her finger on the button to disconnect the call as Carlos dialed a number.

"I'm gonna hit ya, Natalie, I'm gonna hit ya. I'm not kiddin. Do it one more time an I'm gonna hit ya," he yelled.

"No, Carlos," Natalie answered. "As long as you dial, I'm going to put my finger there."

Natalie realized she had made a mistake as soon as she heard what she had said. But she had made a statement and she had to stick by it. Carlos dialed! Natalie put her finger on the button. Carlos swung at her hand but missed on purpose. After a few more misses he finally aimed for her finger and caught it. Natalie ran out of the room, blaming herself for what happened.

Carlos was still so angry at Natalie the next day that he refused to go with her to pick up the sunglasses he had been impatiently awaiting. Since Natalie had a free period, she went up to the office to dictate. Carlos followed a few minutes later. The top half of the Dutch door was open. Carlos took out his knife and demanded over the door: "Lemme in."

"No," Natalie answered. "Now you know I'll have to tell Herbie that you took out a knife."

"Shut up, I cut ya throat if ya do," he threatened, then laughed as if he knew he wouldn't really do it. He climbed over the door, then slowly closed it.

"You scare?" he asked, looking as mean as he could. "The doors close."

At that moment the fire alarm rang. Everyone left the building and the incident ended.

After the fire drill Natalie returned to the office to continue her dictation. Carlos followed close behind. He took off his belt, scowled at her, and hit her with it.

It stung. Natalie was hurt physically, but more shocked emotionally. She picked up the phone to call Herb. Whack —she felt her arm sting again. Feeling rejected rather than afraid, she held onto the phone.

"I'm gonna hit ya again if ya try ta call anyone."

Natalie got to the door and rushed downstairs toward the rec room, followed by a belt-swinging Carlos.

Jack and Bill stepped between the two of them. Natalie retreated to her room, then returned upstairs to tell Herb what had happened. Herb and Natalie went into Phyllis's office where they could record their conversation about Carlos.

After a few minutes Carlos appeared at the half-opened Dutch door. He didn't seem as angry as he had been before. He looked like he had regained control, at least Herb thought so. Natalie wasn't sure, perhaps because she was the one Carlos was after. Carlos postured himself.

"I'm takin off my belt, Natalie," he announced.

"What should I do?" Natalie asked Herb.

Herb was ready to gamble. Carlos seemed in control.

"Go on out," Herb told her. "He won't hit you again."

Carlos raised his belt.

"Yeah!! C'mon out if ya wanna get hurt."

"Go ahead, he won't hit you," Herb urged.

Natalie heard herself say, "I'm coming out, Carlos, because I trust you," but she wasn't eager to go.

"Wha ya gonna do if I hit er?" Carlos asked.

Herb thought Carlos needed an excuse to back down. So Herb gave him one.

"I'll call the police, but I know you won't."

"Then I won hit er in school," Carlos answered, saving face.

Natalie walked down toward her office. Carlos followed asking, "Why dya tell? Why dya tell?"

"You know I had to tell," Natalie answered. "That's the rule and I don't think you were really angry at me for telling."

Carlos smiled, but didn't answer. Instead he said, "I'm gonna tell em you hit me firs, so I kin hit ya back later."

"You can tell anybody anything you want," Natalie answered. "I'm not going to argue with you, Carlos; in spite of what you are doing, I still like you."

We couldn't understand why Carlos had been so violent with Natalie. She had told on him before. He knew Natalie had to tell the rest of the staff. He hadn't been punished for anything. Why? Why? We thought he had used the telling as an excuse for what he had wanted to do anyway, but why?

Carlos wouldn't tell us anything Wednesday when it happened. He cut school Thursday. When he returned Friday he was just as secretive. Henry talked to him for a while but all Carlos would say was that he was quitting school. Why should he come, he argued. School was boring. Henry took him to Herb. Carlos began the same complaints.

"Of course you don't want to work," Herb interrupted. "Because Natalie isn't here today. You act like you're angry with her, but I know you still like her and want to work with her."

"Yeah, I wanna fuck er—fuck er," Carlos announced.

"Oh, no wonder you've been acting so nasty to her lately and refusing to work," Herb replied. "Maybe that's your way of keeping away from her. You can still work with her next week anyway even if you feel like that."

Carlos smiled silently, then walked away.

HARD TIMES

An unhappy, irritable George returned to school after the vacation in a nobody-loves-me mood, nobody at home or in school either. Natalie tried to talk to him, but he wouldn't see or hear her. George only wanted Henry; he only wanted to curse Henry. He only wanted to punch Henry. He wanted to, but he couldn't. He was too depressed to work up enough steam for even a small scene. All he could say was that none of us liked him because we hadn't taken him on any of the trips during the vacation. Henry reminded him that he had told us he was going out of town. But George hadn't gone out of town for the vacation after all. He had been in New York all the time. He had missed the trips and blamed us. It didn't make any difference to him that he had told us he would be out of town. It didn't make any difference to him that he had our phone numbers and he could have called any of us. We were to blame.

He wanted the allowance we owed him and his tokens, that's all. He got them and left.

After a few days, as we gave George smiles, food, sunglasses, and attention, he forgave us for "what we had done to him." As he did, he began to complain to Henry that he was being picked on by his parents. He didn't get enough to eat, his father wouldn't give him his allowance, and his mother wouldn't let him have the leather jacket he wanted.

Henry made an appointment with Mr. and Mrs. Jackson. However, when Henry arrived at their house, he learned that George's father refused to talk to him. George, his mother, brother, and aunt were there.

George took offense right away by bringing up the leather jacket and allowance he wasn't getting. Mrs. Jackson told Henry she refused to get George the jacket because he would look like a hoodlum in it. George claimed that his father wore a leather jacket. Mrs. Jackson looked embarrassed. Henry said that he was sure that her husband's jacket wasn't styled quite like the one George had in mind. No, that wasn't true, Mrs. Jackson admitted, her husband's jacket was just like the one George had in mind.

Henry didn't say it, but he wondered if Mrs. Jackson also thought that her husband looked like a hoodlum. Whether she did or not, Henry could see the motion picture projector, hi-fi equipment, photography equipment, and other furnishings which George claimed his father had stolen from his truck.

Mrs. Jackson confirmed that George hadn't been receiving the allowance his father had promised him. Initially Mrs. Jackson and her husband were each giving George a dollar and a half toward the three dollars George was supposed to get from them. However almost immediately after they had agreed to give George the allowance, Mr. Jackson accused George of stealing thirty-five cents and refused to give him any allowance until George told him what he had done with the money. Mrs. Jackson continued to give her son a dollar fifty because she doubted that George had taken the money. In fact, she added insensitively in front of both boys, she thought George's older brother had taken the money.

Henry asked Mrs. Jackson if she had defended George against her husband's false accusations. George liked that and smiled appreciatively. Mrs. Jackson, noticing George's smile, looked toward Henry and said: "Sometimes I think that George wants you to be his father. Don't you?"

Too embarrassed to really deal with the statement, George looked away and mumbled a denial.

Changing the topic, Mrs. Jackson asked Henry to help George's older brother. His girl friend who was pregnant was pressuring him to marry her. He was undecided about what to do.

"All three of my children are in trouble," Mrs. Jackson said to Henry. "George, his brother, and my daughter."

Henry thought Mrs. Jackson was trying to sidetrack the conversation. So he answered: "Well, if you want to discuss it, why don't you come to the office next week?"

HAPPY TIMES

When George came to school the next day he wanted to talk to Henry about his "back taxes," which was what he called the fifteen dollars in allowances his father hadn't given him. George felt we should give him the money because we had guaranteed him seven dollars a week. George wanted a definite answer. Henry told George that even though he thought it would be right for us to give him his back taxes, Henry would have to discuss it with the staff during the afternoon meeting. George wasn't satisfied, but he let it drop for a while—a short while.

Just before lunch he started a campaign to make sure we made the right decision. Henry and Herb were talking in the hall. George walked up to them.

"You betta gimme my money, mothafucker. Else I'm gonna kill you. I'm gonna break this here school up, mothafucker. You betta gimme my money."

"We told you we couldn't tell you anything definite until after the meeting," Herb answered. "You know some kinds of decisions require a meeting first."

George wasn't satisfied.

"Listen, nigger," he told Herb, "I want my money now. You hear nigger, now."

Herb wasn't going to budge.

"You know we'll make up our own minds, whatever you say. If we give you the money, it won't be because of your threats. I want you to understand that. We'll make up our own minds. Don't think we'll pay attention to threats."

Neither was Henry going to yield to George's threats.

"Maybe that's what you have to do at home to get something, George, but the whole world's not like that—we certainly aren't. Threats aren't necessary and they don't work here either. But if you can't wait till this evening when I call you, you can wait for an answer in school during our meeting. We'll discuss it first thing."

That seemed to satisfy George.

During the meeting Bill and Norm were initially opposed to giving George the fifteen dollars in cash. They thought we should buy him something, whatever he wanted, with the money. Another group thought we should give George the money outright. They weren't a majority either. A compromise was reached. George could have the cash in three weekly installments of five dollars each, or he could have it all in one lump sum if it was used to buy something he wanted.

Henry left the meeting to tell George about our decision. George thought about the two alternatives. He also thought about his father. He was concerned about taking the money when his father didn't want him to have it. However, he wasn't concerned enough not to take it.

"How bout a bike? Could I get a bike?" he asked Henry.

"Fifteen dollars toward a bike? George, where would you get the rest of the money you need?" Henry reminded him.

"Yeah, that's right. Okay, gimme five each week then. But you betta have it."

Henry smiled.

George was happy about the results of Henry's visit. His mother had agreed to get George the leather jacket he wanted and we had promised to pay him his "back taxes." We were pleased with George's new mood. We were even more pleased about the real academic progress he was making with Ed and Jack in math and social studies.

Jack had finally learned how to work with George. He was able to engage George into an academic situation by talking to him, telling him stories, explaining things to him, and showing him films. Jack had also made an agreement with George. He would give George credit for social studies regardless of the amount of time George spent in class, as long as he attended regularly. He only had to attend for as long as he could sit in class—fifteen, twenty, twenty-five minutes, it didn't matter. George didn't even have to go to Jack's room. They could have class in the gym, the hallway, or even out in front of the building.

George and Jack turned out to be a good match. They

were both interested in things like the Reconstruction period, the black revolution, and white racism. George wanted to know more about things he had heard, things such as proportionally more blacks than whites being sent to Vietnam and getting killed there. Jack was able to help George find out the facts about these and other questions which were important to him.

Unfortunately, all sorts of disruptions occurred during most of the rest of the day.

PAINFUL TIMES

Despite George's academic progress, he had been acting much more disruptive . . . less dangerous, but more disruptive, and at the wrong time. We were accepting new students into the program at the rate of one or so every week. We were no longer able to give George as much individual attention as before. And we had become much less tolerant of George's disruptions.

In our changed situation we could only contain George when Henry was physically present in the school. When he wasn't, George was more disruptive than we could endure. We had to make a decision. It made us feel guilty, but we made it. Even though Henry and Jack disagreed, we decided to exclude George from the school building when Henry was out. That meant all day Wednesday and Thursday afternoon. We would still give him a program during that time. Perhaps we would find a big brother or volunteer to take him on trips. Until we found someone, one of us, probably Ed, would take him.

Jack couldn't accept the decision. After the meeting he tried to convince Bill that we were about to make the wrong move.

"Jack," Bill answered, "you have the same problem I had when I first started here. I was afraid, no . . . guilty about my anger. I couldn't let the boys know how I felt when they bugged me. But they knew anyway. I used to feel impotent and shitty when I didn't defend myself or at least get back at them. My feelings came out though. I took it out on them anyway. When I saw George walk up to you and punch you in the face for no reason—smiling, and you didn't do anything or even say anything . . . that was me two years ago with Charlie. I'm not that way anymore. George punched me like he hit you . . . only once. I gave him a shot right back, automatically, without thinking. I don't think he ever held that against me. You better set limits or they'll walk all over you. Everyone gets angry—even you."

"Maybe you're right," Jack answered without meaning it. "I can't say for sure. If so, you're only teaching George that you can't use force against people that are stronger than you. You're still teaching him to use force. I'd rather try showing him that I don't hate him. Maybe then he won't have to feel so hostile. Isn't that what Herb and Henry are doing?"

"Within limits," Bill explained. "Not punching people . . . not hard, anyway. You know what helped me realize that? The meetings. Hearing other people say they were angry without feeling guilty. . . . After a while I learned to accept my necessary anger. It's a common problem. You'll see . . ."

"I still like the Summerhill approach," Jack answered.

BAD TIMES

Like many of the other boys, Harold was depressed when he returned to school after the vacation. He claimed that his parents had been giving him a bad time. Although we believed that the extended Easter vacation together had been difficult for him and his family, we thought that the major reason that Harold was so depressed was that he was coming to grips with his educational difficulties. He was making academic progress but feeling depressed at the realization of the long road ahead of him.

As he often did when he was depressed, Harold started to steal. Four subway tokens from Phyllis, a cheap tool from Norm, a paintbrush from Bill . . . nothing worth anything. We wondered what we should do about it. We thought it would pass with his depression. We treated Harold especially well, bought him a new pair of glasses, and whenever possible protected him from being rejected.

Despite his depression, Harold was able to attend all of his classes regularly. He was doing extremely well in biology and math. He was progressing rapidly in English. And he and Jack finally had a breakthrough in American history.

FIGHTING TIMES
Harold continued his involvement with the "Diggers" and the "peace movement" after the vacation. He arrived one morning with a scraped and black-and-blue face, which he said he received while walking in the Village with his girl friend. He claimed three guys made wisecracks about his peace button. One of them told him to take it off, or else. Harold refused. The three guys jumped him, then ran away after Harold knocked some teeth out of one's mouth.

Harold had been growing bigger and stronger. He was easily the strongest student in the school. But it didn't seem likely that "three guys" would run from him. His story sounded a little bit like Carlos's fight with the two men in Palisades Amusement Park to us. However, we didn't say anything.

OBNOXIOUS TIMES
Harold was behaving too well in school. Something obnoxious had to happen. It did. Harold had been coughing so much after the vacation that we asked the school doctor

to examine him. The doctor arrived during the warm-up and began to question Harold. Without signaling what he was about to do, Harold quietly reached under his chair and brought up a paper plate full of green phlegm which he had saved for the doctor and put it right up into the doctor's face. The doctor looked like he was about to throw up. When he had regained his composure, he brought Harold up to the office for an examination. Harold had a serious case of bronchitis and infected lungs, which was probably the result of his constant smoking.

PROBATION REPORTS

Since Larry hadn't gone on any of the vacation trips, we were concerned when he missed the first Monday of school. When he showed up Tuesday, we were all relieved. Larry spent most of the morning boasting to Norm and the others that he had spent most of the vacation stealing, earning money from queers, and procuring girls for men. Later in the day, Larry told Henry that his mother had been told that the management planned to follow through on the eviction notice. Henry checked Larry's story, found it was true, and sent a letter to the management, urging them to reconsider their decision.

Larry's probation officer called Wednesday morning to tell us that Larry was scheduled to appear in court on Thursday for a probation hearing. He told us that Mrs. Keating had given him a bad report about Larry. He wanted to hear from us before deciding on a recommendation. We gave him as positive a report about Larry as we could, within the limits of accuracy, and hoped for the best.

When Larry arrived, he was understandably nervous about his impending court hearing. He told us that his mother had been threatening to ask the court to send him away. We explained that we had given the court a good report about him, which the judge would probably accept.

Larry didn't show on Thursday. He was busy in court. Friday he called bright and early to tell us that he had been taken off probation, even though his mother had said he was a thief and an addict.

When Larry arrived in school he was flying and shouting, "I'm free. I'm free."

When he calmed down, he suddenly became concerned.

"If I'm not in court," he asked, "can I still come to school?"

Larry felt concerned, but we were relieved. He was worried that he might not be allowed to attend. We were worried that he might not want to attend.

FREEDOM'S FRUITS

Monday morning Larry and a phone call from his mother arrived one after the other. Larry announced that he had had "a piss poor weekend." Mrs. Keating filled us in on some of the details when she called.

"The boy has no respect for me," she told Herb. "He says he's off probation and I can't do anything to him. He comes home at four in the morning and curses me. He called me a prick and a fuck. Is that the way a boy should talk to his mother who loves him? I ask you. The other night he jumped on top of me while I was sleeping. Do you know what he did? He pinned me down with his body and squirted shaving cream all over me, all over my face too. I just don't know what to do with the boy. Now I lock my room at night so he can't bother me. I don't know what to do. If something doesn't happen, I'm going to have the boy taken care of."

"Taken care of? What do you mean?" Herb asked.

"I will just have to take him back to court and have him sent away. He has no right saying things like that to his mother. I'm too nervous even with my door locked. Just because he's off probation the boy has no right. Does he?"

We took a supportive tack with Mrs. Keating: Larry had no right doing what he did. As long as he was a minor she could bring him to court. No one should expect her to tolerate such behavior. We took an insightful tack with her: she should also realize that getting off probation had given Larry a sense of freedom which he was testing out at home, hopefully temporarily. Larry's problems would take some time to overcome. We didn't expect dramatic changes overnight. His behavior was already improving, wasn't it? No more daredevil stunts, no more physical attacks. And he was attending school pretty regularly. We also took a cooperative tack with her: we would continue to work toward Larry's improvement but we would also lay down the law to him about his behavior at home.

Later we took a hard but cooperative line with Larry. He was a minor and subject to his mother's discipline. She could take him to court. No more cursing, no jumping on her, no lying on top of her, no squirting her with shaving cream. We, in return, would try to keep his mother calm and him out of court.

FREEDOM ALMOST LOST

Larry missed school Tuesday. We called him at home Wednesday morning. Why had he missed school, we asked. He was in bed, sick. What was the matter, we asked. His stomach was bothering him . . . he felt groggy . . . he had a headache . . . he had a cold. Was he taking anything, we asked, implying drugs, alcohol, and such? Yes, aspirin. Was he doing anything like drinking or taking drugs? No, he was sick. Did he have a fever? No.

But something was bothering Larry. Finally he got around to what it was. He had to go to the precinct Friday afternoon about the time he had been picked up for drinking. His mother was supposed to go with him. She had refused. So he was worried.

Don't worry, we told him. The incident had occurred while he had been on probation. Now that he was off, the past wouldn't be held against him. If his mother wouldn't go with him, Henry would speak on his behalf.

Henry called Mrs. Keating at her office. Larry had told us the truth. She wouldn't go to the precinct. She couldn't "take the boy anymore." She couldn't wake him in the mornings because he yelled and swung at her when she tried. She was going to "leave the boy alone." Yes, she admitted, things were better between them at home. No more drinking parties. Even Johnny had kept away, but she was "through with the boy."

Henry called the precinct. The officer told him that Larry had been caught drinking wine some weeks previously. As a matter of routine police procedure, Larry had been asked to report with his parents to be given a "scolding." Henry told the officer that Larry was in our special school. The officer offered to delegate the responsibility to us. Henry accepted. Larry didn't have to report to the precinct. The matter was closed.

HEADY CONVERSATIONS

Larry didn't show Thursday. But he came the next day and spent most of his time talking. First Herb.

"Am I schizophrenic?" he wanted to know.

"What do you mean?"

"Would you call me schizophrenic?"

"Why do you want to know?"

"Do I have a split personality?"

Herb wanted to avoid a direct answer about labels. He wanted to deal with Larry's concern. So he told Larry that like the other boys in the program, he had problems which some people might label one thing or the other. But whatever the label, Larry was changing and dealing with his problems.

After he had dealt with what he thought was Larry's concern, Herb asked what had brought up the question. Larry told him that he was going to take a trip on mescaline or peyote, but only if he wasn't schizophrenic.

"It's dangerous for schizophrenics," Larry explained. "They freak out."

"Would it be dangerous for you?" Herb asked.

"Maan, that's what I'm askin you. That's why I wanna know if I'm schizophrenic."

Herb explained about labels again.

"You know, Herbie baby, I'm still high from some pills I took last night. But I'm no addict, man. I don't take shit or speed. There's nothin wrong with me. I'm off probation, I got *no* problems."

"If you're happy with yourself, if you don't think you have problems, if you don't want to change, then we're your enemy because we're involved in a conspiracy to change you."

"You mean you want me to be just like you guys?"

"No, we don't want you to fit a mold. We want you to be a happier you."

"I am a happier me. I've changed a lot since comin here."

"You're completely happy with yourself? Come on, don't you want to change in some ways?"

"No."

Larry was talking like he had no reason to come to our school. So Herb confronted him. He asked Larry what he wanted to be. A doctor, Larry answered. Herb saw he had an opening with Larry. He told him that he was doing absolutely nothing in the program to become a doctor. Larry immediately denied that. Well, what was he doing, Herb asked. He was reading science books at home and going to some classes. That wasn't enough to earn a year's academic credit, Herb insisted. That, Larry agreed, was something he wanted us to help him change.

Was he happy hanging around with Johnny, Herb asked. No, Larry answered. He liked hanging around with Johnny but disliked him. That was a second thing he was less than happy about.

"What about pills?" Herb asked.

"You think I'm an addict?"

"That's not what I asked. I'm asking whether you're happy fooling around with pills."

"No."

"That's another way we can help you change. See," Herb concluded, you're not crazy, and you're not perfect either. You just have problems . . . like all the guys in the school."

After he finished with Herb, Larry moved on to Bill and Ed. He walked tall, but it was only a pretense. First big drug talk; he had been high on goof balls the day before. That was why he hadn't come to school. He had even taken three that morning. But Bill and Ed didn't have to worry. He never got high on three pills. No more drinking. Pills were his big kick—no heroin, only "ups." He didn't want to become an addict.

Next big girl talk; he had a twenty-two-year-old nympho with her own apartment. He also had a prostitute that gave it to him for free. She had been eleven years old when he had first "violated" her. That made him feel bad. It was his fault that she became a prostitute. His sister, the nurse, was on his back about drugs. He didn't mind because she cared about him. What she said was a drag, but she said it for his own good. Sometimes he purposely popped a pill before he saw her just so she would worry about him.

Larry's mood suddenly dropped. He was down. He said he knew why he took pills. Something was wrong with him.

He was crazy—mixed up. When he was high on pills or on a "mind high" he understood himself. He felt better and didn't worry that he was crazy. He looked at Bill.

"You gonna tell Henry?"

"We don't have secrets here," Bill answered.

"I know. It's just sometimes I like to tell other people things. Henry's always askin why and I can't stand it."

After their conversation, Phyllis's daughter, Marcie, walked into the gym. Larry took to her immediately—like a protective big brother. He taught her to play Ping-Pong, shoot basketballs, and play the piano. When Marcie left the gym, he told Ed that he wanted to have his own kids some day. He would give them the best he could. He started to mention something about his mother who had never cared for him properly, but he quickly broke it off as soon as he realized what he was saying.

Finally it was Henry's turn. Henry asked the kinds of questions Larry had expected from him. Larry seemed almost pleased that Henry did.

POT PARTY

Larry missed a "pot party" on Thursday by cutting school. But Don, Willie, Manuel, and Sam, one of our original students who had returned, were present.

Don had been building up to something for a while. April started off badly for him. After the vacation he and Lisa came to school very uptight about something. Henry got together with them as quickly as possible. Neither of them had been home since Saturday. Lisa and her parents had quarreled. Since Lisa didn't want to go home to face them, they hung around Greenwich Village for a couple of days. However, that wasn't what was bothering them. Sunday night they had witnessed a murder. A marine had been shot practically right next to them. Lisa was afraid that she would be called as a witness. Don couldn't explain why he was upset. He just kept repeating, "He was shot. I didn't do it. I didn't kill him."

The whole thing seemed unlikely to us. However, when Henry checked the newspaper, he found an article which confirmed their story. Don and Lisa might well have been standing next to the marine when he was murdered. But they didn't have anything to do with it. Still, it took a whole week for Don to finally believe that he wouldn't be blamed or involved.

Don felt better the following week, but not much better. On Monday he came in around lunchtime with a buddy. They ate by themselves and left together shortly afterward. Tuesday was no better. Mrs. Russo called around nine o'clock in the morning to tell us Don had just come home and was preparing to go to bed. Henry talked him into coming to school. However Don spent most of the day sleeping in the rec room. Wednesday he was wide awake and alert. He wanted something from us. It was his anniversary. It had been exactly one year since he had started going with Lisa. Henry had promised to help him finance an anniversary gift. He had come to collect his money, that was all. He collected half of it, then left. Thursday he brought a bag of pot to school.

Willie was the second pot party-er. The beginning of April produced no surprises from him. From time to time he played around, wrestled with Herb, or pretended that he didn't want to go to class. However, he was still far from relaxed and spontaneous. He took his psychological tests but protested that he didn't need them. We thought he was right, but we asked him to follow our routine anyway. Herb and Henry tried to get close to him, but he wouldn't bite. Everything was regular.

The second week was different. Willie was hostile, not playfully hostile, really hostile. It seemed to have something to do with Sam's return. Something was going on between them, but we didn't know what.

Sam was the third party-er but he didn't smoke. He just hung around. Manuel was the fourth pot party-er.

The party started after lunch. Don, Manuel, and George sneaked out somewhere and got high. Sam went along. Connie was the first one to notice the signs in her afternoon reading class with Manuel, but she wasn't "hip" enough to catch what was going on. She thought Manuel was just tired.

Later in the afternoon Jack came down to the gym. Manuel was trying to play Ping-Pong with Bill. Don was lying on a mat loudly laughing hysterically at the simplest things. Jack began shooting baskets. Don looked up.

"Lemme take a shot, man," he called to Jack. "I can get it in from here. Yeah, I got a big one. I can get it in from anywhere."

Jack threw him the ball. Don hurled it toward the basket from his prone position. It hit off the wall and bounced around harmlessly. Don laughed and shouted, "I almost made it, didn't I?" Jack didn't see anything funny. He realized that Don was high. So he sat down next to Don.

"Man, I got some good stuff. You want some?" Don asked Jack. "Close your eyes and open your mouth and I'll put it in. It's just for you."

Manuel caught the action, came over, opened his wallet, and showed Jack two reefers.

"They fron my bag, man. You wan sone? I always carry a bag jus in case."

Manuel went back to his Ping-Pong game. Jack watched him closely. Jack could hardly tell Manuel was high, he was so repressed. But Don was euphoric. Jack started to deliver his usual speech about pot to Don but caught himself. Manuel and Don left. Jack followed, a discreet distance behind. When he got outside the building they had disappeared.

They returned a few minutes later with Willie. The three of them were giggling, whispering, and having one hell of a good time. Manuel and Don walked into the art studio, Jack followed. Willie split. Manuel turned on the electric wood engraver and began cutting designs in a board. Don took the engraver from him. He ground it into the wood until it began to smoke, as he laughed and recited a mumbo-jumbo poem like a witch would. Bill came over and pulled out the plug. Don moved away and allowed Manuel to continue until it was time for Manuel's math class.

Jack gave Manuel some problems to do, but the session turned into a joke. Manuel added or subtracted whenever he felt like it. The few times that he accidentally came up with the correct answers, he couldn't write the numbers on the paper because the space between the lines had somehow become much too small for him.

Don came into the room. He wanted math too . . . but he was too busy knocking things over and talking mumbo-jumbo to do anything.

Jack gave up on the math just as Willie and Sam came in. Everyone was giving cool signs to everyone, slapping each other's palms and laughing hysterically. Bill came in to continue a discussion with Sam. Don, Manuel, and Willie got their coats and went outside again: Connie followed and saw them disappear into a cellar entrance down the block.

After school we met to decide what to do with each boy. Don was first. Don had flagrantly announced that he had brought a bag of marijuana to school, as if to call attention to himself. He was flaunting his pot. We felt that our best tack would be to completely ignore his behavior, not a single word about it, no matter what. We hoped Don would come to us if we played it cool enough. Then we could use an insightful approach with him.

We wanted to continue our nonconfronting approach with Willie, because we remembered the futility of confronting him directly about the money he had stolen when he bought his jacket. We decided to let Willie know that we were aware that some of the boys were smoking pot without saying he had been one of them. We wanted to tell him we knew what was going on. We weren't accusing him of anything, but we had decided that it should not continue. We hoped that would give Willie the message without pushing him into a corner where he would have to deny being involved.

With Manuel we decided to come right out and say, "You've been smoking pot, that's illegal. You're already on probation. Don't do it anymore."

The boys responded as we predicted. Manuel smilingly said that he wouldn't smoke pot anymore. Willie said okay with a nod of his head. Then, almost as an afterthought, he added that he hadn't smoked any. Don got upset because we ignored him. We had spoken to Willie and Manuel, but we hadn't said a word to him.

He became more open and more persistent in his attempts to engage us in a conversation about pot. First he asked Henry: "You still gonna give me the rest of the money to buy my girl a present? Even though you know how I spent my allowance?"

When that didn't work, he announced, "I gotta leave early with Manuel. We have things to do in the park."

That didn't work either.

When Henry handed Don his allowance and the extra money without comment, Don became more frustrated. Finally he was forced to ask, "What are you going to do about the marijuana?"

"Nothing," Henry replied.

Don was ripening. He would soon be ready for picking.

11 April Happenings

CON

A lot happened during the last two weeks of April. George must have thought he had conned us for his back taxes because after getting the first five-dollar installment, he tried a number of unsuccessful hustles to get more money from us. His major con occurred after a tooth-fixing trip we had organized for a few of the boys.

On the way back to the subway George patted his pockets: "Shit, I don have my fuckin wallet. I must of left it in that dentist's place. I hafta go back and get it."

"Uh! uh!" Jack answered sternly. George had already acted up by grabbing the dentist's hand while he had tried to drill George's tooth. Jack wasn't eager for another scene.

"I'll go," he told George. "You wait here. Order some sodas. I'll pay."

A few minutes later Jack returned empty-handed, wondering if George had lied to him.

"You didn't leave your wallet there. I looked everywhere," he told George.

"Oh yeah, nigger, I had twelve bucks in it. The school betta pay me back."

379

Jack didn't know what to say. Even if George had told the truth and had lost his wallet, did that mean we should replace his money? Jack didn't think so, yet didn't want to commit himself. George wanted an answer, but Jack felt he didn't have the authority to make the decision. So he said, "You'll have to take it up with Herb or Henry when we get back to the school."

George knew Jack couldn't make the decision. So he dropped the issue. Jack was glad. He was already exhausted from keeping the peace at the dentist's. He didn't need any more scenes.

"The school owes me twelve bucks," George announced firmly to Herb when they returned to school.

Herb looked at Jack, bewildered.

"Why?" he asked.

"Cause I lost it on a school trip. It's in the dentist and no one could find it."

Herb hadn't been there. He didn't know what had happened. He looked to Jack for help. Jack explained: "George says he lost his wallet in the dentist's office. I looked everywhere for it, but it wasn't there. The dentist promised to look for it later and let us know."

"Now look here, I want my money," George declared firmly, without any "if" in his voice. "If he can't find it, you betta give it to me."

Herb would have liked to search George to see if he was pulling anything, but he realized he couldn't. Herb didn't think he should replace George's money even if it really had been lost on a school trip. However he felt that was a decision for Henry. So he gave George a noncommittal answer.

"Well, we'll have to call the dentist in the morning and see what we'll do after that."

Jack called the dentist the following morning. George's wallet wasn't there. Hell! What should I do now? Herb wondered. He didn't believe George had lost the wallet.

From the cool way George was acting, Herb felt sure he was trying to con us.

"I won't tell him anything about the call," Herb decided. "Just watch him a while. If he's trying to con us, he'll probably trip himself up."

Herb was right. About an hour later Herb discovered George and Nat in the music room. George was holding a black wallet and counting some money. It was time for some indirect non-putting-in-a-corner-type confrontation, the kind that wouldn't raise George's defenses.

Herb smiled.

"Hey, George, did you get a new wallet already? How did ya know yours wouldn't be found?"

George smiled back.

"So far so good," flashed through Herb's mind.

"Where did ya get the money?"

George knew he was caught.

"I won it from Nat," he answered anyway.

"From Nat? How much you have? Come on, you couldn't have won all that from Nat."

Nat kept quiet. He didn't want to get involved. Besides he knew George was caught.

"Henry gave me it. It's the money I lost," George answered, changing his story.

"Henry gave it to you? You know he wouldn't be so stupid."

George smiled as if to say maybe Henry didn't. That was all the confession George was ready to make. It was enough. Herb turned around and left.

George went to Jack's class and told him with a big grin: "Man, I almost pulled one off on Herbie. He almost gave me the money. He woulda if he didn catch me with it."

"What happened to the money?" Jack asked, as disinterestedly as possible.

"They stole it from me and gave it back."

Jack didn't believe him, but he kept quiet. No more scenes, he told himself.

Later when Herb heard that George had admitted that the money was really his, Herb thought it was time for some direct confrontation.

"Hey, George," he asked, "how did ya get your money back?"

"They gave me it back."

"Come on, no one steals money, then gives it back. You know that. That's not much of a story."

"Yeah, but I really thought I lost it. I couldn't find it till I got home. It was in my jacket . . . in the bottom by the linnig where my pocket was ripped. That's why I didn't know I had it."

That seemed more plausible. Whether it was the truth we didn't know, nor did we really care.

JUSTICE FOR THE PEACE MOVEMENT

Harold had a happy April. He had a new girl friend, "a cool chick, pretty, intellectual, and a peacenik." His girl friend was all the things he wanted to become. She was rich, she lived on Park Avenue, and she attended Hunter College. Harold told us that she knew he was only in high school, but it was all right because she was younger than he was. Besides they enjoyed the same things—peace rallies at Hunter and folk sings in Central Park.

We were pleased that Harold was happy, but skeptical about the accuracy of his story. We were even more skeptical when Harold returned to the school after a weekend with a story of police insensitivity and injustice. According to Harold he and his girl had been peacefully singing songs and playing the tambourine with a group of peaceniks in Central Park on Sunday.

"All we were doing were thinging. Thith cop come over

and gave uth a ticket for nothing. I'm not gonna pay it. I'm gonna get the Thivil Liberty Union into it. Down with the fuzz."

We asked him what the others were going to do.

"They paying . . . not me. I'm gonna fight."

"Why?" we asked.

"There were no thign againth muthic in the park. The fuzz didn't give uth warning. We didn't give em a hard time or anything. It weren't fair."

Knowing Harold, it was hard for us to believe that he had been as innocent as he portrayed himself.

Later in the week Harold triumphantly announced that he had been in contact with the Civil Liberties Union. He claimed they were considering handling his case. Ceremoniously, he took out his wallet, slowly extracted a folded newspaper clipping, and read aloud an article which described the case of one Harold Stern who was contesting a summons he had received in Central Park.

"Mr. Thtern," Harold read, "vowed that he would take his cathe to the Thupreme Court."

The final blow to our skepticism came from Ed who happened to have been at a party with one of the policemen who had given out the summons to the group. Ed described Harold to the policeman.

"Oh, that kid," the policeman said knowingly. "Sure I remember giving him a summons. He was dressed in a T-shirt, no shoes, and a medallion around his neck, and he was playing the tambourine. They didn't make any fuss, but we had to give them summonses. Afterwards, your kid walked off arm in arm with a girl."

Yes, Harold was really coming along. Even more so than we realized. The very next day a woman called the school. She told us that her son was in serious trouble in court. She knew Harold very well. She had observed a miraculous change in him. Since we had done such a wonderful job with Harold, she wanted to see if her son could be referred for the same kind of help. That was real therapy for us. Just when we needed it.

LARRY'S LITTLE SCHOOL

We had a hint of big doings when Mrs. Keating called Henry to tell him that Larry hadn't been sleeping at home. She said she didn't know what Larry was doing, but Johnny had told her that Larry was mixed up with homosexuals.

The next morning brought another call from Mrs. Keating. She had awakened in the middle of the night to find one boy sleeping under Larry's bed, another one behind the couch. She kicked them out, and Larry left with them again.

"I don't know what to do about the boy," she told Henry. "He's just impossible. Now he's threatening to run away from home unless I let his friends sleep over. I think I will just have to have him sent away."

"Mrs. Keating," Henry answered, "you know we're trying to help your son. There's always time to send him away. But you and I know that's not necessarily the answer. If you can do what we told you and do it right, maybe Larry will also. Be patient and sit tight, won't you?"

Larry called Henry later in the day.

"Where the hell have you been?" Henry demanded. "Here you go around promising and then you disappear again. You can't take our medicine. Always running away. What building are you swinging from now?"

"Okay! Okay! If you really want me, I'll be back. I'll be back. I don't mind coming to school. I dig it. You guys got a great school. I'll be in in the morning."

But he wasn't.

Henry spoke to Larry again, on the phone. Again Larry

told Henry what a great school we had. Again Larry promised to come in. Again he didn't show. Finally, on Friday,
Henry convinced Larry to meet him for dinner Saturday
evening in a midtown restaurant.

Here I go again, Henry thought to himself. Meeting a
kid Saturday evening . . . Saturday evening when I should
be doing personal things.

Larry was beaming happiness when he met Henry for
dinner. He told Henry that he was extremely proud of himself. He was about to move out of his mother's apartment.
He hadn't seen his friend Johnny in weeks. He had turned
over a new leaf. Then he hesitated.

"What gives, Larry?" Henry asked. "Something funny's
going on. You've turned over a new leaf but you're not
coming to school? You're as pleased as if you had swal-
lowed a canary."

Larry smiled extra brightly. Then he said, "You know,
man, there are lots a kids in trouble. You guys aren't the
only one who can help em . . . I wanna help em too."

"Maybe someday you will."

Unable to contain himself any longer, Larry let his secret
burst out.

"Not someday, now. I'm workin with a bunch of kids.
We're all sleepin in the same place. I give em allowances
like you guys and lunch."

Then Larry showed Henry his bank book. He was down
to his last dollar. His "program" was about to run out of
funds.

Henry interrupted, "Not seeing Johnny's great. Wanting
to help kids is great too. But how can you help kids when
you need help yourself? Furthermore, running a program
for kids takes money. How much do you think it takes to
run our school for a year?"

"Ten thousand dollars?"

"The staff alone gets paid much more than that."

"But I do it for nothin. You guys only do it because you get paid."

"Is that why I'm here Saturday night?"

Larry understood Henry's argument but continued to talk about how groovy it felt to help kids. Henry agreed that it was groovy. "But for you, Larry baby," Henry added, "it's also unrealistic. You still have your own problems."

Larry agreed but pleaded with Henry to give him another week with the kids. If he could have one more week, he promised, he would return to the school. That would just be more fantasy, Henry told him.

Monday brought no Larry. Instead Johnny showed up looking for him. Johnny hadn't seen Larry for weeks. Like us, he didn't know where Larry was. Johnny was all dressed up. He claimed he was going to an interview with a famous TV personality who wanted to give him a job. He was looking for Larry to take along. Maybe Larry could get a job too. We told him he would have to get in touch with Larry himself, then politely ushered him out.

The next day we received a call from the guidance counselor of the school which Larry's "students" attended. She had a lot of questions to ask us. Did we have a boy named Larry Keating in our school? What kind of school were we? Did we know Larry had visited her? Could we explain what was going on? We knew almost nothing. She knew even less.

Larry finally returned to school on Wednesday. He looked different. It was his glasses. He had lost them. Without them he looked funny. He told us that he had been taking care of some twelve- and thirteen-year-old boys with the money he was getting from a couple of gay men. He wasn't having homosexual relationships with them, he insisted. Just spending time with them. In fact, Larry added, they had a sailboat and they were going to take him sailing on the weekend.

During lunch Herb asked Larry why the guidance teacher had called us about him. One of his boys had run away from home, Larry answered. He was only twelve years old. Larry had been afraid that detectives were after him on a morals charge—corrupting the morals of a minor—because he had been seen with the boy. Larry had decided the best thing to do was to turn himself in to the guidance counselor, before he was picked up. He was sure they would think he was doing bad things, even though he was just trying to help the kids.

Herb called the guidance counselor that afternoon and heard a very different story. She told him that a strange boy (Larry) had walked into her office and said, "I heard you're looking for me."

"Looking for you? I don't even know who you are," she had replied. Larry introduced himself. Then he'd said,

"I don't have anything to do with the kids runnin away. I'm not contributing to the corruption of the morals of minors. The kid was up my house, but he only took a shower and left."

Herb then asked her about the boys Larry was hanging around with. Apparently they had been involved in drinking and truancy long before they met Larry.

Before Larry left for the day, Herb told him what we had been told by the guidance counselor. Larry suddenly remembered the facts more clearly and brought his story in line with hers. We were surprised that Larry wasn't anxious when we confronted him with her version of the story. We were even more surprised when Larry became much more involved in his academic work and attended school much more regularly than we had expected.

NO BIG DEAL

During the weekend Stanley called Herb in a panic. He could hardly talk coherently. He and his sister had an argument. They argued and he pushed her . . . easily, nothing serious. She telephoned the police. He ran out of the house to call from a drugstore. He was worried about the police.

Herb told Stanley not to worry. It was just one more time that his family called the police to intimidate him. Herb reminded Stanley that he was eighteen years old. He wasn't a minor. They really couldn't lock him up or send him away. His sister certainly had no legal authority over him. Besides, the police wouldn't be concerned about a family squabble. It was no big deal. They had much more important things to do.

Herb encouraged Stanley to go back to the house so that his family wouldn't feel that they had intimidated him. Stanley agreed to go home instead of to his girl friend's house where he had been planning to hide out.

Stanley called back about an hour later from the same drugstore. He said that when he had gone home, his sister had told him the police were after him. She was checking in with them every hour in case he returned. Herb told Stanley that sounded like a lot of nonsense. Stanley disagreed. He thought his sister was trying to get him committed to a hospital. Herb explained why Stanley's sister couldn't hospitalize him. He wasn't crazy. He hadn't done anything. Family squabbles were only family squabbles. He encouraged Stanley to go back to the house again and to call him from the house if anything happened.

Stanley called back again. Herb wasn't home, so Marilyn answered. Stanley told her that his sister had charged him with attempted murder. Marilyn asked Stanley if he was worried about it. Stanley laughed and said, "Shit, no!"

ROTTEN LOUSY KID

Carlos was having the same kind of problem as Stanley. We had been worrying about Carlos for a while. However, when he missed three days of school without contacting us, we really became concerned. What was going on? Repeated telephone calls to his home produced nothing. No one would tell us anything. Finally in the middle of Sunday night, Henry received a frantic telephone call from Carlos's sister.

Things had been getting worse and worse at home. Carlos was coming home drunk. Carlos was misbehaving again. Carlos was threatening his father. Mr. Rivera wanted Carlos put out of the house. Mrs. Rivera was upset. The whole family was upset. Henry asked Carlos's sister to bring the whole family to see him. She'd try and let him know.

Unfortunately things moved at a much faster rate than we could handle. Carlos's sister called again Monday morning. Her father had already brought Carlos to the police. Carlos was in jail. He was going to have a hearing Tuesday.

We had to act quickly. The court couldn't force Carlos's parents to keep him at home if they insisted that they wanted him out. We had two alternatives. We could convince Carlos's parents to keep him at home. If not, we had to convince the court to send Carlos someplace besides a state training school.

First Henry called Carlos's probation officer. He described our approach with Carlos and the progress he was beginning to make in our program. He explained why a state training school wouldn't be helpful to Carlos. He asked the probation officer to send Carlos to Youth House as a temporary alternative to a state training school. That would give us time to convince Carlos's parents to take him back home.

Then Henry called our agency's court worker to alert her to the impending hearing. She would act as a friend of the court and present our point of view. Lastly Henry called the Riveras. However they refused to meet with him until the Friday after the hearing.

The following afternoon we received a report from the court worker. At the hearing, Carlos had cried, pleaded, and begged his parents to take him home. However, his parents had refused to take him back. Fortunately the probation officer and the judge accepted our recommendation and sent Carlos to Youth House. But only temporarily. If Carlos didn't go home, he would have to go to a training school.

Our work was cut out for us. We had to get the Riveras to change their minds. It wouldn't be easy. They had refused to see Henry until after the hearing. They had just refused to take Carlos back. The last time Henry had spoken to Mr. Rivera he had tried to mislead Henry. Would the next time be any different? We didn't even know what had happened at home. Henry had a real job on his hands.

During the next few days Herb worked with Carlos's probation officer and Youth House social worker. Natalie and Ed visited Carlos in Youth House, and Henry went after Carlos's parents.

Herb told the social worker the real reason why Carlos had been placed there and what was going on in the family. After the worker understood the situation, she agreed to help us to convince Carlos's parents to take him back. In fact, she said, Carlos's mother had called her, but she had decided not to return the call until after she had spoken with us. It looked like we were making some headway. The probation officer, judge, and Youth House social worker were with us. Perhaps, with a united front and Henry's persuasive powers, we would be able to swing it.

The following day, Henry was supposed to see the Riveras and Ed and Natalie were scheduled to visit Carlos. As we expected, the Riveras refused to see Henry, but they did make another appointment for the following Monday.

Natalie and Ed had better luck. Their first visit to a "lock up" was a shocking experience for both of them. The building was large and ugly with long corridors and heavy clanging doors which required a big, long, heavy key to open. It was a depressing place, especially coming from our school.

They had brought peanuts and cigarettes for Carlos to make his stay a little less intolerable. Carlos seemed concerned.

"What's the matter?" Ed asked.

Carlos told them about the rules, all of them, including the one about only four cigarette breaks a day. If he was caught smoking any other time, even with them, he would lose the privilege. He had been in Youth House twice before, he explained. He knew what happened when kids broke the rules. So he was going to follow all of them.

Carlos looked frightened. He sat on his bench like a mouse. They could hardly recognize the boy who was rocking back and forth and nervously looking down at the floor as "our Carlos."

After a while Carlos told them his side of the story. His father had come home drunk. As soon as his father walked in, Carlos's sister had run up to him to complain that Carlos had beaten her up. It was a lie, he claimed. He had hit her once, on the back, that's all. His father started yelling at him, bullying him, pushing him around. Later his father told the judge that Carlos had beaten up his sister.

Natalie asked Carlos if he had threatened his father with a knife as his father had claimed in court.

"No," Carlos answered. The whole incident started because a guy told his father that he was drinking, pushing dope, and hanging out with queers. That was a lie too. He had gone to the movies with a friend on Friday, Saturday, and Sunday. His father wouldn't believe him. They got into an argument. Carlos felt so angry he was afraid he would hurt his father so he gave his mother his knife to hold just in case. So, he claimed, he couldn't have threatened his father with it.

Natalie and Ed told Carlos that we would do all we could to help him. They explained that we had already given good reports about him to his Youth House social worker and his probation officer.

Carlos was too anxious to take in what they said. He felt the only one who could help was his mother. She had called him at Youth House. She had told him she would be taking him home soon. Still, he said, he was glad that the school was on his side. Then he pathetically promised to attend school every day and never give anyone trouble if he returned. Natalie smiled as she advised him not to make promises he might not be able to keep. He shouldn't worry, she told him, he would be welcomed back without any promises.

It was about time for Natalie and Ed to see Carlos's social worker. As they said their sad good-byes, Carlos told them pathetically that they shouldn't have brought him anything because it would probably be taken away from him. However, when Ed saw the way Carlos clutched at the bag like it was his most valued possession, Ed knew they had done the right thing.

Carlos's social worker confirmed his story about Mrs. Rivera. Mrs. Rivera had called her and had tearfully told her that she wanted her son back. However the social worker was still worried about Mr. Rivera. He was the one who had brought Carlos to court. If he didn't change his mind, Carlos couldn't be sent home.

The worker asked Natalie and Ed if we could do anything about getting Carlos into a treatment center rather than a training school if it became necessary. Yes, they replied, the school would cooperate if necessary. But, they added, they still thought Carlos should be sent home.

The social worker was less optimistic. She reminded them that Carlos had been sent to Youth House twice before. The judge would have to consider that. Yes, Natalie agreed. But the third time Carlos had been sent there for home problems, not delinquent behavior. That wasn't the same thing. The social worker agreed. It did make a difference, especially in light of the progress Carlos had been making in the school.

The social worker seemed convinced. She would recommend that Carlos should go home. She couldn't promise anything. Someone still had to change Mr. Rivera's mind. We would work on it, Ed promised.

Henry had his meeting with the Riveras. The following week Carlos was back in school. Someone must have been doing something right.

ACADEMIA

When we looked up from these crises we noticed that we were running an academic school. Harold had a full academic program: English, math, biology, and two periods of social studies. So did Don, when he attended classes, and Larry, after he had closed down his own school. Willie wanted to follow their lead. Willie told us that he had decided he didn't want to come back to our school in September. He wanted to go to regular school instead. So he needed a full academic program to keep up and graduate. We told him he could change his program if he wanted to. However, we privately doubted that he could handle biology, English, algebra, and social studies when he was still having problems in biology.

When Willie started his new program, Jack gave him a diagnostic math test to determine if he was really ready for algebra. No! He wasn't ready for algebra. He made careless errors in two of the three addition problems and in most of the subtraction and multiplication. He didn't know how to do division or use fractions. He didn't even try the more difficult problems.

When Willie realized where he was at, he asked defeatedly if he could take "business math." He had tried algebra in regular school, he admitted, but he had had so much trouble with it that he had been switched to bookkeeping.

Willie had a good head on his shoulders. However, he had been so defensive about his academic problems and the public school had been so incapable of helping him overcome them, that he was very far behind educationally. Willie was just beginning to admit his difficulties to himself. So it would take a while for him to catch up educationally. Willie had said he planned to leave after the summer. That wouldn't be enough time. Fortunately, he stayed longer.

Jack had an excellent set of programmed math books which fit Willie's needs. Jack could work with Manuel and Willie together and give them both all the individual attention they needed.

Willie didn't have the same success in English. During his first English class, Connie asked him to spell some words for her. As Willie wrote them down, he asked her to tell him which letters stood for which sounds. They got into an argument when Connie told him "E" stood for the short "e" in elbow.

He's just like George, stubborn and defensive, she thought to herself.

Willie did the same thing when he made oral reading mistakes. He read "column" as "columb" with a "b" sound at the end.

"That's not right, Willie," Connie told him. "It's pronounced column. There isn't any 'b' in it. It's spelled COLUMN."

"No it isn't," Willie insisted. "It's spelled COLUMB. I always see it that way."

Connie was tempted to prove to him that she was correct. She had the dictionary in front of her. Should I? she wondered. No better not. He's still too defensive, she thought to herself in the language that had seemed so strange to her a few months earlier. In the next class Willie attended, even getting twenty-three out of twenty-five correct on a reading comprehension test which Connie had rigged so he would do well, didn't help. Willie was too threatened by his difficulties. We had to transfer him out.

Yet, while Willie was doing so poorly in English, he was doing magnificently in music. He had progressed to playing complicated songs like "Stranger in Paradise." He was figuring out the harmony and picking out chords by himself. Willie was also doing extremely well in art and math. The contrast was almost too frustrating for us to accept.

Willie's cooperative facade worked too well. We often forgot that he had serious academic problems, and we often forgot that we needed to use the same patience with Willie's not so obvious problems as we used with the other students' more obvious ones.

Nat and Manuel had also become consistent academic performers. Nat was doing so well he was rapidly becoming a non-Nat. He was able to concentrate for whole periods of reading and social studies. He was even working on arithmetic. Nat liked to get into a corner by himself with his programmed texts to reduce the stimulation of things around him. So we reserved the telephone booth downstairs in the hall for his use whenever he felt too excited to be able to work with other people around.

Manuel was doing even better. Yes sir. He finally earned his return engagement to that plush restaurant we had taken him and the boys to before Easter vacation. Connie had promised Manuel she would take him to lunch there when he was able to read for Herb without getting all nervous and "mistakey," and he had done it.

Connie told him that he had done it. Manuel grinned ecstatically, pounded his fists on the desk, and demanded, "I wan T-bone steak, bread—that hot bread, orange soda an a big bowl a Jell-O . . ."

Quiet Manuel was demanding. Quiet Manuel was different, taller. At least he seemed so to us. Connie became ambitious with Manuel. She started him on "English 2600," a programmed grammar book. He was succeeding with that too. If Manuel earned a lunch for reading, we owed him a week of dinners for math. Manuel had finished arithmetic and subtraction with Jack. He was working on the multiplication tables and addition of fractions in a programmed text.

It was wild. Manuel and Nat were both working in programmed texts, texts with words that a few months ago they hadn't been able to read.

[Jack had been a social studies teacher. We had made him into a math teacher, and he had turned himself into a reading teacher. Jack had made it. He had gotten down where the boys were at, but he had also brought them up to where he was at.]

There were many beautiful people, but Stanley was the most beautiful of them all—at least at the time. He passed his driver's test.

And he bought himself a new burglar alarm.

And he had a job playing drums in a rock 'n' roll band out in the suburbs.

And his parents were talking to him.

And it was true—not a fantasy.

And it was the end of April.

[Ain no problem kids, just kids with problems. Dig?]

Epilogue: June

BAM! BAM! BAM! Someone hammers on the door, disrupting our morning meeting.

"We still have ten minutes, Harold," Bill calls out calmly.

A foot against the outside office door makes a loud *thunk*. It sounds as if all twenty-three boys are banging at our door, but it's only Harold.

"Ten minutes till coffee," Herb shouts in a voice louder and angrier than Bill's.

The banging stops. Jack continues the discussion.

"Okay . . . I want to say something first. When Ed left at the end of the semester there was no one to move toward George and be with him, one to one, when he was acting out. Henry was too busy. I felt guilty so I took over for Ed, telling myself I could handle it. But every move George made toward me angered me. I just couldn't take the physical contact, his going from playfulness to aggressiveness. I was afraid of some of the things I saw in George and he sensed my fear."

"Come on! Come on! What's your vote?"

"You're just talking yourself into a 'yes' vote, Jack."

"I know."

"Okay, Norm. How do you vote?"

"I pass my vote."

"Oh no!" A concerted yell from all of us.

"You can't pass. You have to vote. Don't you think we should get rid of him?"

"I thought we should of gotten rid of him the first week."

"Bill, you're last?"

"I'm afraid he's going to kill someone—I'll hurt him to make sure he doesn't."

"Okay," Herb announces. "It's settled unanimously. George goes. Henry, what did you tell him yesterday?"

"I told him he was suspended from school until further notice. I'll call him today and make an appointment to see him and his mother."

Herb still feels uneasy. Although he said it was settled, he keeps talking.

"If we had unlimited resources we could help George. But we don't——" he says with a shrug.

"It's over, Herb," Henry interrupts.

"Okay," Herb agrees, then asks, "Who's got coffee?"

"Jack and I," Natalie answers.

Jack grabs the tray with the coffee, milk, and cake, leaves the room, and heads to the first floor and the dining room. On the way down he hears pounding in the music room. "It's Nat," he thinks to himself as he keeps walking down the stairs into the dining room.

The dining room is empty. Jack pours himself some coffee, sits down, lights a cigarette, and broods.

"I've just voted to kick a kid out of the best school in New York."

Jack thinks of George the day before, when George was losing more and more control, tightening and relaxing his grip around his marble-based trophy. He thinks he should feel bad that George is leaving, but he only feels relief.

Natalie comes down. "Some of the boys are in the gym," she tells Jack.

"Ugh. Let them stay there," Jack answers.

"What's this bit with you now?" Natalie asks, sensing Jack's mood. They talk about George. Harold walks in.

"Hi, Harold!"

Pow! A strong jab to Jack's bicep.

"Harold," Jack hears himself complain. He knows he sounds just like Harold's mother but he says it anyway. Harold smiles and plops down on the chair. He's fulfilled for the time being.

A new boy, Sam, sits down, pulls out a cigarette, and turns on Harold saying, "That's bright! Boy, you really know how to act!"

"Hi, Sam," Natalie cuts in.

Manuel comes in, then Willie. Some more new students follow. They shove another table over beside the first one. Nat comes in, puts his arms around Natalie, hugs and kisses her. The day is in full swing.

Herb comes down to say: "Ding-a-ling. Time for class."

Natalie and Nat leave immediately. Nat's really serious about his classes.

"Harold, Sam, Pete, social studies," Jack calls out as he gets up to go.

The dining room is emptying out, different students are going with different staff. Nat and Natalie, Connie and Manuel, a mob with Bill for art, another mob with Norm for shop. Herb heads up to the gym by himself; he would have had George. Jack leaves with his group. Harold stops off at the bathroom.

Jack starts the class without Harold. They're discussing the Arab-Israeli war. Before they can get into anything, Harold walks in.

SAM: Get the fuck out of here.
HAROLD: Fuck you.

Don't say anything. It's only their game. They're doing their thing. Nothing serious, Jack reminds himself. He has learned not to lecture the boys. The class resumes. Harold gets into the discussion and they finish the period without further disruption. Then it's time for Jack to clear them out of the room.

It takes five minutes, but they finally start out. Harold stops to knock on Connie's door. Jack is right behind.

"Who is it?"

"It's Harold," Jack calls out, even though Harold puts his finger to his lips. Harold feigns anger, goes at Jack, tries to jab him in the stomach. Jack sidesteps, puts his arm around Harold's shoulder. They head downstairs where Jack drops Harold off with Bill.

Connie was just finishing with Manuel when Harold knocked at her door. They had been reading another book about horses, reading on a page with a picture of an adult horse.

Manuel reads: "It's Pinto's birthday. He is three years old today . . ."

"Tha's crazy," he tells Connie. "A three-year-ol horse's jus a baby. He can be so big."

"Horses are different from people," Connie tells Manuel. "When they're three, they're fully grown. Different animals grow at different rates. By the time dogs are your age, they're just about finished living. They're fully grown after only two years."

Manuel looks puzzled. It's only just beginning to make sense to him. Connie continues the explanation until it's clear. At least she thinks it's clear until Manuel tells her, "They have ponies in a park. Like midget. People don let them grow. They bang on they head so they can grow big. Like you bang on a nail."

There's a knock on the door.

"Who is it?" Connie asks.

"It's Harold," Jack answers.

They ignore him.

Manuel continues. "I saw sone reeal small horse at this horse show once. They got hit on a head like the people in a circus."

"That's not why they remain small. You can't keep people from growing by pounding them on the head. All you do is hurt them. The reason they're small is . . ."

It's the end of the period, but Connie keeps Manuel for a while because she thinks they're doing something important.

Carlos is working on his sculptured head and talking to Bill as Jack drops Harold off. Bill and Carlos are just finishing their conversation. Carlos had been telling him a story. A week before, he and two friends had been walking in East Harlem, toward 116th Street, when they heard a couple of explosions. One of his friends said, "They mus be shootin off firecrackers."

"Nah, thas not firecrackers, man, thas a gun," Carlos answered.

Carlos and his friend started toward the sound. As they did, a man appeared running out of the alley with a gun in his hand. As the guy came near, he pointed the gun at them. They didn't move. He cursed them and ran off. As soon as he was out of sight, they went around the corner into an alleyway. Somebody had called an ambulance.

Harold moves closer. Carlos continues.

"There was this kid on a groun shot right between the eyes." Carlos points to the spot on his clay head. "Blood all over. Another guy was shot in a arm. When he saw us, he took off. We mus a been the only witness. Now they're afta us. My mother won lemme go ou'side cause they're lookin fo us with guns. My friens gonna join the Job Corp. Me an my cousin gonna P.R."

Bill studies Carlos. He doesn't look scared, but he does look serious.

"I gotta see Henry fa money," he tells Bill. "I gotta have

money fore I leave. They only got me a one-way ticket. Wha if they won lemme come home from P.R.? Henry gotta gimme money ta come home. He betta gimme the money."

Carlos finds Henry and tells him the story. Henry checks with Mrs. Rivera. It's true. Mrs. Rivera believes Carlos is in danger. Her husband is only getting Carlos a one-way ticket in case Carlos wants to say in Puerto Rico. We have a new crisis on our hands.

After Carlos leaves, Henry thinks back to the morning meeting and our decision to discharge George. Henry feels depressed. He knows that we were helping George. Then he reminds himself that like everything else the school isn't perfect.

"It's one of the best damn places I've ever worked in. But it's not perfect. It's a good thing I have my private practice so all my professional satisfactions don't have to come from the school. . . . Nothing's perfect . . . fuck it."

Harold starts his math class with three other boys. They're all using different books. Bill has his hands full. Harold is moving along, but he isn't going to finish the course by the end of June.

Natalie is looking for her next period student who isn't in school yet. She looks in Bill's room. She sees the mob and hears the radio blaring. She looks in Norm's room—another mob. Nat and Carlos, where are they? Oh, oh, trouble, her internal alarm tells her. She heads back upstairs.

Nat and Carlos are hanging, jumping, and riding on Herb and Henry outside Phyllis's office. Nat had been trying to get in the office because he's not supposed to be there. Now Nat is trying to grab Henry's keys, his wallet, his glasses, trying to play his "look-what-I've-got-play-with-me-and-I'll-give-it-back" game. Herb breaks away from Carlos.

Carlos joins Nat against Henry. Finally, they all agree that Natalie should take Carlos and Nat to a nearby fruit store for cherries.

At eleven thirty Jack heads downstairs to the gym in his sweat clothes. He's filling in for Ed. Norm is sitting on the steps in the hall outside the gym talking to a new student. The student goes into the gym. Jack tells Norm that he still feels bad about George.

"Do you know what your trouble is, Jack?" Norm asks. "You got too much guilt. That kid only touched me twice. The first time he kicked me in the shins and I didn't do anything. The second time he punched me in the chest. That was the last time. I rapped him so hard he never even looked at me angry again. That kid lost control, sure. But he knew who he could do it to and get away with it. He wasn't psychotic."

Henry joins the group. He and Jack talk about their Memorial Day school trip to Washington, D.C. Jack tells Henry, "I really got close to George in Washington. He was beautiful then. I think I understood him for the first time that weekend. If only we hadn't had to leave Washington."

"Yes, George was beautiful," Henry agrees sadly. "But spending all weekend with him was one of the most difficult things I ever did in my life."

Jack goes into the gym. Norm returns to shop where he has six boys for biology. Henry goes back upstairs. Three boys are waiting for Jack. They play basketball until fourth period. We now have four periods in the morning in order to have more time for academic work.

Don is still trying to get started in Natalie's English class. He has been trying for six weeks. He has started umpteen different books and put each one aside. This time he picks up *Catcher in the Rye* and asks her if he can start it.

"Yes, but first let me tell you something about the book."

They talk about the meaning of the title and a few other things. Don reads and laughs through the first few pages. He lifts his head.

"This is a crappy book."

Natalie keeps quiet because she wants Don to continue reading. He goes back to the book.

"It's a shitty book."

Again she doesn't respond. Again, it works.

"My mother would throw a fit if she knew I was readin this."

"Why?" Natalie asks, without realizing that she is being sucked into conversation.

"It's dirty."

"I'm sure your mother knows you use worse language."

"Yeah but . . ."

The reading stops for a long while as they talk.

Don goes back to reading. He sees himself in the story.

"This kid tries to make himself believe things just like I do," he tells Natalie. "I gotta show this to Henry. The kid's just like me."

It's the end of the period. Don asks for an assignment.

"Read up to Chapter Eight and we'll discuss it tomorrow," Natalie tells him.

"That's too much. *Up* to Chapter Six, I can do that much," Don answers.

Natalie agrees, but she's not optimistic that he'll read any of it. Don takes the book and leaves.

Nat is with Henry. He's still doing well academically. He wants to talk to Henry about the summer.

"Ah needs twenty-five dollar."

"Why?"

"Foh the lady collectin foh the trip down Virginia."

Nat is his usual vague self.

"What kind of trip?"

"A club trip."

"What lady?"

"The lady who run the club."

"What kind of club?"

"The club ah belong to."

More questions and answers. Finally, Henry understands the details. Nat wants money for a deposit for a Labor Day weekend trip to Virginia that a lady is organizing for the teen-agers in his neighborhood. Henry tells Nat that it sounds like a good idea but he will have to discuss it with the rest of us during the staff meeting. Nat understands the process, but he is impatient.

"Then you hurry up bout it . . . hear?" he insists.

It's time for lunch. The mob rushes down to the dining room. Four tables are pushed together with sixteen or seventeen people around them. Four new students are seated at a table off to one side. Norm and Bill are eating by themselves in the studio. Don and two of his friends walk through the door. Almost all of the kids are in school.

Everyone is eating and everyone is talking. The place is alive with activity; Nat grabbing across the table; Don "ranking" Lenny; Carlos talking with Henry; Herb kidding a new boy about finally getting out of bed. Bill and Norm come down after lunch. They organize most of the kids into a volleyball game in the back yard. Connie and Natalie also play. Marilyn goes to the music room with Larry and Willie.

Don is in a therapy session with Henry. They're talking about Lisa. Herb, working in his office, thinks of how much Sam reminds him of Nat and George. Sam has George's anger but Nat's ability to control himself. Nat's ability to control himself? That rings funny to Herb. It reminds him how far Nat has progressed. Herb is also upset about George. But we had no choice, he tells himself. George isn't like Sam. Sam will never hurt anyone.

By the time classes resume, the boys have knocked themselves out playing volleyball. Willie stays in the music room for his lesson, Nat has social studies with Jack, and Harold and another student have English with Connie. Natalie is with two new students. The rest of the boys are spread out around the second floor with Norm, Bill, and Herb. That is, everyone except Larry who is talking to Henry about his impending eviction. We still haven't been able to settle that problem.

One more period passes. Then Herb walks around the school calling out "Ding-a-ling." We still have a flexible schedule. It's time for the afternoon meeting. It takes a good fifteen minutes to give the kids their allowance and carfare. Norm talks with Sam for a few minutes on the front stoop. Nat and Carlos play a sort of I-won't-leave-until-you-love-me game with Natalie before she can convince them to go. Connie walks down with Manuel. Finally the boys are gone and we head to our meeting. Natalie sees the book Don has left and rushes out to give it to him, but too late.

The psychologist reports on one of the new boys. We listen and question. Then there's the day's events, the exchange of information, talk about next year, the need for another social worker and a full-time science teacher, Sam's overwhelming tensions, his need to be fed, Nat's becoming too attached to Natalie, Carlos's trip to P.R., Harold's increasing use of physical strength to show that at last he can't and won't be pushed around, Willie's starting to act out more, Larry's eviction. . . . What shall we do? There's not enough time to discuss all the problems, but we have to deal with them. The room is too small. The staff is too small. We're starting to pick at each other. We don't know it at the time but in a few months we will be planning a third version of our program. We will be moving into our own quarters. We will have a larger student body and a larger staff, more space and more equipment.

At the moment our minds are on the more immediate problems. What are we going to do for a trip Friday? Are we going to take the boys bike-riding *again?* We still have another week of school before we start the summer recreation program.

It's the middle of June. It's hot. We're all tired. It's four thirty. So we stop. It's been a long day. Most of us head for home. But Henry isn't finished. He still has Carlos's return ticket to worry about.